SAGE was founded in 1965 by Sara Miller McCune to support the dissemination of usable knowledge by publishing innovative and high-quality research and teaching content. Today, we publish over 900 journals, including more than 400 published in partnership with more than 300 learned societies, more than 800 new books per year, and a growing range of library products including archives, data, case studies and video. SAGE remains majority owned by our founder, and after Sara's lifetime will become owned by a charitable trust that secures our continued independence.

Los Angeles | London | New Delhi | Singapore | Washington DC | Melbourne

Revolutionary Violence VERSUS Democracy

Revolutionary Violence VERSUS Democracy

NARRATIVES FROM INDIA

Edited by

Ajay Gudavarthy

SAGE

Los Angeles | London | New Delhi
Singapore | Washington DC | Melbourne

First published in 2017 by

 SAGE Publications India Pvt Ltd
B1/I-1 Mohan Cooperative Industrial Area
Mathura Road, New Delhi 110 044, India
www.sagepub.in

SAGE Publications Inc
2455 Teller Road
Thousand Oaks, California 91320, USA

SAGE Publications Ltd
1 Oliver's Yard, 55 City Road
London EC1Y 1SP, United Kingdom

SAGE Publications Asia-Pacific Pte Ltd
3 Church Street
#10-04 Samsung Hub
Singapore 049483

Published by Vivek Mehra for SAGE Publications India Pvt Ltd, typeset in 11/13 pt Century Schoolbook by Fidus Design Pvt. Ltd., Chandigarh and printed at Chaman Enterprises, New Delhi.

Library of Congress Cataloging-in-Publication Data Available
Name: Gudavarthy, Ajay, editor.
Title: Revolutionary violence versus democracy : narratives from India / edited by Ajay Gudavarthy.
Description: New Delhi, India ; Thousand Oaks, California : SAGE Publications India, 2017. | Includes bibliographical references.
Identifiers: LCCN 2017033115 (print) | LCCN 2017040220 (ebook) | ISBN 9789386446961 (Web PDF) | ISBN 9789386446978 (ePub) | ISBN 9789386446954 (print pdf : alk. paper)
Subjects: LCSH: Democracy—India. | Political violence—India. | Communism—India.
Classification: LCC JQ281 (ebook) | LCC JQ281 .R49 2017 (print) | DDC 954.05/3—dc23
LC record available at https://lccn.loc.gov/2017033115

ISBN: 978-93-864-4695-4 (HB)

SAGE Team: Abhijit Baroi, Sandhya Gola, Deepti Thapa and Ritu Chopra

To Trevor Stack—endearing and enigmatic

Thank you for choosing a SAGE product!
If you have any comment, observation or feedback,
I would like to personally hear from you.
Please write to me at **contactceo@sagepub.in**

Vivek Mehra, Managing Director and CEO, SAGE India.

Bulk Sales

SAGE India offers special discounts
for purchase of books in bulk.
We also make available special imprints
and excerpts from our books on demand.

For orders and enquiries, write to us at

Marketing Department
SAGE Publications India Pvt Ltd
B1/I-1, Mohan Cooperative Industrial Area
Mathura Road, Post Bag 7
New Delhi 110044, India

E-mail us at **marketing@sagepub.in**

Get to know more about SAGE

Be invited to SAGE events, get on our mailing list.
Write today to **marketing@sagepub.in**

This book is also available as an e-book.

Contents

Introduction: Is Violence Necessary for Revolutionary Change Today?

Political mobilisation across the globe is undergoing transformation. Amidst the many changes, one of the pertinent questions that is resurfacing is the issue of relevance of political violence, or more specifically revolutionary violence, and its efficacy in forging radical social/political change. As democratic sensibilities spread in terms of fuller participation, wider and more open sense of difference of opinion, more microscopic interest group formation, complexities related to the question of representation that get articulated as issues of organisational hierarchy and hegemony of leaders over followers, scepticism about all forms of constituency-based mobilisation and long-term goals of organised movements as against the more immediate interests of those involved in those organisations, the question of use of violence as a legitimate and also effective means of bringing about social/political change has come under stress. Michel Foucault, reflecting some of these concerns, questioned the legacy of 'moral authority' of the leaders when 'the intellectual spoke the truth to those who had yet to see it, in the name of those who were forbidden to speak the truth; he was conscience, consciousness, and eloquence'. He sarcastically argued that intellectuals would state 'what freedom consisted of, what one had to do in political life, how to behave in regard to others, and so forth' (quoted from Miller 1994, 188). Along with such new found democratic sensibilities, the issue remains if the costs of using violence actually match up to the gains it brings for the social groups in whose name it is being deployed (even if one were to make a cold cost and benefit analysis of revolutionary violence), or it merely ends up using the subaltern social groups as cannon fodder for the ostensibly higher goals of those in the leadership ranks. Further, given the nature of the changes under the neoliberal economic order which is faceless and dispersed unlike the previous feudal regimes or national governments that were authoritarian in nature, it becomes pertinent to ask who exactly are the targets of this kind of violence and what does it yield. In a post-Westphalian reality, definitive targets get replaced by series of networks.

We could also argue in terms of further changes in the nature of democracy brought about by new social media where ideas can be more freely expressed and the battlefield of ideas is ever-expanding, even if the scope to realise them is shrinking. If one considers politics in the final sense as a conflict of ideas, then violence might come across as a less viable strategy in allowing for contesting ideas. Again, Foucault, representative of much of this kind of 'modern' political sensibility, argues for politics represented by an intellectual who refuses to 'issue blueprints for the future' and who is 'incessantly on the move' and 'doesn't know exactly where he is heading nor what he will think tomorrow' (quoted from Miller 1994, 189). Similarly, electoral politics, unlike in many of the Western countries, seem to be at the peak of their dynamism with, for instance, voter turnout in India increasing with every general elections. There is a sense of empowerment in terms of a self-belief that a vote can alter destinies and can deliver more effective modes of governance. Democracy in this sense has emerged as an ever-expanding field representing a kind of global 'politics of hope'.

However, alongside all of these changes, there seems to be social groups that are necessarily, structurally at the receiving end of some of these palpable changes. They seem to fall through the net of development and governance. It is such groups that are still persisting, and justifiably so, with more extra-institutional modes of resistance. Even if these subaltern social groups do not hold lofty ideals about meta-structural transformation and idealistic imaginations to fight for the emancipation of all of humanity, and even if they lack an effective imagination of alternative models of development, they seem to need more violent modes of protest for mere survival. Violence is an everyday reality for many who fall through the cracks of restless growth stories across the globe, and they might believe that violence alone makes them heard. Much of the ongoing political battle in Central India is one such story. Tribals who are recklessly displaced and forcefully impoverished through an ongoing process of 'primitive accumulation' cannot but resort to more violent forms of protest because they are seen to be dispensable and without stakes of any kind in the new urbanised development model pursued by all of the 'mainstream' political parties and ideologies (Corbridge, Harriss and Jeffrey 2013). Democracy and constitutional governance makes very little sense for both the resisting groups and militant political mobilisation by the Maoists, as well as the state. It is a literal everyday battle over claiming and reclaiming sovereignty, in its territorial and more philosophical sense of inalienability of the 'people' residing in these territories.

While democracy initiates a complex process of inclusion and exclusion, keeping the majority in the waiting lounge of development, there continues to be a minority that is necessarily, structurally produced, which the promise of democracy fails to lure. Democracy presents not a linear and a clear line of mobility but a rather crooked line that offers a range of choices whose outcomes are not clearly visible. It could combine the space for cultural assertion with economic dispossession as is the case with majority of *Bahujan*—social groups such as the Dalits and the backward classes in the vast rural hinterlands of India. Or the open net of reservations that might not be all inclusive but produces a vocal and visible middle class among the subalterns. Or it could demand cultural subjugation with an elusive promise of economic integration, as is the case with the minority Muslim population in India or those in majority in Kashmir. For such groups, democracy becomes a ground, a template of negotiation, a game of getting included bit by bit. This could create a 'politics of hope' as much as a 'politics of anxiety'. There cannot be a clear assessment that such social groups can make or afford about their future. It is a surreal combination of hope and despair. They might feel empowered, powerless and dormant, all at the same time. Will there be a terminal point where this game of inclusion–exclusion can no longer be played effectively by those controlling the institutions of constitutional democracy? Or a tipping point where such subaltern groups move beyond mere 'contextual negotiations' and dream something larger in terms of more fundamental and sustainable change to their everyday existence? Maoists in India constitute one such political formation that is of the view that structural conflicts cannot endlessly sustain and self-propel themselves, and therefore, a more robust mobilisation against the very idea of the current economic and political system is not only feasible but a necessity. For them, revolutionary violence is a necessary mode of political mobilisation to counter the invisibilised violence of the current political system. It continues to believe that social groups would eventually get exhausted with the inclusion–exclusion game of modern democracy and begin to speak the language of revolution. However, revolution for them without deploying violent means makes very little sense, even in the current phase of capitalist growth. This book, based on the experiences from the ongoing armed political conflict lead by the Maoists in India, is an attempt to contextualise and throw light on this perspective and its relevance. It is important to comprehend this articulation, even if to understand the nature and limits of democracy.[1]

---

[1] Among recent literature on the Maoist politics, see Jeffrey, Sen and Singh (2013) and Gudavarthy (2014).

Political Economy of Violence

State formation in India, unlike Europe, was established by entering into accommodation with feudalism and not obliterating it. D. D. Kosambi refers to this as shifts in the mode of production taking place through 'adjustment and not displacement'. The coexistence of multiple modes of production creates a unique social formation in India, with a distinct historical space for culture and other social aspects. Whether Maoists ascribe a similar place for culture in their strategy of revolution or not, they, however, subscribe to this formulation of Kosambi in regarding India still remaining a 'semi-feudal semi-colonial' social formation. Kosambi observes, and this remains true for most of India even today, that 'the country had an immense feudal and pre-feudal accumulation of wealth which did not turn directly into modern capital' (1964, 10 cited in Chattopadhyay 2002). He further argues, 'the older cults and forms were not demolished by force but assimilated. Superstition reduced the need, for violence. Much more brutality would have been necessary had Indian history developed along the same lines as that of Europe or the Americas' (1964, 21).

Within this mosaic of cultural mediation, caste played the primary role of mediating the relations between the economy, polity and social dynamics. In other words, the caste system absorbed and processed the matrix of violence between the various domains. Here, he argues, 'caste is class at a primitive level of production, a religious method of forming social consciousness in such a manner that the primary producer is deprived of his surplus with the minimum coercion' (Chattopadhyay 2005, 59). In other words, there was a continuous trade-off between culture and violence. This precisely was the critique that Ambedkar offered against Marx's formulation of India belonging to an Asiatic mode of production, wherein he argued that what caste represented was not 'merely' division of labour but 'division of labourers'. The practice of untouchability, unique to Indian cultural ethos, was a mode of violently regulating social and economic life without the direct coercive intervention or necessity of modern governmental mechanisms. If you will, it was a case of violent regulation being outsourced by the state. It was deeply bio-political in nature and demarcated areas or spheres of operation that Foucault, in marking the character of modern power, ascribes to the governmental regulatory power of the modern state based on census and other technologies.[2] Here, one could argue that in an India of 'our modernity', there was a convergence between the hierarchies in tradition with regulatory governmental powers of the modern technologies. Much of post-colonial writing on India rightly theorised that 'the new caste politics therefore defies characterization in terms of the easy dichotomy of mordernization theory. It is not a wholly modern practice, since it is based on caste; equally it is not wholly traditional, as it puts caste to an unprecedented modern use' (Kaviraj 2010a, 228). However, what this description fails to extrapolate is the fact that these dynamics are not lateral or horizontal but a case where hierarchies internal to the ladder-like structure of caste enter into an alliance or convergence with the regulatory mechanisms of modern politics. 'Secularisation of caste' is as much a story of mobilisation of a traditional institution of caste for modern purposes of electoral mobilisation as much as a continuation of traditional, rigid and violent caste distinctions. Without capturing the latter, we cannot comprehend either the role of caste or the interface between culture and violence in modern India. Within the interstices of social change is the unchanging reproduction of structures through 'silently violent' means. The idea and

---

[2] Much of post-colonial theory and rendering of history overlooks this aspect of caste and instead intriguingly adopts a Western reading by laying emphasis on modern governmental regulation as being new and a coercive aspect of social life.

practice of 'community' is as much a mobilising force as it is a repository of tremendous reproduction of violence—both physical and more insidious forms. Without accounting for this mode of violence, one will fail to contextualise the idea and practice of revolutionary violence.[3]

The underlying communitarian subtext was politically articulated by Gandhi through his 'politics of accommodation' during the anti-colonial national movement.

> As the nationalist movement grew and looked for a mass basis, Gandhi provided a link between powerful sections of the bourgeoisie and the peasantry through the doctrine of nonviolence, trusteeship, and the glorification of the Indian village community. For this and other reasons, the nationalist movement did not take a revolutionary form. (Moore 1984, 316)

A more sympathetic reader of Gandhi could well argue that what he was looking for was a mode of social change that does not undermine the collective, fraternal and communitarian aspect of Indian social life. Non-violence was a way of devising change without the threat of the process of individuation that accompanies modern industrialised societies.[4] Community, as in village republics and not in civil society, was the necessary mediating institution between capital and state. Instead of becoming a source of 'passive acceptance', community could, as Gandhi was experimenting, become a rich resource for 'passive resistance'. Community was the only institution that could undermine capital without the adversities of violence.

---

[3] Post-colonial scholarship, on one hand, undermines these inherent forms of violence in community and, on the other, partly exaggerates the violence in the regulatory mechanisms of the modern state. In doing this, it misses on many of the sociological aspects of the functioning of community and instead captures more of an imagined idea of community outside modernity.

[4] In a sense, Ambedkar also laid stress on the idea of fraternity, though it is one of the modern associational kinds and not that of the communitarian variant emphasised by Gandhi.

Gandhi argued, 'It is my firm conviction that if the state suppressed capitalism by violence it will be caught in the evils of violence itself and fail to develop nonviolence at any time' (Moore 1984, 375).

It was not that Gandhi did not pay heed to the hierarchies that community produced, but he wished to address them differently. This was to be achieved essentially outside of the 'political' domain and through both cooperative– social means and personal self-motivated transformation. Individual here does not talk the language of rights against the collective but as a corporeal entity representative of self-imposed change. Gandhian 'gradual revolution' meant a separation of the political from the social. 'Politics of accommodation' required a separation of 'the techniques of political organisation from the method of social reform'. Politics was a domain of assertion, while social was a domain of change through cooperation and consensus. Gandhi therefore altered periods of mass movement (political) with 'constructive work' (social). In other words, 'the approach amounted to an indirect attack on the normative and institutional foundations of traditional, social and economic and political hierarchies' (Frankel 1988, 25). Electoral mobilisation at the village level to the Panchayats was envisaged as the institutional mode of preserving the collective, yet forging social/political reform. In this sense, as Maoists today concede, elections are perhaps the largest impediment to a revolution, along with caste. Democracy and revolution have become mutually exclusive.

It was this model of politics crafted by Gandhi that was followed by the post-Independence Congress. It developed a mechanism of reconciling contradictory social groups into a political alliance, making it difficult for them to enter into conflicts. It was a patronage system working itself on 'faction chains'. Rajini Kothari referred to this as the

'Congress System' where, 'a system of patronage was worked out in the countryside, traditional institutions of kin and caste were gradually drawn and involved, and a structure of pressures

and compromises was developed ... and an intricate structure
of conflict, mediation, bargaining and consensus was developed
within the framework of the Congress'. (1964, 1163)

'Congress System' was representative of what Rudolph
and Rudolph (1987) referred to as 'persistent centrism' in
Indian politics. They noted or predicted in the 1980s that

> Significant as the changes since 1975 have been, they are not likely
> to alter the centrist character of Indian politics in the foreseeable
> future. In the absence of state fragmentation, revolution, or
> international cataclysm, the social and institutional determinants
> of centrism are likely to prove more powerful and durable than
> those supporting class or confessional politics. (59)

The political process was oriented towards consensus and
compromise, and not conflict, as Gandhi had envisaged.
However, this was based on a system of patronage, and
it brought competing social groups together politically
but not socially. The mutual prejudice and conflicting
attitudes continued. What it lead in course of time was
distancing and ghettoisation of social groups from each
other. Political alliances such as the later day 'Bahujan
Samaj' could not rework the prejudices between the Dalits,
OBCs and the Muslims, which in a sense prepared a
working ground for more right-wing mobilisation based
on religious/confessional consolidation. This also worked
towards more violence within the system as there were no
political alternatives for groups that were being mobilised,
or political representation did not translate into social and
economic mobility. This porous existence of many of the
subaltern social groups created a pressure cooker kind
of situation where mobility had to be achieved within
the set limits of this dual existence where the political
representation was pitted against social and economic
stagnation.

Therefore, the question that remains to be answered
in the Indian context is 'Can there be any method of
transforming the entire social structure other than a direct

attack on the propertied castes and classes?' (Frankel 1988, 27). In this sense, does not revolutionary violence continue to present that alternative to 'gradual revolution' and continues to remain relevant for various social groups in India? However, one could also ask if we really understand what it means to transform 'the entire social structure'. Does history, having initiated the democratic change that is 'molecular' in nature, offer us an opportunity to go back to talking of changing the 'entire social structure' without taking into consideration the changes already initiated by the processes of democracy? Does resorting to violence represent the forceful negation of acknowledging those changes? Or does it serve the purpose of highlighting the inadequacy of that change without necessarily bringing about a change in the 'entire social structure'? In this sense, could one argue that democracy and revolutionary violence mutually contribute to make the process of transformation more self-reflective rather than obstruct each other? Where and how do we locate and focus the nodal point of transformation?

One way to approach the idea of transformation could be to analyse if the fragmented nature of 'social reform' is dissipating social power into smaller fragments or reconfiguring itself into larger 'multitudes'. Recent events across the globe including the Occupy movement in the United States, Arab Spring in the Middle East or Brazilian Spring in Latin America represent a new kind of cross-class alliances against the idea of the 'system'. There is something fundamentally wrong with the social and political system as it deepens a sense of crisis, helplessness and worthlessness at the individual level and dysfunctional institutions at the level of the collective. Corruption has emerged as an 'empty signifier' that could galvanise various social groups, including those that have relatively benefited from the new kind of growth, and there has been even deeper dissatisfaction with the very nature of representation. Questioning representation has become a new mode of refashioning issues related to economic inequalities and those related to recognition and dignity. These uprisings or springs have been mobilising without resorting to violence and stand as a challenge to the idea of forging change through revolutionary violence. They have succeeded in installing a feeling of 'we are the 99%'—something revolutionary movements across the globe have failed to achieve after the era of mass revolutions in the 1940s. Perhaps, China was the last of the violent insurrectionary movements that mobilised a new collective with a common revolutionary imagination, after which revolutions have remained compulsively fragmented and represented a bare minority.

Could these new modes of mobilisation that configure into 'the people' as an effective political formation, beyond the constitutional claims to sovereignty by nations, represent an effective alternative to change through revolutionary violence? Do they not initiate the same kind of structural change without the costs of violence? Or could these springs, on the contrary, be a desperate reminder that revolutionary change cannot be achieved without more robust extra-institutional means? They offer us a symbolism or simulacrum of a revolution without a revolution. Alain Badiou argues, for instance, that

> the Occupy Wall Street movement's slogan 'we are the 99%', with its supposed capacity to unite people, is completely empty. ... Far from being the 99%—even symbolically—the courageous young folks occupying the Wall Street represented no more than a small clutch of people ..., whose fate is to vanish as soon as the 'movement' party was over. (2015).

In India, the crisis has been deepening for a long time and had been best articulated as the failure of 'passive revolution' and the way political crisis deepens with the success of a new kind of predatory growth and capitalist order.

> It is not a condition of 'abnormality' which could be expected to disappear with a change in leaders or parties. It is coming to be

a condition of stressful, violent normalcy of this late, backward, increasingly unreformist, capitalist order. It is different even from a standard Gramscian case; because here even a passive revolution has not succeeded, but is lapsing into failure. (Kaviraj 2010b, 142)

If crisis is all-pervasive, does it necessarily mean revolutionary violence remains the only viable means of overcoming it? Or does this kind of a crisis also create a crisis in revolutions in making them potentially authoritarian and sharing the same characters of the 'system'? Or does crisis push more of an unequal social order since the subaltern cannot afford protest beyond a level of distress? And it also blocks effective alternative visions. Although Marx pronounced that 'revolutionary subject is made in course of revolutions', it does not actually explain how they come into being. One could perhaps more consistently argue that revolutionary militancy does manifest an urge or a spirit to break the routinised forms of violence, whether they actually have an alternative vision or not.

Violence in Indian democracy needs to be observed and understood even outside the context of revolutionary violence of the Maoists.[5] It is more pervasive, and often the Maoists have become a symbol that has been useful to the ruling elite to block out many other kinds of violence entrenched in the political system. Violence of the Maoists blocks the possibility of focussing on more generic 'crises of governability'. As Atul Kohli remarks,

> Issues of changing values and new patterns of stratification, including the emergence of class conflict, are important for understanding a situation of increasing socioeconomic conflict. The social mobilization that results from these processes of socioeconomic change typically outpaces the institutional

---

[5] I referred to Indian democracy as a *'Violent Democracy'* in my previous book (Gudavarthy 2014).

capacities for accommodation, thus contributing to crises of governability. (1990, 31)

There are many other forms of violence endemic to democracy in India that have nothing to do with the Maoists. Caste- and religion-based violence can account for a much larger number of deaths than what Maoists would have committed in more than three decades of their mobilisation. Even if we were to reduce violence to a mere headcount, the number of Sikhs killed in the anti-Sikh riot in Delhi in 1984 and the number of Muslims killed in Gujarat in 2002 would account for a much larger figure than that ascribed to the violence committed by the Maoists in three decades of their militant mobilisation. Yet, why does the Maoist violence become or come to be represented as more endemic and the other kind of violence more episodic? One is structural, the other an aberration? One is outside law, the other within the legal means and limits set by democracy? One is committed by gun-wielding militias, the other by those representing political parties and democracy itself? In fact, the violence by the Maoists has helped eclipse other kinds of violence and the possibility that 'the relationship between violence and democracy is enabling rather than inherently oppositional'. Further, for instance, in relation to the violence related to caste or religion, 'democracy, civil society, and Hindu nationalism have coexisted very comfortably, working in tandem rather than in opposition ... the structures and discourses of constitutional democracy, civic nationalism, and civil society were used to justify, condone and allow the violence in Gujarat to continue' (Basu and Roy 2007, 13).

Democracy, in a sense, concentrated in the idea of a popularly elected government was often the justification invoked in the context of violence in Gujarat. In fact, the government under whose watchful eyes Gujarat carnage took place was elected repeatedly—thrice to be precise with a considerable majority—precisely because it 'dared' to allow riots to let loose.[6] The tipping point in liberal democracy for the principle of majority to convert into a majoritarian norm is not as wide as we often perceive. Has not this process of entrenched violence in a democracy got accentuated with a new kind of convergence between a neoliberal economic order, fragmented and vigorously competing inward-oriented identity politics and a majoritarian ethos of religious nationalism? If democracy is inherently violent in the modes of governance, then why does the debate on revolutionary violence stand out in 'violent democracies' like that of India? What kind of a conceptual difference do we draw between routinised violence and episodic/organised violence of the Maoist kind? Would it not be a possibility to argue that episodic/organised violence of the Maoist kind is a way to highlight and grasp the sources of routinised violence?

Genealogies of Revolutionary Violence

With a long history of 'politics of accommodation' that got expressed in the crisis of 'passive revolution' in the economic sphere, 'gradual revolution' in the social sphere and 'silent revolution' in the political sphere as the central template around which Indian politics moved, the 1990s brought in neoliberal reforms to the already existing slow pace of change. A shift took place from Nehruvian development state to an 'interventionist state' that was not

---

[6] I explored this limit of civil society in my book *Politics of Post-Civil society* (Gudavarthy 2013) and argued that much of what is considered undemocratic and hegemonic actually grows within the corridors of civil society. I tried to conceptualise how current political movements are possibly going beyond civil society in order to negotiate and undermine the structures perpetuated and reproduced by the state and civil society in tandem (Gudavarthy 2013).

a welfare state but formulated a large number of welfare policies. Ironically, with neoliberal reforms, the state came to the centre stage with a large number of rights-based legislations, though the extent of their effective implementation can be questioned and debated about (Jayal 2014). This 'double movement' of the expanded role of the private and global capital in the economic sphere and extended role of the state in the political sphere led to a process of 'accumulation by dispossession' and further entrenched engagement with the state. It was no longer a centrist polity of the Nehruvian era but a centrism that accentuated disparities, instead of accommodating and moderating them.

This shift had its own kind of impact on the protest politics. It led to sharp decline of the trade union movement, collapse of the farmers' movement, a rise in distress migration, swelling of the informal and unorganised sector and decline of the Left parties and their ability to mobilise. Streets vacated by the subaltern groups were occupied by the urban activism of the middle classes around corruption and issues of governance. Within this changing matrix was the unabated armed and militant protest mobilisation organised by the Maoists. Alongside the Maoist movement were those more visible protests against various developmental projects such as the POSCO in Odisha or displacement induced by developmental projects such as Polavaram in Telangana or setting up of nuclear power plants in Kudankulam in Tamil Nadu. Development became the single most contested idea, which shaped the content and contours of protest in the contemporary Indian political map.

It is in this broad context that various essays in this volume revisit the question of revolutionary violence. Varavara Rao, in his lead essay that also lays out the nature of current Maoist politics, argues that 'As Mao-tse-Tung put during the Great Proletariat Cultural Revolution in China that it is a "three in one" or a triangle struggle, the base being the class struggle and the scientific experiment and development are its other angles'. Militant armed struggle and development are considered the key cornerstones for advancing the Maoist movement for establishing 'Maoist Guerrilla zones', and therefore, the question of violence needs to be understood in the context of its revolutionary (read Class) content. He argues that establishing a 'Janatana Sarkar' is the concrete form that the New Democratic Revolution is taking in much of Central India. Violence by armed squads cannot be made sense of outside this context, which would only empty it of its essential political content. It is to promote an alternative model of development that is more local and participatory in nature and also aims to transform the nature of ownership relations in the area. Village development committees strive to implement land reforms, provide irrigation and protect water resources, supply seeds and manures and provide primary education and health facilities. As part of this, he argues that the Maoist party is fighting against repression 'with brave heart and sacrificing their lives to transform the future generations into new human beings'. Finally, he hopes that the leadership would become more organic as the 'ideological hegemony' would loosen its vice-like grip, and therefore, in essence 'there is no difference between the people and the party'.

This basic model of class struggle in one of India's most underdeveloped areas raises serious questions about how much and how far can this mode of revolutionary struggle be extended. Would it be applicable outside the pockets that Maoists are currently holding? It could well be argued that the Maoist movement receded from the plains mostly due to unabated state repression but also due to changes in the nature of agrarian political economy, essentially expansion in the non-farm sector and increasing commodification of land and land relations with the conversion of agricultural land into real estate. In spite of persisting agrarian crisis, Maoists could not take hold in many of the states. Could it be a manifestation of the new calculation that 'masses' at large are making about the costs they need to pay for supporting an armed rebellion? It could be possible that revolution has lost its old idealised imagination and can be conceived as another service-delivery mechanism, given the nature of activities that village development committees headed or organised by the Maoists partake in. Similarly, violence obstructs basic participatory ethos, given the sensibilities that a democracy creates. Would it not be then appropriate to argue that in such contexts revolutionary violence looks more obstructionist than empowering? In only those contexts where the reach of the state is limited and there is utter neglect or reckless displacement that the Maoist modes of organising hold value.

It is in this context that Anand Teltumbde's contribution further theoretically contextualises the essence of revolutionary violence. Drawing mostly on classical literature by Marx, Engels and Lenin, he argues that violence is not exalted but a structural necessity given the nature of the state–capital interface, which creates what he refers to as 'structural violence'. He argues,

> Structural violence has a causal relationship with revolutions. It is important, therefore, to recognize the existence of structural violence, which is far more indirect and insidious than direct violence. Structural violence is typically built into the political, social, and cultural institutions that map up the societal structure.

However, Anand strikes a note of caution in arguing that 'no revolution so far has confirmed to basic Marxist scheme', and it cannot, more so now, as capitalism has creatively reconfigured itself. However, revolutionaries seem to be stuck to the idea of 'fidelity to the event'. 'It is a paradox of kind that the behaviour of bourgeoisie reflects dialectical materialism while that of proletarian revolutionaries, mechanical idealism'. These observations of Anand Teltumbde offer us an occasion to raise a series of questions. First, given the nature of Indian polity that we traced in the previous section, what fundamental differences or distinctness should an 'Indian Revolution' have? Can armed methods coexist with more popular modes of mobilisation that Maoists in their earlier phase did experiment but could not hold on to due to state repression and Maoists' own insistence on armed means being of primary or even exclusive significance? The emphasis gradually shifted to more militarised means. Is this shift more strategic or structural? Can violent means coexist with a more participatory approach, including that of partaking in electoral politics? Is it a realistic proposal for the Maoist party to forge alliances with other mass struggles? Did these experiments in popular alliances with other struggles against land acquisition or displacement fail because Maoists often follow their involvement with attempts to convert them into more militant forms?

Some of the above questions continue to dictate much of the dilemmas surrounding revolutionary violence. This emanates partly from the collapse of various kinds of discriminations and exclusions into a monolithic term of 'structural violence'. For instance, can we consider unemployment as 'violence' and equate it with deaths due to famine or drought induced through colonial policies or deaths due to extrajudicial killings? While one might strike a connect between the two, would it be analytically helpful to collapse the two except for drawing a rhetorical legitimacy for the use of counter-violence? The other significant reason for the inability of the Maoists to combine more militant means with other kinds of available spaces or the immediacy with which they convert open demonstrations into more militant modes is that their understanding of non-violence is drawn from radical theoretical literature in general and from its invocation by Gandhi in particular. 'For example Franz Fanon's 1963 *The Wretched of the Earth* portrays nonviolence as a doctrine that served imperial interests, deeming armed struggle legitimate in the face of colonialism' (Hallward and Normann 2015, 24). Similarly, Herbert Marcuse arguing against the liberal precept of tolerance makes a case for 'right to intolerance', or Walzer refers to non-violence as a 'disguised form of surrender' (Hallward and Normann 2015, 24). If revolutionary violence continues to hold sway and comes across given the massive proportions of dispossession as one legitimate mode of protest, it is equally relevant to argue given the transformations in late capitalism that they need to be combined with other forms of protest. There has been, by and large, no alternative imagination of what this kind of combinatory modes of struggle could look like.[7]

Within this intensifying debate on the possible limits to revolutionary violence and growing criticism from the civil rights and other organisations, Maoists reinvented kidnap as one such militant-revolutionary strategy that is overtly less violent but could possibly be as much of a revolutionary strategy. G. Haragopal, who was himself a mediator on three occasions in Koyyur in Andhra Pradesh, in Odisha and then in Chhattisgarh when the Maoists kidnapped officers of the Indian Administrative Services, observes that 'this form of resistance unexpectedly came back with the Malkangiri Kidnap in Odisha in 2011, after a gap of almost two decades'. Haragopal lays out a detailed narrative around how the mediation between the Maoists and the state governments took place and how on all the occasions that the Maoists abducted an officer, they laid down a string of demands related to the tribals. Mostly, the demands were related to issues regarding land for the

---

[7] Arundhati Roy, in more figurative than substantive terms, refers to this possible combinatory form as Maoists becoming more of 'Gandhians with guns' (2010). I attempted formulating one such combinatory strategy through the idea of 'refolution' (Gudavarthy 2013).

tribals, adequately compensating those already displaced due to developmental projects, release of those illegally detained and inclusion of smaller or lesser-known tribes in the list of Scheduled Tribes (STs).[8] This way, the Maoists succeeded in raising an important debate on development and those who are being dispossessed due to such developmental activities. This, in a sense, was also one of the purposes of the Maoists in using kidnap as a specific strategy with much less bloodshed. It is not a coincidence that on all the three above-mentioned occasions, the Maoists released those kidnapped unharmed, even though on more than one occasion, the demands made by the Maoists were not met by the respective state governments.

However, how far are these innovations sustainable, given the larger goals of the Maoist movement? As Haragopal observes, 'One of the problems, of course, with the Maoist movement is their public pronouncements of protracted armed struggle, overthrow of the Indian state, as if that is the only preoccupation of the movement'. If such novel combinatory strategies have to succeed, Maoists would have to interrogate the prioritisation of their demands and strategy. Should the capture of state power necessarily be the central demand around which the entire revolutionary strategy needs to be formulated? Or, on the contrary, is it possible to visualise revolution more as a process, not an event, where questioning and reconstituting sovereign power could be one such process and not necessarily the starting point? Violence is also essentially about sovereignty and challenging the state's monopoly over the use of violence. Challenging the sovereignty of the state also makes the state less dialogic and become more lawless. If sovereignty is imagined more

---

[8] This was also a rare occasion where print and electronic media were compelled to cover the news of the tribals on their prime time and front pages.

in terms of 'power to the people', then mobilising larger multitudes around complexly interconnected issues would expand the revolutionary imagination, rather than restricting it to the idea of ceasing power through violent means.

Why Maoists feel capture of state power is essential for any revolution to proceed from political to social and economic transformation is partly clarified by the 'righteous lawlessness' of the state by floating vigilante organisations such as the Salwa Judum (SJ), where the arbitrary power to carry out extrajudicial violence is outsourced to the non-tribals in the tribal belt. Here is a case where democracy is not just connected to violence or exceptionalism but explicitly depends on it. It is democracy that intervenes through the most brutal forms of violence and extraordinary laws. It is instructive here to refer to Alain Badiou who reminds us that 'today the enemy is not called Empire or Capital. It's called Democracy. What today, prevents the radical questioning of capitalism itself is precisely belief in the democratic form of the struggle against capitalism' (quoted from Zizek 2007, 7). This again is the line of the argument by the Maoists: democratic forms do not sustain themselves when fundamental questions of ownership are raised, since sovereignty is connected more to the issue of private property and control over resources rather than the idea of 'the people'. People become dispensable not only in 'remote' tribal belts that are struggling over questions of survival and economic dispossession, but a policy of exceptionalism can also be adopted in border states like Kashmir, which is more about identity and self-determination. The state responds in both the cases with extraordinary laws and extrajudicial violence.[9] The most self-evident argument that security

---

[9] It is appropriate to recollect here that while Kashmir continues with its long-time demand for *azadi*, essentially meaning self-determination, Nagaland under Muivah has been recently willing

forces developed in justifying such dispensability of 'the people' is one of 'collateral damage', which is elaborately discussed in the survey by the Human Rights Forum (HRF), with reference to various incidents including the infamous killings at Sarkeguda, Edesmetta and Kotipalli.[10]

This dark side of democracy raises a few pertinent questions as to what could be the possible equation between a democracy that is porous and incrementally inclusive and one that is blatantly violent. How can revolutionary struggles reconcile these two dimensions of democracy? Maoists have mostly not responded to the inclusive part of democracy and treated it as a hindrance to revolution and a legitimising tool of the ruling elite, even though the beneficiaries of those inclusive policies have preferred not to view it in those terms. This gap between the Maoists and those included into the portals of democracy remains to be bridged. This could also well be the reason that Maoists use more of violent measures to validate their reading of democracy as essentially being violent. However, even if this were to be largely true, Maoists as part of their revolutionary strategy need to take the more porous dimension of democracy seriously, if only to undermine the possibility of a process of revolution becoming a statist project and revolutionary violence arbitrary, like that of the state. HRF's survey report observes that 'brutal violence by the Maoists has resulted in the death and maiming of not only a number of police and paramilitary personnel but also unarmed civilians. At times, they have deliberately targeted and killed civilians'. This is a clear indication that revolutionary violence can become as arbitrary in

---

to enter into a dialogue to drop the demand for secession and be reintegrated into India.

[10] Refer to Human Rights Forum 2010. These securitised discourses on collateral damage also enter the political lexicon; for instance, the lynching of a Muslim in Dadri for being suspected of eating beef was referred to by the Finance Minister Arun Jaitley as a 'stray incident'.

the name of revolution, as any other kind of violence. It is, therefore, necessary to critically interrogate these forms of violence, even if one does not reduce it to a simple-minded criminality or an issue of 'law and order'.

In the next section of the book, we have included three such essays that critically interrogate the nature and consequences of revolutionary violence. Neera Chandhoke concludes her essay on a note of caution.

> In sum, we have to be aware of the indeterminacy and the unpredictability of this avatar of politics, and the incapacity of human beings to control violence, or rather the relentless impulse of violence to control those who handle it for definable ends. Any study of revolutionary violence has, therefore, to track the dilemmas, the quandaries, and the political predicaments that stalk the practice of revolutionary violence.

In other words, we might have to recognise certain autonomy to the logic or path dependency that might be forced in the very use of violence as a means. Does violence then have a life of its own? For instance, violence invariably invites fear and silences the majority from partaking in such methods of politicisation. Similarly, violence invokes secrecy and lays social processes vulnerable to everyday machinations that we time and again witnessed with violence related to the executions of those identified as 'informers' by the Maoists. Violence also disables us from grasping the sense of political consciousness. For instance, in many of the Maoist strong holds can one be reassured that social groups have moved away from caste and communal prejudices? The Mahbubnagar district of Telangana, where the Maoists till recently had a strong hold, soon after became a constituency where a candidate from the BJP won Assembly elections. It was strongly argued by many in Telangana that being a centre for Maoist activities, Mahbubnagar would be representative of progressive and secular sensibilities. Why did those who held such beliefs fail to assess the political consciousness?

How did 'the people' who were widely believed to hold sympathies for the Maoists soon turn and respond to more sectarian kind of mobilisation? Did the nature of Maoist mobilisation leave little open space to deliberate any or all of these issues?

It is in this context that Sumanta Banerjee in his essay argues for a 'post-Maoist political strategy' of revolution. He argues that

> Maoist leaders had remained crippled by a limited understanding of these complexities of the vast heterogeneous Indian society. Unable to formulate a multi-pronged strategy for these various layers of our society, the Maoists concentrated mainly on the most exploited layer—the tribal poor in the inaccessible forest and hill areas of the Dandakaranya region of central India and Jharkhand in the east.

Along with the various changes to the nature of class divisions that Banerjee points out, there are complex issues of recognition and representation that are not only co-primary as Nancy Fraser points out (Fraser 2000) but also work many a time at cross purposes. These microscopic processes cannot easily be coalesced into larger structural analysis, and even if one manages to do that politically, they still need to be negotiated on their own set of terms. For instance, not only is there no larger class unity that can be found among the working class and the peasantry, but there is also a growing phenomenon of intra-subaltern conflicts. They could include conflicts between the OBCs and the Dalits, various sub-castes of the Dalits, Dalits and Muslims, and OBCs and Muslims, among others. Each of them has a specific and particularistic cultural context and history and also potential to reconfigure many other kinds of conflict, including that of the nature of class conflicts. There cannot be a supra-class struggle that can override many of these conflicts. This kind of articulation of contradictions, in a sense, was also the unique contribution of Mao during the Chinese revolution. As Zizek remarks,

This is Mao's key point: the principal (universal) contradiction does not overlap with the contradiction which should be treated as dominant in a particular situation—the universal dimension literally resides in this particular contradiction. In each concrete situation, a different 'particular' contradiction is the predominant one, in the precise sense that, in order to win the fight for the resolution of the principal contradiction, one should treat a particular contradiction as a predominant one, to which all other struggles should be subordinated. In China under the Japanese occupation, patriotic unity against the Japanese was the predominant thing if Communists wanted to win the class struggle—any direct focusing on class struggle in these conditions went against class struggle itself. (2007, 6)

It is pertinent to ask what possibly could be the role of violent resistance in the post-Maoist strategy with issues related to recognition and dignity. Would not it be more productive to generate certain symbolic representations of values rather than violent mobilisation? It is therefore believed that Ambedkar rejected the idea of resolving the caste question and caste-based discrimination through violent means as he did not believe that violence can actually transform the cultural patterns of domination that exist at both material and symbolic plains.[11] Similarly, we could ask if violent means would not obstruct the emergence of heterogeneous modes of mobilisation and push the politics to more monolithic imagination of a single party emerging as a catch-all formation. Similarly, we could ask if violence also makes it difficult for the politics to shift strategies where necessary and instead begins to dictate it. For instance, the shift of the Maoist party from plains to the forests and to exclusively mobilising the tribals is actually out of a compulsion to wage an armed rebellion, as it became difficult in the plains both due

[11] Point borrowed from the presentation made by Gopal Guru in a seminar on 'Understanding Maoist Politics' organised by the Centre for Political Studies, JNU, 24–25 February 2014.

to state repression and due to changes in the agrarian economy. Maoists, instead of revising their strategy and looking for novel modes of mobilisation, preferred to move to more backward regions with a forest cover that allows them to carry out an armed mobilisation with the support of the tribal population.

It is along a similar line that K. Balagopal, who was once a staunch supporter and considered an ideologue of the Maoist politics, began to critically interrogate them. While he agrees that the Maoists or the then Naxalite movement had a social base among the landless and later in tribal areas, it has over a period of time become more militarised. He argues,

> A blanket condonation of the use of violence by a group that lives by its own norms, which are enforceable only by itself is no doubt unacceptable in any society, even when it is declared to be for the good of the oppressed, but the contrary argument that a positive response from the government would perhaps have delegitimised the argument for revolutionary violence was never considered.

It is a fact that the state responded primarily through repressive measures; however, a movement that proclaims itself to be political and radical should have thought of the possible consequences of increasingly militarising the struggle. Here, Balagopal observes that some of the consequences of this were armed squads becoming a substitute for struggle by the subaltern themselves, Maoists ending up killing more of their own social base than that of their enemies, increasing acts of violence that had no relation to or bearing on the immediate demands of the landless or tribals they represented, inability to respond to a generational change where the newer generations had a different set of aspirations born out of the relief that Maoist struggles in the past brought, degeneration into factious violence and creation of 'renegades' or surrendered Maoists who then became a law unto themselves in targeting the sympathisers of the Maoists. Many of these

observations raise serious questions about certain consequences of revolutionary violence where in spite of politics
they begin to border on arbitrariness.

Part of the explanation can be drawn from the fact that
violence needs an extreme justification, and in this, accepting anything short of extreme criticism is not possible.
Maoist methods would work in conditions of extreme
deprivation where violence is a necessity for survival
but where intermittent relief is possible, without a
structural transformation, and then Maoist movement
has no other mode of analysing it except as a compromise
or a manipulation by the state. This inability to link
relief with revolution, reform with revolution has been
a long-standing limitation of the Maoists. This has also
incapacitated them in understanding what kind of relief
identity politics provided to those suffering harsh caste-
based exclusion and stigma. Similarly, under neoliberal
conditions, the state is today in a position to also provide
a reversal of those in terms of compensation and other
measures (Sanyal 2010). Humanitarian aid or micro-
credit and self-help groups are examples of providing
concrete and immediate relief, even if they are part of
the same structural conditions. Maoists have mostly
been either at worst dismissive or at best indifferent to
these intermediary processes but have not attempted
a more positive theorisation in terms of the everyday
micro-processes. This has in itself made the Maoists more
dependent on a singular focus on armed mobilisation,
which in turn blinds them to micro-processes. This is a
vicious cycle that is difficult to break once it takes off.

The third section of the book focuses on these micro-
intermediary processes—a space between revolution and
the everyday. Who gets attracted to the Maoist movement
and why? What are the processes beyond the macro-lens
of class struggle and ideological frames? How do these
micro-processes get hooked to the modes of revolutionary
violence, and what impact does that violence have on their

individual lives and psyche? How is this impact different from that of those who are engaged in other kinds of non-revolutionary violence? Chitralekha attempts to shift the template and says,

> I argue in this paper that entry into the armed *dastas* (squads/ platoons) for many participants, in fact performs not just as means of access to the public sphere, but also as sites for construction of individual identities along pathways not always predictable by the imperatives of the collective. Quite different from dominant discourses on Naxalite politics and goals that emanate from or revolve around narratives of the Maoist leadership or ideologues, narratives of guerrillas—including those from the most oppressed classes—often ruminated with urgency, not so much on the formal struggle for equalization of group identity or resources, as on a deeply individual quest for recognition and self-actualisation.

Not deprivation but struggle for recognition is the matrix around which much of the micro-foundations of power and everyday struggles of the Maoists could be explained. This adds a fresh dimension in not only understanding the Maoist struggles but also the contours and nature of revolutionary violence.

Chitralekha points out that there are three types of cadre; she calls them drifters, opportunists and the committed; however, the question that remains relevant for all is, 'Where does the readiness, even eagerness to participate in violence derive from? How is the "readiness" to kill accomplished with such ostensible ease?' If one begins to explore a dimension, as Chitralekha does, below the known terrain of political mobilization, then we might have to raise a different set of questions regarding revolutionary violence. One of them could be that the possibility of what we call 'revolutionary violence' may not be as distant and distinct from other forms of violence. Or, to rephrase it, we could legitimately ask what could be the processes that keep this kind of violence of the Maoists necessarily revolutionary. Beyond the lens of political consciousness and political education, we need to put on board the fungibility of such violence into various other kinds of sectarian forms, and it is therefore only legitimate to ask of the Maoists what, if any, considerations have they included in their political programme.[12] These have been historical events and not mere conceptual generalizations.

> Swept up in the vortex of a political 'limit-experience', it was all but impossible to sort out what was genuinely creative (hence, in Deleuze's terms, truly 'revolutionary') and what was merely a blind reiteration of the most viciously destructive impulses (and thus, in Deleuze's view, a deadly reinforcement of the most rigid power relations, hence potentially 'fascist'. (Miller 1993, 240)

Foucault too, who keenly followed the French Maoists after 1975, began to address 'the fascism in us all'. French philosopher Andre Glucksmann argued for potential links between guerrilla violence and state terrorism of Stalin. These potential subterranean links need to be discussed as part of the revolution-making exercise.

Along similar lines, Lipika and Uday in their contribution attempt to negotiate the issue of agency and ask if the Maoist mobilization propels agency or mutes it. They argue for a more nuanced problematisation of agency in terms of 'antinomies of agency'. They argue,

> As such, those who deny subaltern agency in the Maoist insurgency as well as those who assume an excess of it are both

---

[12] One of the most notorious cases in the recent history has been that of a Maoist leader by the name Naeem, who not only surrendered but also became a 'serial killer', targeting those associated with civil rights organisations close to the Maoists. In one of the incidents, he killed Purushottam, general secretary of the Andhra Pradesh Civil Liberties Committee (APCLC), by beheading him in broad daylight in Hyderabad. This did lead to a debate in Andhra Pradesh as to what leads to such 'degeneration?' Is it an aberration or the danger of further ranks joining gangs is real? Maoists, as in many others instances, did not further reflect on these insidious underlying processes.

misled into error. By mistaking the terms of propaganda to be descriptions of empirical reality, as we have shown, a vast swathe of writings on the Maoists tends to paper over the complexity of micro-political realities.

As we pointed out earlier, micro-foundations of power relations lead to what can be variedly referred to as 'competing sovereignties', 'shared sovereignties', 'overlapping sovereignties', 'multiple sovereignties', or in Lipika and Uday's words, it could as well be termed 'non-sovereign agency', where agency is located within and not outside given power relations. To allude to previous literature on the question of agency, one could argue that it is 'not being entirely subsumed, as in Spivak, under the power of dominant discourse, or being, as in Guha, entirely voluntarist' (Nilsen and Roy 2015, 12).[13] Here the backward–forward movement in subaltern politics cannot be viewed exclusively in terms of compromise and limitations, as Maoists often do but a necessary or inescapable mode in which real-time politics move. This, in turn, can only be agreed upon when Maoist politics moves out of pre-designed scientific propositions of unilinear directions and comprehends politics essentially as an open-ended power negotiation where a given structural condition offers manifold possibilities, even as it restricts the workings of an 'autonomous domain'.

Democracy as a political imagination has expanded and entrenched itself over the last century but revolution as an alternative imagination has not ceased to exist and with it comes alternative ways of mobilising, even as collectives are attempting various other modes of protest. It is in this context that this book attempts to raise certain

---

[13] Reference here is about Spivak's position in her celebrated article 'Can the Subaltern Speak?' and Ranajit Guha's formulation in inaugurating Subaltern Studies.

critical issues that lie at the interface of democracy and revolutionary violence.

References

Badiou, Alain. 2015. 'True and False Contradictions of the Crisis'. Accessed 10 June 2016. https://www.versobooks.com/blogs/2014-alain-badiou-true-and-false-contradictions-of-the-crisis

Basu, Amrita, and Srirupa Roy, ed. 2007. *Violence and Democracy in India*. Calcutta: Seagull.

Chattopadhyay, B. D. 2002. *Combined Methods in Indology and Other Writings*. New Delhi: Oxford University Press.

———. 2005. *Combined Methods in Indology and Other Writings*. New Delhi: Oxford University Press.

Corbridge, Stuart, John Harriss and Craig Jeffrey. 2013. *India Today: Economy, Politics and Society*. London: Polity.

Frankel, Francine. 1988. 'Introduction: The Paradox of Accommodative Politics and Radical Social Change'. In *India's Political Economy: The Gradual Revolution (1947–2004)*, 3–28. New Delhi: Oxford University Press.

Fraser, Nancy. 2000. *Adding Insult to Injury*. London: Verso.

Gudavarthy, Ajay. 2013. *Politics of post-Civil Society: Contemporary History of Political Movements in India*. New Delhi: SAGE Publications.

———. 2014. *Maoism, Democracy and Globalisation: Cross-Currents in Indian Politics*. New Delhi: SAGE Publications.

Hallward, Carter, and Julie M. Normann. 2015. *Understanding Nonviolence*. London: Polity.

Human Rights Forum (HRF). 2010. *Terrible Costs of Inhuman Counter-Insurgency*. Hyderabad: HRF.

Jayal, Niraja. 2014. *Citizenship and its Discontent*. New York, NY: Harvard University Press.

Jeffrey, Robin, Ronojoy Sen and Pratima Singh, ed. 2013. *More than Maoism: Politics, Policies and Insurgencies in South Asia*. New Delhi: Manohar.

Kaviraj, Sidupto. 2010a. 'A State of Contradictions: The Post-Colonial State in India'. In *The Imaginary Institution of India: Politics and Ideas*, 210–34. Ranikhet: Permanent Black.

———. 2010b 'The Passive Revolution and India: A Critique'. In *The Imaginary Institution of India: Politics and Ideas*, 100–43. Ranikhet: Permanent Black.

Kosambi, D. D. 1964. 'The Culture and Civilisation of Ancient India'. *Historical Outline*. Accessed 18 July 2017. https://www.scribd.com/document/341746639/indian-histpory-and-culture-pdf

Kohli, Atul. 1990. *Democracy and Discontent: India's Growing Crisis of Governability*. Canada: Cambridge University Press.

Kothari, Rajini. 1964, December. 'The Congress System in India'. *Asian Survey* 4 (12): 1161–73.

Miller, James. 1993. *Passion of Michael Foucault*. New York, NY: Anchor Books.
———. 1994. *Passion of Michael Foucault*. New York, NY: Anchor Books.
Moore, Barrington. 1984. *Social Origins of Dictatorship and Democracy: Lord and Peasant in the Making of the Modern World*. Boston: Beacon Press.
Nilsen, Alf and Srila Roy, ed. 2015. *New Subaltern Politics: Reconceptualizing Hegemony and Resistance in Contemporary India*. New Delhi: Oxford University Press.
Roy, Arundhati. 2010. 'Walking with the Comrades: Gandhians with a Gun? Arundhati Roy Plunges into the Sea of Gondi People to Find Some Answers...' *Outlook Magazine*, 29 March. Accessed 18 July 2017. https://www.outlookindia.com/magazine/story/walking-with-the-comrades/264738
Rudolph, Susanne and Lloyd Rudolph. 1987. *In Pursuit of Laxmi: The Political Economy of the Indian State*. Chicago: University of Chicago Press.
Sanyal, Kalyan. 2010. *Rethinking Capitalist Development*. New Delhi: Routledge.
Zizek, Slavoj. 2007. *Mao on Practice and Contradiction*. London: Verso.

PART I

PART I

1

Janatana Sarkar: An Alternative Model of Development

Varavara Rao

Today in Dandakaranya, the revolutionary masses under the leadership of the Communist Party of India (Maoist) (CPI [M]) are experimenting on an alternative people's development model with the support of four-class United Front and People's Liberation Army headed by Krantikari Janatana Sarkar, the revolutionary people's committee, fiercely fighting against the war on the people, particularly from November 2009, in the name of Operation Green Hunt. This is not a development programme alone but also an experiment based on class struggle and United Front. As Mao Tse-tung put during the Great Proletarian Cultural Revolution in China, it is a 'three in one' or a triangle struggle, the base being class struggle, and scientific experiment and development being its other dimensions.

In Dandakaranya, this struggle started with the establishment of grama rajya committees (GRCs) as the primary units of power; today, it has evolved into Krantikari Janatana Sarkar. It comprises village-level revolutionary people's committees (RPCs) to area-level RPCs. Today, depending on the basic programme of New Democratic Revolution and the level of development in the movement, it is advancing in the direction of forming higher level divisional Janatana Sarkars. The councils of the delegates of these Janatana Sarkars are paving the way for them to implement its concrete programmes and policies.

In a similar manner in Bihar and Jharkhand, the struggle started with the formation of revolutionary peasant committees, called krantikari kisan committees

(KKCs), as the primary units of power. Today, they have formed area-level KKCs. Now they are advancing further to form people's government with four-class United Front, transforming the KKCs into RPCs in order to implement the basic programme of New Democratic Revolution.

The RPCs are taking a concrete shape in Maoist guerrilla zones and playing an effective role, as of now, only in areas where there is a strong party capable of leading the people's war, where there is a strong People's Liberation Guerrilla Army (PLGA) under the leadership of the party and its three forces are consolidated and strong, where the people of the area are well organised in the form of mass organisations and people's militia and steeled in class struggle, and where the leadership of the village party organisation is established up to the village level. Based on these foundations, this embryonic political power of the people in the guerrilla zones is valiantly fighting against the power of the ruling classes and destroying its armed forces and wiping out its power, and in that space, RPCs are being formed.

Background

The Naxalbari struggle envisaged the economic struggle for land to the tiller, the guerrilla form of struggle to protect it and the political programme of seizing the state power. After its setback in Naxalbari and Srikakulam, it has taken a mass line in Jagtial Jaitra Yatra, and the Dandakaranya Perspective was drafted with the formation of the Communist Party of India (Marxist–Leninist) (CPI [ML]) (People's War). After the Indravelli massacre, the Party consolidated its hold in Dandakaranya, and within a decade, while the ruling classes at the centre and in states have taken up imperialist globalisation as a policy of development, the Party has creatively adopted an alternative development scheme.

In 1995, at the special conference of the CPI (ML) (People's War), this alternative development scheme was planned with GRCs having political power and village development committees for implementing land reforms, providing irrigation and protected water, supplying seeds and manure and providing primary education and health. To start with, it was taken up in Dandakaranya, the then larger Bastar, particularly south Bastar and north Telangana. In hundreds of north Telangana villages, it was implemented during 1996–99, but since it was mostly in the plain areas, it was ruthlessly crushed by the then Chief Minister N. Chandrababu Naidu who himself claimed to be the chief executive officer of the World Bank and turned Telangana into a laboratory for imperialist globalisation. I need not go into the details except to say that the central leadership of CPI (ML) (People's War), namely Nalla Adireddy, Arramreddy Santosh Reddy and Seelam Naresh, along with Laxmirajam were lifted from Bangalore on 1 December 1999 and killed in a fake encounter in Koyyur forest in Karimnagar. They were among the architects of this alternate people's development programme. They were also responsible for talks with the Telugu Desam government in 2002, which could not materialise. One can understand the reaction of the Party—the attempt on Chandrababu Naidu's life—in response to the killing of the top leadership of the Party.

In Dandakaranya, too, it was not smooth sailing. First, the scheme was met with severe repression from different *abhiyans* (campaigns) by the state, the ruling classes and reactionaries and then the anti-constitutional vigilante force named Salwa Judum (SJ), which was the brainchild of Mahendra Karma, leader of the Congress party, and was implemented by Raman Singh, the BJP chief minister for two successive terms from 2004. By withstanding the *abhiyans*, the SJ, the burning of hundreds of villages, destruction of houses and granaries, rapes of women and killing of hundreds of Adivasis and Maoists, the

Party gained strength and extended to more areas. The repression culminated in a full-scale war: about 3 lakh paramilitary forces were dumped under different names, and finally in 2011, the military base also came in Maad area and the paramilitary forces are using all military infrastructure, including army planes and bombs, to crush the movement. The people under the leadership of the Maoist Party are fighting against this repression with brave heart and are sacrificing their lives to transform the future generations into new human beings.

Janatana Sarkar's Functioning Today

GRC: It comprises the Party and the mass organisations of the Party. This committee is mainly run by the Party committee.

Sarkar: In the Sarkar, people's participation is more, and the role and responsibility of the Party is less. This is the United Front of four classes. There are no landless people now in Dandakaranya, but there are rich peasants, in a relative sense, with most of the people allotted land by the Party.

GRCs are in extended areas, too. In nine divisions and at the zonal level, there are Sarkars. For the people in Dandakaranya, Sarkar means Janatana Sarkar, and to distinguish it from the outside government, they call it *looty sarkar*.

If there are 350 people in an area, about 50 people may be in the age group of 40–50 years, and the rest are youngsters. The average revolutionary's age is 25–30 years. All of them are local people. In the Sarkar committees, there are no outsiders. All of them are local people. Men and women are equal in number in GRCs, and women are more in number in education and health departments. The women in these committees see it as a reflection of the outside society and demand and ask why it is so and why these fields alone are to be seen as suitable for women and why not defence, agriculture and other committees.

There are nine departments in Jantana Sarkar: (a) agriculture; (b) people's education and culture; (c) public health and social welfare; (d) forest protection; (e) people's defence; (f) finance; (g) public relations; (h) trade and industry and (i) people's judicial department.

There will be nine members in each committee. In an area committee, the report of the committee is to be given but not the personal opinion of the member who represents the committee.

Agricultural Department

Revolutionary land reform is the main task of this department, and it is an ongoing process.[1] Since the first phase of distributing the land to one and all, there are no landless people in Dandakaranya, and now the task is to level the land for cultivation and slowly but steadily bring people out from slash and burn (*Podu*) cultivation habits. In Maad area, it is still seen in some places. In levelling the land, there is a possibility of cutting the forest, and it contradicts the policy of the forest department, which protects the forest and looks after the environment. At a recent conference, the forest department complained that during this year's land levelling programme, 2,000 trees were destroyed and the agriculture department has promised to compensate with replantation.

Land is distributed according to the nature of the soil quality. If earlier the land without quality was given, now it will be compensated.

---

[1] See the Revolutionary Land Reforms CPI (M) Party document, 2011 (unpublished).

The criteria for land distribution are: (a) landlessness, (b) the families of martyrs—even if the land is not levelled they should be given the land and (c) the families of political prisoners.

Levelled land is given only to the landless people. Since there are no landless people now, the criterion is the yield of the cultivation. The land of rich peasants and those who commit crimes against people will be taken back. But it happens very rarely. Such action will be taken at the GRC level, depending on the gravity of the crime against broad masses of the people.

Land levelling workshops are conducted—when to do or how to do it and who to include. The committees of agriculture and forest departments attend these workshops. They discuss about improving skills for cultivation, digging *kuntas* (small tanks) and tanks. Questions such as 'is it necessary to have tanks', 'how can we get water' and 'how do we preserve the tanks' are reviewed. (A 20-page document was released in 2000 in this regard.) Land distribution workshops are also conducted.

Where the tanks are not useful for cultivation, they are converted into fish ponds. The tanks are constructed to divert and attract the water from canals, and natural water flows in hills and forests; it is seen that in the command area of the tanks, there are lands for cultivation. Using fertilisers is not encouraged. They are not in use at all. Leaves of forest trees and cattle dung are the main manure. The cattle are tied in the fields only for the collection of cattle dung. Rice, corn and other grains like pulses, which are necessary during famine, are grown. These days, vegetables and fruits are grown in plenty. Horticulture and forest gardens are seen everywhere. Every household has a vegetable yard.

Cultivation is done on: (a) cooperative basis and (b) collective basis.

Four or five families together form a batch (team). It is seen that every batch has cattle and agricultural tools.

The families of martyrs are placed in strong teams. For the parents of jailed people, a cooperation committee and work teams do the needful. Cooperative teams are formed to help neighbouring teams.[2]

Since the people in cooperative teams are not going for agriculture labour work as in the old system, they receive help from the Party fund if they are faced with scarcity of food. Maad still follows the *Podu* cultivation system, while the rest of Bastar has reached a stable cultivation stage. Every household has agricultural land, and vegetables are grown in one's land. A kind of importance or primacy or influence is possible sometimes for a family which is supposed to have founded the village or hamlet.

There are many factors for improving yield. Planting paddy is not in vogue in many areas. People, particularly women, are used to throw seeds on fields. They say that they get backache if they bend their bodies in the fields for planting. This is the main reason for low yield. To rectify this, prolonged education is needed. This is a major problem for production. Only 4—5 batches among 10 know planting. But they do not bluff. They are transparent; they often say, 'May be we may learn in future. We will think about it'. Killing wild animals is prohibited. All the cattle are not used for cultivation since they have plenty of cattle. Beef eating is prevalent. The skin of goats is used for making drums.

Collective cultivation: While distributing land, Sarkar allots some land to itself. Suppose there is 400 acres of land; 370 acres will be distributed, and 30 acres will be kept with Sarkar. In this land, people collectively work under the leadership of a Sarkar committee.

The yield from this field is distributed in three parts: (a) redistribution for the common interests of the village (b) to conduct Sarkar and its medical activities (functioning

---

[2] For instance, team A will help team B and vice versa.

of Sarkar and public health), and buy agricultural tools and (c) manage Sarkar's treasury (the granary). Grains from the granary will be distributed to those who do not have food and to those whose yield is less. Some yield will be kept for use during the plucking season of the *ippa (mahua)* flower. The rest is for the expenditure of the PLGA. This is in view of the PLGA giving protection to the people who are participating in work and also for looking after public welfare.

Though cotton production is prohibited in a few places, it is under cultivation in some places. This is treated as a violation of the rule. In some places, the agriculture committee also violated this rule. This generally happens in roadside villages where the market has entered and where there is no GRC. In border villages, the market has entered. About these violations, Sarkar and the Party think that the farmers have to be persuaded and educated.

There is some crime, and Janatana Sarkar views it as an issue that harms the Party and the class interest of the people. An informer is one who causes harm to his own class of people and to the Party, which represents that revolutionary class. The state is entering there in the form of army and market, and Janatana Sarkar is fiercely resisting the army and educating the people about the disaster of the entry of the market.

Generally, Janatana Sarkar decides the prices in the outside *sandy* (weekly traditional market) also. Adivasi people go to these outside *sandies* and the sahukars (traders) there buy the forest produce from Adivasis at the rates fixed by Sarkar. Sarkar gathers information about the rates outside. Sarkar uses *sandies* for political campaigns and distribution of pamphlets. Sarkar tries to win over small traders. They allow and encourage the *sandies*, but they want their hold on it. Naturally, there is a conflict. On one hand, police will have an eye on *sandies* and try to control them. Police would go there in the name of arrangements for surveillance. The Party will also be present there for political campaign and protection of Adivasis who go there for selling and buying. Scattered *sandies* are prohibited by the outside government, particularly in interior areas, and Adivasis are forced to go to the *sandies* set up near military camps of Bhadrachalam, Cherla and such towns. Using shampoo is discouraged. Presence of mobile phones is there, but they are used only to hear songs and watch movies. The defence committee does not allow signals. Some areas on the Andhra border get signals.[3]

Adivasis are gradually learning water-harvesting methods. In some areas, tanks are dug only for growing fish. Small canals and streams are not used in large numbers, may be because water is available in plenty. If proper water-utilisation methods are adopted, cultivating two crops is also possible. In some areas, two crops have already started. Groundnut and vegetables are grown in some areas during winter. That two crops are essential to achieve self-sufficiency is the understanding of the Party and Sarkar, and they are trying to inculcate it among people by education. They believe it is a process.

Mahua gathering is prevalent in the cultivation season. The rates of the forest produce are decided by Sarkar. *Mahua* oil is extracted from *mahua* flowers. A very old ancestral instrument is used for extraction, but now the Party has introduced a new instrument. There are small rice mills but no flour mills. On the whole, for two to three months, essential food items are not available. This is the time the Party is seriously engaged in increasing the production, taking every care to educate the people as a continuous process. During the harvesting season, menstruating and pregnant women are not allowed to participate. The Party is trying to educate and convince Adivasis to overcome this taboo. This discrimination is there in Sarkar's committees also. It is not that the

---

[3] Chetna Natya Manch (CNM) has written songs to propagate Party programme.

youngsters are defying their *riwaz* (custom). CNM has written many songs about this.

Education

People have not reached the stage of education and employment. There are Sarkar schools at the village level, and midday meals are also provided. At the area level, there are ashram schools. Sarkar committees are looking after them. Sarkar is very serious about children's education, and the education department is visiting villages to encourage parents to send children to schools. There is a big campaign about it. There are no government schools in the interior forest. Where there are government schools, Sarkar is persuading teachers to come there and stay in the villages. Sarkar is promising them that they will be provided with house and land. They can go and get salary from the government. In spite of this, if the schools are not run, Sarkar is taking them and teaching the children. Getting teachers is a big problem. Panchayat-level schools are not functioning. Day and night, Sarkar schools are protected by people's militia and parents of the children to give education to children. Where the raids on villages and schools by the paramilitary forces are intense, the system of mobile schools is in vogue. To say that schools are being destroyed by the Maoists is completely a false propaganda.

Syllabus is prepared for up to 4th and 5th classes in Koya (colloquial Gondi), in Gadchiroli and in some Bastar and Maad areas. There are magazines for these areas. The Dandakaranya Committee has prepared textbooks for up to the 4th class. Students are not failed. In the evenings, there are games and cultural programmes, where Adivasi art forms and CNM art forms are taught. Students are taken to fields and forest as part of education. Once in 15 days, they are taken to fish ponds. Education is linked to nature and production.

There is a basic communist training school. It teaches about the Adivasi movements and their culmination into political movements. It is a six-month course. Every year, a different division has to take its responsibility. The students above the age of 16 or 17 are allowed to join this. The syllabus comprises of philosophy, political economy and mathematics. Communist Manifesto as *Darshan Shastra* is mandatory in the syllabus. Classes are conducted in the afternoon. In the evening, the students are asked to speak. There are interactive sessions. Along with their dialects and languages, the lessons are in Telugu and Hindi. Their school is attached to the village collective agriculture farms.

Health and Medicine

There is concentration on tribal medicine. The agriculture department grows age-old medicinal herbs. There are two books—*Tribal Medicine* and *Modern Medicine*. They use both of them. In the villages, there is a priestly class called *Vadde*, and they practice traditional medicine. A workshop was conducted for these *Vaddes* to explain to them medicinal herbs instead of mantra and tantra. *Vaddes* in some places are antagonistic. (There is a story in *Dandakaranya Kathalu* about this).

Women are more in number in the health department. They treat injured people and also conduct surgeries. In every mobile team of cattle trainers and fishermen, there is a doctor and there are health teams to tour the villages. For the villages and militia, there are doctors without fail. In every conference, there will be a medical tent. Youngsters aged 18–20 years are learning and practising medicine. It is more because of their care and service that there is high recovery of health, and they use doctors with sensibility, human approach and service motive. It is entirely opposite to the outside world.

Department of Justice

This is to resolve contradictions among the people, and it also deals with the enemy. Right from the quarrels between a man and his wife, every individual and collective issue is taken up. People from the whole village will be invited and involved. There are no extramarital relations and dowry. If the husband comes drunk, it will be reported immediately. Men will try in some cases for second or third marriages, but slowly such cases are drastically coming down. Drastic change has come in man–woman relationships.

The punishment is in the form of labour. If somebody misuses the Party money, he or she will be asked to dig a *kunta*, without anybody's help. If a man beats his wife, he also is asked to participate in labour and production without anybody's help. If a loss is caused to people because of exposure to the enemy, such persons will be socially boycotted.[4] Similarly, dealing with government officers (see–Tomorrow–Vernon) and to elect or to remove, committee meetings are organized in a democratic manner. The Party refers to this as 'village-level democracy'.

Public Relations Department

This is the department to connect Sarkar with the children, women and CNM committees. This is the committee to link Sarkar with Party organisations.

Janatana Sarkar expects from the outside world the following:

1. Condemnation, opposition and resistance from the outside world against the low-intensity conflict (LIC)

---

[4] See 'Siksha', a story by Midko in *Dandakaranya Kathalu*.

policy of the state, the carrot and stick policy. In the recent surrender of a Dandakaranya spokesman, an NGO and government top brass were involved, and they attempted to rehabilitate him.

2. Humanity is falling for imperialist globalisation, and this needs to be thwarted.
3. Reformist Revolution—There is a need to condemn the recent government policy of sending the students of the Tata Institute of Social Sciences (TISS) to conflict areas as part of Mahatma Gandhi Rural Employment Scheme.
4. Naked and ghastly killings, destruction, burning of villages and huts, mass rapes, encounter killings and inducting converts to poison food and kill—There are recent examples of such practices from Andhra Pradesh.
5. The Party expects the outside world to understand the alternative people's development model and its attempt to create new human beings. To stand by and propagate it or at least observe and understand.
6. There is a dire need of teachers and doctors; any help in this regard will be very useful.

One can easily see that the political culture and values of Sarkar are in complete contrast with those of the outside world. Along with the PLGA, the political culture is a safeguard for Janatana Sarkar. The political conscious-ness, practice and class struggle are seen even among the ranks and files not only in the cadres but also in broad masses. But we cannot say that at present a leadership will emerge from them to lead the class struggle. The ideologi-cal hegemony is very strong. It is therefore important to understand that there is no difference between the people and the Party.

2

Examining the Logic of Revolutionary Violence

Anand Teltumbde

All men recognize the right of revolution: that is, the right to refuse allegiance to, or to resist, the government when its tyranny or its inefficiency are great and unendurable.
—Henry David Thoreau

Introduction

The title of the chapter is premised on the commonplace notion that violence is an integral part of revolutions. It is particularly contextualized by the Maoist movement in India which has been associated with continual violent episodes by the Maoists against the security forces and local people being seen as informers or government agents, which have resulted into huge loss of life on both sides. The movement claims continuity with the Naxalite movement that itself was born into violence way back in May 1967[1]

---

[1] It happened during the agitation of peasants against the *jotedari* (share cropping) system in a village called Naxalbari in West Bengal, in which most of the produce was taken by landlords leaving little for the peasants. Egged on by a handful of Marxist ideologues, and supported by the workers of surrounding tea gardens, they decided to fight back and began their sit-in on stretches of farmland. The infuriated landlords and the state government called in police. On 23 May 1967, a police inspector was killed by an arrow that came from a crowd of people. The police retaliated later two days, that is, on 25 May, firing on another crowd, killing 10 people, including 7 women and 2 infants. With

and inspiration from the Chinese Revolution under the leadership of Mao Zedong who had variously centre-staged violence famously saying, 'Political power grows out of the barrel of a gun' (1938, 224) and 'The seizure of power by armed force, the settlement of the issue by war, is the central task and the highest form of revolution' (1938, 219). While the movement evolved from such revolutionary infatuation of early days, where its leaders toed the blatantly violent line of *khatam* (annihilation of class enemy),[2] to emphasizing the importance of mass organizations,[3] it could not give up its emphasis on armed struggle. The movement grew since then to many states although not to the extent blown up in the government propaganda.[4] Episodes of violence followed all along with a wide range of low-intensity guerrilla tactics against government institutions, officials, security forces and

---

this began the 'armed struggle' called the Naxalite movement. See Hiro (1976, 150).

[2] On 1 May 1969, the establishment of the new party, Communist Party of India (Marxist–Leninist; CPI [ML]), was announced by Kanu Sanyal, at a gathering on the Shaheed Minar grounds in Kolkata. In March the following year, the CPI (ML) state committee was established, and in May, the first party congress took place in which Charu Majumdar's line of *khatam*—annihilation of class enemies—was endorsed unanimously (Chattopadhyay 2010). Later Sanyal rejected Charu Majumdar's advocacy of individual assassination, which, according to Ashim Chatterjee, former CPI (ML) Central Committee member and top Naxal leader of the 1970s, was 'anarchism of the Bakuninist kind'.

[3] K. Seetharamaiah, the founder of the CPI (ML) People's War Group in Andhra Pradesh in 1980, which is the main precursor of the current Maoist party had emphasised building mass organisations restricting the annihilation line (Chakrabarty and Kujur 2010, 46; Kujur 2008, 3).

[4] Chakrabarty and Kujar state that by 2006 it spread to 509 police stations comprising 7,000 villages in 11 states, namely Andhra Pradesh, Chhattisgarh, Bihar, Jharkhand, Odisha, Maharashtra, Uttar Pradesh, Madhya Pradesh, West Bengal, Tamil Nadu, Karnataka and Kerala, covering 40 per cent of country's geographical area affecting 35 per cent of the country's population (2010, 38).

paramilitary groups. But the violence significantly picked up with the Chhattisgarh government launching the movement of Salwa Judum[5] (SJ) in 2005 against the Maoists in order to clear the area of them for the industrialists with whom it had signed MoUs.[6]

There was no looking back therefrom. The government's response to the challenge posed by the Maoists was in terms of flexing its military muscle. Under the state blitzkrieg that it was the biggest threat to India's internal security,[7] the government opened a virtual war against them, intensifying further violence. While both sides (the security forces and Maoists) contributed to the resultant violence, the former perhaps more because of its fire power, it was entirely attributed to the latter. The burgeoning middle classes who were always skeptical about the violent methods of Maoists but somewhat appreciative of the cause they espoused and their sacrifice for many decades completely turned against them. They have already given their verdict by terming them terrorists who should be brutally rooted out. Unfortunately, these developments have not been unique to India. Most movements relying overtly on armed struggle since the later years of the previous century seemed to have met similar fate as

[5] SJ was a civilian militia mobilised and deployed as part of anti-insurgency operations in Chhattisgarh, India, aimed at countering Maoist violence in the region. The militia consisting of local tribal youth received support and training from the Chhattisgarh state government.

[6] It is noteworthy that the SJ campaign was started on the very same day on which the state government of Chhattisgarh signed an MoU with the TATAs to set up a steel plant in Lohandiguda in Bastar. Essar is also setting up a steel plant in Dhurli/Bhansi region of Dantewada. Both these parties have also demanded lease and mining rights for the vast iron ore reserves in Bailadila (Saha 2007).

[7] Prime Minister Manmohan Singh said, 'I have been saying for the last three years that Naxalism remains 'the biggest internal security challenge facing our country' (PTI 2010). The government deliberately amplified the scale of the movement through the willing media to influence public opinion.

the Maoists do today. Notwithstanding the moralistic arguments against violence, at the sheer strategic level, a question arises why the revolutionary movements are still obsessed with violent methods.

This chapter basically seeks to understand the underlying logic of violence in revolutionary struggles and assesses the present Maoist violence from the viewpoint of its goal of ushering in a structural change in favour of the oppressed people. It is divided into four parts. The first part deals with the meaning of violence as it tends to be used in partisan terms. The second part discusses the genesis of revolutions and revolutionary violence in the particular context of Marxist theory, as it supposedly informs the Maoist movement. The third part reviews what Marx and Engels had to say about the role of violence in revolutions. In the light of this discussion, the fourth and the last part seeks to assess the Maoist movement in India.

Violence: Direct and Structural

There are two ways of conceptualizing violence—a narrow, 'minimalist conception' and a broader, 'comprehensive conception' (Bufacchi 2005). 'Minimalist conception considers violence narrowly in terms of physical force and 'bodily response and harm' (Glasser 1998) and hence is criticized for 'taking no account of the wider contexts of social relationships in which violence occurs, or non-physical harms (especially psychological), and the possibility of violent outcomes that were not consciously intended' (Bourdieu 1977, 192; Henry 2000). The 'comprehensive conception' of violence broadens the definition to include 'anything avoidable that impedes human realization, violates the rights or integrity of the person and is often judged in terms of outcomes rather than intentions' (Felson 2009). Felson (2009) extends violence to cover social harm or deprivation of resources. Norwegian peace researcher Galtung (1969) had proposed the concept of 'structural violence' to include physical and psychological harm that results from exploitive and unjust social, political and economic systems. It is not caused by individuals but is inflicted by structures that prevent people from realizing their potential. For instance, it would be difficult to attribute violence to the worldwide system for the trade in goods but it is well correlated with infant mortality, infectious disease, and shortened lifespans. Unemployment, job insecurity, cuts in public spending, destruction of institutions capable of defending social welfare, dispossession and violation of rights—these are all social harms that could be encompassed within 'structural violence'.

Structural violence has a causal relationship with revolutions. It is important, therefore, to recognize the existence of structural violence, which is far more indirect and insidious than direct violence (Galtung 1969). Structural violence is typically built into the political, social and cultural institutions that map up the societal structure.

Those who abhor violence want peace but peace could be far more insidious than even direct violence. History is replete with examples of such negative peace. For example, both ancient Egypt and imperial Rome practised slavery, were rigid despotisms and had extended periods without wars. The peace that prevailed there was not without violence as for the majority of people, it was there embedded in the system. India also is superficially painted as a peace-loving country but with its society characterized by the caste system fraught with exclusions and misery, it will rank as one of the most violent countries in the world. With this perspective of violence, the examples of positive peace may be very scarce. When the victims of structural violence try to resist it, they are accused of violating peace by the vested interest in the status quo. It is rather easy to condemn such struggles of poor for social and economic justice as destructive of the status quo, conveniently forgetting that the status quo is responsible for millions facing hunger, disease, misery, torture and the unequal effect of police powers that are organized to protect property rather than people.

Structural violence includes deprivations of food, health care, education, and other resources necessary for human life and development that leads to physical disability, the destruction of human potential and death. It can be far deadlier than direct violence as it is capable of affecting a far greater number of people, which is never possible in direct violence. It has the effect of denying people important rights such as economic opportunity, social and political equality, a sense of fulfilment and self-worth, and so on. When people starve to death, or even go hungry, when they suffer from diseases that are preventable, when they are denied a decent education, housing, an opportunity to play, to grow, to work, to raise a family, to express themselves freely, to organize peacefully, or to participate in their own governance, a kind of violence is occurring even if bullets or clubs are not used. Violence is done when the optimum development of each human being is denied because of race, religion, sex, sexual preference, age, or whatever. From the structural perspective, violence traces the ways in which the distribution of wealth and power is effected through policy instruments (Chasin 1998; Iadicola and Shupe 1998) devastating lives of people over a long period of time as no weapons of mass destruction may be capable of doing. In the Indian context, Gupta (2012) rightly observes that policies and programmes aimed at providing nutrition, employment, housing, health care, elder support, and education end up killing many of those in whose name they are launched. He particularly highlights the violence of poverty resulting from the bureaucratic processes.

Revolutions and Revolutionary Violence

Revolutions are germinated in this structural violence. Revolutionaries are inspired to change the structures of exploitation, oppression, dispossession of people to usher in a better society. It is not a piecemeal solution to some discrete acts of violence but to the condition that gives rise to such violence. Since the structural change necessarily alters the prevailing social relations, those who are comfortable in the present and abhor the fear of unknown tend to resist it. Violence is thus born in the contention between the revolutionary forces and the forces of the status quo. The violence involved here is of direct and physical type, which is visible and measurable as wounded or dead or damaged property. The main custodian of the structure and the status quo is the State and it necessarily rushes in on behalf of those who wish to resist the change with all its might in the name of preserving law and order. The resultant violence is attributed to revolutionaries and not to those who resist it. The State, which assumes monopoly of violence, in reality is the real initiator of violence but is scarcely seen as such. It is accorded legitimacy to unleash violence by the entire intelligentsia, media and other dominant sections of the society.

Revolutions, on the other hand, conjure up images of storming of Bastille or guillotining thousands of people, destruction of property, etc. Indeed, they are constructive destruction; to make space for the new to emerge. As episodes in time they seem bloody, unjust and mindless but within the reference frame of history, they become the mother of entire human progress. Without revolutions mankind could have been stuck at the basic level of existence. The violence in revolutions which is of direct type is approximately proportional to the prevailing quantum of structural violence but would amount to a dot in the sea of the latter. That should settle the question of efficacy of revolutionary violence raised by the agents of the status quo with moral veneer. Revolutions being episodic moments representing eruption of suppressed energy of vast majority of victims cannot possibly be controlled. But the question whether violence is an essential correlate of revolutions may be answered in terms of counter-conditionality whether the response to the revolutionary upsurge by the State, the custodian of the status quo, is violent or not.

Marx and Engels, constructed a theory of revolution after discovering the basic law of dialectics governing all phenomena in universe. It is explained in terms of three broad and interconnected laws in particular relation to societal progress. The first is the law of quantity and quality, which states that the society does not progress in a slow evolutionary manner; the continuous build up in contradiction creates episodic periods leading to political and social crises where it demands a concentrated application of energy to resolve them by giving birth to a qualitatively new and next higher phase of the society. The second law is the interpenetration of opposites, which tells us that dialectics applied to society does not have the same degree of precision as it does in the science laboratory. The roles that myriad conscious forces in the society, such as individuals, political parties and social movements, play are not scientifically pre-ordained. The third law, the law of negation of negation, as Engels stated, is 'extremely general and for this very reason, extremely far reaching and important, law of development of nature, history and thought' (1976a). It deals with development through contradictions, which appear to annul or negate a previous fact, theory, or form of existence, only to later become negated in its turn. This theory basically deals with societal leaps from one stage to the next higher stage.

In the realm of natural science, the proof of these laws is amply corroborated. Whether it is Newtonian or Einstein's relativistic universe, these laws seem to hold good. In the context of quantity transforming into quality (qualitative change—a Hegelian jump), a familiar example of phase transition of ice into water and into steam by application of heat may suffice. When water is heated, its temperature rises up to 100 degrees centigrade. Further application of heat does not show up in the rise of temperature but is absorbed as latent heat (used for breaking up the water molecule) and when this absorbed heat reaches 540 calories per gram per degree—its latent heat of vaporization, it starts transforming into steam. The reverse process of cooling of water takes place in a similar manner and would require extracting 80 calories per gram per degree—its latent heat of fusion, to transform it into ice. The phase transition in physical matter corresponds to the societal transformation through revolution, with an important difference that unlike the former, there is an involvement of live human agency that is subject as well as an object of revolution. The latent heat that is required to break the bond of the old phase is the force required to break the bonds in the older society. This force is ordinarily imagined as the revolutionary violence required for bringing about the revolutionary change.

In the Marxist theory, every socio-economic formation is marked by its specific mode of production, which relates to the productive forces existing in a given period (i.e., technology + appropriate human knowledge + raw materials) and the relations of production between people, relations reflected mainly in the property laws dominant in that period. If the relations of production are in consonance with existing productive forces, a given social formation is said to be in equilibrium. But this equilibrium is relatively short-lived, as the very relations of production would push for further development of the productive forces but would fail to keep pace with its development. The inertia of the relations of production is due to the interests of specified social groups, which, with respect to their relationship to the productive forces, are termed classes. Some of them are interested in preserving the existing state of things, which guarantees them various privileges, whereas others are interested in changing them. When this contradiction reaches its peak through the conflicts between the contending classes, a period of revolution begins, ready to give birth to the new socio-economic formation which would push the forces of production to develop further. This change from one formation to another is thus always a sui generis revolution, which is brought about by the application of a bout of enormous energy.

Marx and Engels on Violence

We do not get precise guidance from Marx and Engels, as in many other matters, as to the form of this energy. Usually it is seen manifested into violence. Did they see inevitability of violence in social revolutions? The answer to this question cannot be given in a straightforward manner. Marx and Engels made very few direct references to violence, as such, in their writings. As young men, both were influenced by Jacobin elements of the French Revolution[8] and the revolutionary struggles in the first half of the nineteenth century. The prevailing notion of revolution was heroic fighting on the barricades with gun in hand. Marx clearly believed in a violent, armed revolution as the culminating point of class struggle. He said in one of his early works that the weapon of criticism cannot replace criticism with weapons and stressed the necessity of resisting physical force with physical force (2000 [1844]). It culminated in the violence being sanctioned as the means of transiting to socialism in *The Communist Manifesto.*

In the beginning of 1845, both Marx and Engels were yet to develop in a comprehensive form the materialist conception of history to see the inevitability of a violent

---

[8] A political club of French Revolution, later under the leadership of Robespierre, unleashed the terror not only against counter-revolutionaries but also against former allies of the Jacobins, such as the Cordeliers and the Dantonists (followers of Georges Danton). See Mellersh and Williams (1999, 55).

change or otherwise. Marx tended to see violence as a necessity relative to Engels, who was not opposed to the idea of peaceful change. In a speech in Elberfeld on 15 February 1845, while initially outlining the inevitability of a violent upheaval, he had made the following remarks:

> If, gentlemen, these conclusions are correct, if the social revolution and practical communism are the necessary result of our existing conditions, then we will have to concern ourselves above all with the measures by which we can avoid a violent and bloody overthrow of the social conditions. And there is only one means, namely, the peaceful introduction of communism. If we do not want the bloody solution of the social problem. … then, gentlemen, we must apply ourselves seriously and without prejudice to the social problem, then we must make it our business to contribute our share towards humanising the condition of the modern helots. (Marx and Engels 1844–45)

In Principles of Communism, written at the end of 1847, Engels asked himself the question: Will it be possible to bring about the abolition of private property by peaceful methods? (Question 16) and gave the following answer:

> It is to be desired that this could happen, and communists certainly would be the last to resist it. The communists know only too well that all conspiracies are not only futile but even harmful. … Should the oppressed proletariat in the end be goaded into a revolution, we Communists will then defend the cause of the proletarians by deed just as well as we do now by word. (1847, 89)

One can easily see that Engels was not averse to the idea of peaceful change. In fact, he wished that such a thing were possible. But since changes are brought about by historical circumstances, if they are not congenial to a peaceful change, then the change had to be violent. For example, if the proletarians' efforts for change are forcibly suppressed, as Engels says was being done in all 'civilized' countries during his time, then they will be 'goaded into a revolution', that is, they will be forced to resort to violent methods of bringing change.

In their analysis until 1848, a peaceful change was not even remotely possible, given the historical and existing circumstances, and that the change, therefore, had necessarily to be violent. This inevitability of the violent nature of revolution was determined by the very structures of the bourgeois system. In the *Poverty of Philosophy* (1847), Marx says that '[I]t is only in an order of things in which there are no more classes and class antagonisms that social *evolutions* will cease to be *political revolutions*.' Till then on the eve of every general reshuffling of society, the last word of social science will always be: 'combat or death, bloody struggle or extinction. It is thus that the question is inexorably put' (1847, 212).

The shift towards moderation in their thinking came with actual participation in political activities in post-1848 revolutionary upheavals in Europe. Exiled from Brussels in March, Marx went to Paris and involved himself in the political activities of the German expatriate workers who had formed an armed body called the German Legion, with the aim of installing a republican government there. Marx vigorously opposed this plan arguing that conditions were not ripe for armed imposition of a republic in Germany. The Legion, however, persisted with its plan and was badly defeated. In June, the workers of Paris, finding the conditions worse than those before the February revolution, revolted against the bourgeois-republican government, but were ruthlessly crushed. Thousands of workers were killed. Although Marx thought that the June uprising was premature, he still upheld it just to be on the side of the workers (Marx 1948; Marx and Engels 1848). The suppression of the June uprising proved the beginning of the end of the revolutionary upheavals in Europe in the years 1848–49. It marked the triumph of reaction over revolution. The June defeat was followed by similar occurrences elsewhere. These events forced Marx and Engels to revise their tactics of cooperating with the 'radical' democratic bourgeoisie. They were totally disillusioned with the vacillation of the latter and turned their sight towards the proletariat's own organization and leadership. Enraged by 'the purposeless massacres perpetrated since the June and October events, the tedious offering of sacrifices since February and March, the very cannibalism of the counter-revolution', they abandoned their faith in peaceful political activity and pinned their hope on revolutionary violence. In an article, 'The Victory of Counter-revolution in Vienna', published in the *Neue Rheinische Zeitung* on 7 November 1848, Marx wrote: 'The counter-revolution will convince the nations that there is only one means by which the murderous death agonies of the old society and the bloody birth throes of the new society can be shortened, simplified and concentrated and that is by revolutionary terror.' As a result, he was expelled from Prussia on 16 May 1849. In his last contribution to the *Neue Rheinische Zeitung*, on 19 May, Marx addressed the authorities in a defiant mood. He wrote: 'We have no compassion and we seek no compassion from you. When our turn comes, we shall not make excuses for the terror.'

In March 1850, the Address of the Central Committee to the Communist League, drafted by Marx and Engels incorporated their bitter experience of the revolutions of 1848–49 and marked a further shift in their changed attitude towards the bourgeoisie. With the belief that a new revolutionary wave was imminent in Germany, the circular asked the League to arm 'the whole proletariat with rifles, muskets, canon and munitions—at once'. 'Arms and ammunition must not be surrendered on any pretext; any attempt at disarming must be frustrated, if necessary by force.' During this phase, Marx and Engels were willing even to let the workers kill those individuals of the ruling classes who have been particularly harsh in their dealings with the people, if it serves to advance the momentum of the revolution. Although it was allowed as a tactical measure in a revolutionary phase, it reflects their attitude towards violence. Still the Blanquist elements in the League disagreed with Marx and believed that a few daring individuals armed with weapons could force a revolutionary uprising in Germany, and accused Marx of being a reactionary. In response, Marx lashed out at his opponents saying, 'Instead of the materialistic view of the Manifesto they bring forth the idealist one. Instead of the real conditions they point to the will as the major factor in revolution.'[9]

In one of his articles written for the *New York Daily Tribune*, Engles wrote:

> Never play with insurrection unless you are fully prepared to face the consequences of your play. Insurrection is a calculus with very indefinite magnitudes, the value of which may change every day; the forces opposed to you have all the advantages of organisation, discipline and habitual authority; unless you bring strong odds against them, you are defeated and ruined. (1976b, 377)

It was the clear support to the theoretical and tactical position of Marx against the Blanquists. In another article published in the *New York Daily Tribune* on 25 August 1852, Marx wrote:

> Universal Suffrage is the equivalent of political power for the working class of England, where the proletariat forms the large majority of the population (and) where, in a long, though underground civil war, it has gained a clear consciousness of its position as a class.

Marx here points out the possibility of a peaceful transfer of power to the working class in Britain due to the peculiarities of the British conditions. In the first volume of the *Capital*, written and published during this very period, Marx wrote, 'Force is the midwife of every old society pregnant with a new one. It is itself an economic power.' It is no doubt true that the Marx of the post-1845

[9] 15 September 1850, in a meeting of the Central Committee.

period believed that revolutions were the result largely of circumstances, and that he accused people like Willich of treating will as a major factor in revolution. Yet he nowhere entirely denies the role of will. As he writes in 1851 in his famous pamphlet *The Eighteenth Brunnaire of Louis Bonaparte*: 'Men make their own history, but they do not make it as they please; they do not make it under self-selected circumstances, but under circumstances existing already, given and transmitted from the past'. In other words, even if men have to act 'under circumstances... encountered, given and transmitted from the past', even if they cannot choose the circumstances, yet they can choose as to when and how to act within the limits imposed by circumstances.

Marx and Engels saw the possibility of a peaceful transition to socialism in the United States, where the strong military and bureaucratic machinery of the state was still non-existent at that time. Marx's letter to Kugelmann (12 April 1871) shows that the smashing of that machinery was a prerequisite of a people's revolution on the Continent of Europe. In his Preface to the English version of *Capital*, Engels wrote in 1886 that Marx's studies had led to the conclusion that, 'at least in Europe, England is the only country where the inevitable social revolution might be effected entirely by peaceful and legal means' and continued that he 'hardly expected the English ruling classes to submit, without a "pro-slavery rebellion", to this peaceful and legal revolution' (Duncan 1973, 162). On 3 July 1871, that is, after the Paris Commune, Marx said, in his interview to *The World*, that the problem of revolution had its specific aspects in every part of the world, that the workers were taking these into account and approaching to its solution in their own way. For instance, in England the working class could choose the path along which it would add to its political power. There a rebellion would be a stupidity, since the goal could be attained more quickly and more surely by peaceful agitation. In 1891, in his criticism of the Erfurt programme, Engels admitted the possibility of a peaceful development of a socialist revolution in such countries with an advanced parliamentary system as those in England, America and France.

Lenin later said (in The State and Revolution) that the conditions which had made Marx treat England, the United States and the Netherlands as exceptions had ceased to exist, but he did not exclude the possibility of a peaceful transition to socialism in the new epoch, and he even strove to put that idea into effect at one stage of the Russian Revolution. In the same work, he stated that a violent revolution was a necessity; nevertheless in his polemics with Otto Bauer he admitted a possibility of a peaceful transition to socialism in a capitalist country surrounded by socialist countries. In 1917, Lenin often reverted to the issue of a peaceful transition to socialism in Russia and thought that such a course of events would be exceptionally advantageous. His idea was most clearly formulated in his paper 'The Tasks of the Revolution' (October 1917), where he wrote that Russian democracy, the Soviets, the parties of the Socialist Revolutionaries, and the Mensheviks were facing an opportunity, extremely rare in history, to ensure a peaceful development of the revolution.

It is very clear that although attitudinally Marx and Engels were not against any amount of violence being used in the interests of revolution, they never thought it to be inevitability. When Marx wrote that force was the midwife of every old society pregnant with a new one, some people like Kautsky, whom Lenin had praised as the Pope of Marxism, substituted force with violence (Salvadori 1990, 20). Many critics of the communists use this state-ment to paint the proletarian revolution to be an orgy of violence. It should be noted, as did Daniel De Leon (Paul 1922), that Marx did not sum up a revolution in the terms of force. The metaphorical 'midwife' intervenes only at the critical moment of birth. The development leading up to the birth, its time and place, are factors outside the control of the midwife (Paul 1922). Moreover, there is a difference between force and violence. Force is a social power derived from the organization of individuals in such a manner as to enable them to enforce their will upon society. The real force of a revolutionary movement depends upon the way in which it is able to organise great masses of determined workers in every plane of social action, to setup new administrative organs to replace those of the old regime. This is the most important work of the revolution. Insofar as the basic aim of the revolution 'to uproot the economic and political power of the propertied interests' is concerned, it would be sheer stupidity to expect the present ruling class to surrender voluntarily. To suggest that the revolutionary movement could go forward without preparing itself to meet the civil war, which the proprietary class is determined to enforce when a revolutionary situation develops, is foolishness. It is at this moment of danger to the new rising social order that revolutionary force passes, briefly, into the sphere of violence.

In December 1878, Marx stated in an interview to the American newspaper *Chicago Tribune,*

> No socialist need predict that there will be bloody revolution in Russia, Germany, Austria, and possibly in Italy…. The deeds of the French Revolution may be enacted again in these countries…. But these revolutions will be made by the majority. No revolution can be made by a party, But by a Nation.[10]

Marx introduces a new element here when he says that these revolutions will be made by the majority, by the nation as a whole, and not merely by the party. Although, they never believed in a minority revolution, yet it is for the first time that they were saying this in unambiguous terms.

[10] See http://www.marxists.org/archive/marx/bio/media/marx/79_01_05.htm

Marx and Engels viewed the use of violent or peaceful methods essentially as a matter of strategy and tactics to achieve the goal of socialist revolution. What methods were to be used was to be determined largely by the social and historical conditions of a given place and time. One set of methods may suit a situation better, just as the other may prove more suitable in different conditions. At some places bourgeois democratic institutions were so irretrievably advanced and deeply entrenched that the proletariat could use these very institutions to capture power and effect the socialist change. They, therefore, started entertaining the possibility of a peaceful change in such cases. Nevertheless, they made it clear that the working class should not forego its right to use violent methods even at such places because the ruling classes could not be expected to give up their power, even here, without an armed resistance. As for the places where the bourgeois democratic institutions, customs and traditions had not taken root, violent struggle remained the only way to bring socialism. Further, under extremely oppressive conditions, the revolution could take even a terroristic turn.

Maoist Violence in India

India is an excellent example of structural violence, where incidents of direct violence are just its by-products. The vast masses of people were reduced to be automatons in service of the very same oppressive religio-cultural contrivance that reproduce their oppression. The violence is metered out along the entire caste hierarchy and hence was made invisible. Only in the colonial times, after nearly two millennia of imprisoned life, the consciousness of the lowest strata sprouted and brought them face-to-face with their state of victimhood. The traditional ruling classes, who mobilized this mass resentment into an anti-colonial struggle, lured the masses into their project promising heaven to them. But when they succeeded, they resumed their traditional treachery with added tricks picked from the colonial masters. Creating a grand structure of liberal democracy with deceptive slogans of inclusiveness, they variously followed the most illiberal exclusions of the traditional oppressed people. The post-Independence history is testimony to this systematic treachery of the ruling classes and helplessness of people.

India boasts of a constitutional democratic State with deep entrenched institutions, with long-standing religio-cultural and moral fabric creating civilizational paradigm of diversity, inclusiveness, fairness and justice. But in reality it has been its exact antithesis. It has developed into a gigantic contrivance perpetuating structural violence. Millions of lives are devoured by this contrivance every year.[11] In addition, the State kills, maims, and devastates thousands of people in direct violence every year. For instance, there were 14,231 custodial deaths during 2001–10 and 14 custodial rapes. Scores of people are getting encountered with the Maoist or terrorist label (Asian Centre of Human Rights; NCRB). The hedonist 'life styles of the handful rich in city pockets in the sea of misery' is the product of structural violence perpetrated over the last six decades. This is the context in which the Maoist violence should be seen and assessed. Even after its outbreak, the response of the State is worth incriminating. Instead of trying to understand the underlying causes and handle the crime involved objectively, the State only adopts naked terrorist methods to curb this movement. Incarcerating thousands of people in jail without trial, adopting blatant illegal methods to hold them inside jails, slapping fake

---

[11] According to WHO, 1.7 million children died in 2010, and more than half died in their first month of life, mostly due to malnutrition. This feature pervasively applies across all people.

cases on them, denying them bail, re-arresting them after their release, intimidating and harassing human right activists and intellectuals, resorting to inhuman torture of youth, etc., are the endless episodes of this terrorist state. The State systematically blew the Maoist movement out of proportion with its massive propaganda machinery among the middle classes and carried out its menacing plan to destroy it with impunity. Looking back at this stage, anyone can realize the falsehood and mischief of the State.

If one takes a historical glance at their development, this mischief comes out more glaringly. The Maoists, or their previous version in CPI (ML) People's War Group, were never as strong as it was made out to be the biggest internal security threat. While it is true that they ideologically professed armed struggle to bring about the New Democratic Revolution in the country and flaunted their guns and bombs in the minor skirmishes with local tyrants, there was a strategic emphasis on the mass work to begin with. Many mass organizations had sprung up in Andhra Pradesh and elsewhere to work in various segments of the society. It was in no way illegal. But when the State illegally pounced upon these organizations, most of their activists were driven to jungles in self-defence. They were chased there too. For instance, when they reached Bastar, in the mid-1980s, they had to invest huge effort in winning the confidence of the tribals, whose encounter with 'civilization' was only through the experience of exploitation by the forest personnel. The Maoists worked for the development of these people for two long decades without much disturbance, creating education, public health, and self-help infrastructure. But with the opening of Bastar to corporate pirates, the State desperately needed to vacate the area of Maoists and, hence, they resorted to all kinds of measures, mostly unconstitutional like SJ, with impunity. Thousands of people fled and equal numbers were killed, maimed, raped and variously tortured. It obviously invoked violent response from the Maoists, thus escalating the cycle of 'mindless' violence. A judicious view in the matter will still be against the Indian State, which practised anti-people policies all these decades and went berserk to curb peoples' reaction, resorting to unconstitutional means, just at the behest of the capital. Even the Supreme Court has acknowledged it in essence that the Indian State was in the wrong.

While the Indian State can be incriminated million times than the Maoists for violence, it does not automatically justify the violence of the latter. As seen before, the Marxist theory does envisage expenditure of huge latent energy (akin to violence) at the point of revolutionary break out, a point of revolutionary transition; although it does not preclude possibilities of peaceful transitions in certain circumstances. In the course of revolutionary build-up (class struggle), however, the theory does not envisage violence. Unfortunately, the communist revolutionaries in their enthusiasm do not distinguish these phases and flaunt their armed struggle almost with suicidal instinct. The main reason being the theoretical difficulty in knowing precisely whether the conditions were ripe for revolution and reliance on the human agency. It may be tactically expedient to use arms even during this phase, but it can never be strategically prudent to declare it as an armed struggle. To understand these phases is as important in theory as is in practice. Indian situation is far from reaching the revolutionary climax where the strategic choice of violent (or otherwise) means is to be made. Until then it needs to be a multi-pronged class struggle at societal level. Even this struggle may not be non-violent as could be seen from the incidence of caste atrocities. But the question of use of violent methods during this stage is purely of tactical nature. If the perpetrators of caste violence are not punished by the State, it would be tactically expedient to punish them with violence as a part of class struggle.

However, these all theoretical dictums are either ignored in practice or lost in expediency of the obsessive war. Also forgotten is the most important dictum of Marx that revolutions are not made by minorities, or a party, which foregrounds the necessity of preparing the vast masses of people for revolution. The argument that if the majority is in favour of a revolution, it could well be brought about through ballot smacks of ignorance of the bourgeois confines on elections, which has amply shown up in the pathetic plight of the parliamentary left. Marx, however, has not totally discounted the possibility of revolution happening through elections in countries having deep entrenched bourgeois democracy. Indeed, theoretically, it may be possible to do so, but as the experience reveals, it is almost impossible to hold on to revolutionary politics within the vortex of bourgeois politics. In India at least, it does not appear to be a viable alternative.

While the importance of theory for any revolutionary movement cannot be overemphasized, the latter should be able to objectively assess it with its own experience and to progressively contribute to its enrichment. Unfortunately, theory does not remain a theory and becomes an *ism*, with its associated identitarian intoxications. Ism is a holy cow that can only be worshiped. While the basic theoretical framework of Marxism in broad terms may still be valid, it would be an unMarxist folly to believe it or its later variants in Leninism, Maoism, etc., to be blueprints for enacting revolutions. Over the last 150 years since Marx and Engels put forth their theory, the world has changed with accelerated pace and little of that theory today corresponds to reality. Many a basic theoretical postulates should have been revised to correspond to the changing reality but for the fear of being labelled as revisionist or reactionary or renegade, no one, who is in position to do so, would do it. This basic attitude of the revolutionaries must change. They may be reminded that actually no revolution so far has confirmed to basic Marxist schema and is in sight of happening in future. Capitalism has creatively reconfigured itself and is flexible enough to do it because it does not care for ideological fidelity as the revolutionaries do. It is a paradox of the kind that the behaviour of bourgeoisie reflects dialectical materialism while that of proletarian revolutionaries, mechanical idealism.

In the context of violence, the Maoists should have considered basic guideline of Marx that use of a method in revolutionary war is a matter of strategy and tactics. The strategy needs to be formulated with acute consideration of one's own strengths and weaknesses vis-à-vis ones' adversary in the overall context of the environment. No amount of theory may guide in this matter. The states that existed in Marx's or Mao's times were not even a fraction as strong as the states today, and certainly were not part of the mighty imperialist network as they are today. Even then Marx and Engels stressed the need of weighing circumstances before any revolutionary uprising. Over the years, the might of the State has increased manifold with sophisticated technologies of surveillance and weaponry. The class configuration of the society also has undergone a sea change from the one assumed by Marx in his conceptualization of capitalism. The environment is characterized by the defeat of the socialist regime in popular imagination and high pitched propaganda on the virtues of capitalism and free market economy. Is there a class extant when societies are pulverized into discrete self-centred individuals? What propels people to invest in revolutions? Is it absolute or relative deprivation? What is there for people to believe that revolution is feasible? What is the nature of a post-revolution society? Numerous such questions ranging from basic theory to revolutionary practice crave for answers. But the revolutionaries would dismiss them as non-issues. Most of these questions relate with strategy and the decision on what method to adopt for the revolution.

The logic of revolutionary violence mainly lies in the structural violence. Paradoxically, as the logic gets stronger, the prospect of revolutionary violence appears weaker and weaker. Maoist movement in India, with all its follies, represents lone resistance of the people on margins to the devastations by the neoliberal State. No doubt, it has paid huge cost in human blood to sustain itself. While it is surely a serious question for the Maoist movement to consider whether their obsessive reliance on arms has been serving their objective, the very question raised about the Maoist violence smacks of taking sides of their adversaries. While it is easy to criticize Maoists as Maoists, the bigger question arises beyond Maoism: How 'people' should respond to their blatant dispossession and decimation. Maybe, history will bracket Maoist violence with Jacobin terror or any such terror thereafter but historically and morally it may still be superior to the State terror faced by the people. If a revolutionary decides to kill, he is simultaneously risking his own life too. It may, thus, be extra-moral, but not immoral. Maoists may have lost their ideological anchors like the French revolutionaries, but so long as they pose challenge to the present order, their violence, as Walter Benjamin (1986) and Slavoj Žižek (2006) may see, be regarded as divine violence.

References

Asian Centre of Human Rights. 2011. *Torture in India 2011*. New Delhi: Asian Centre of Human Rights.

Benjamin, Walter. 1986. *Reflections: Essays, Aphorisms and Biographical Writings*. New York, NY: Schocken Books.

Bourdieu, P. 1977. *Outline of a Theory of Practice*. New York, NY: Cambridge University Press.

Bufacchi, Vittorio. 2005. 'Two Concepts of Violence'. *Political Studies Review* 3: 193–204.

Chakrabarty, Bidyut and Rajat Kumar Kujur. 2010. *Maoism in India: Reincarnation of Ultra-Left Wing Extremism in the Twenty First Century*. Oxon: Routledge.

Chasin, Barbara H. 1998. *Inequality and Violence in the United States*. Atlantic Highlands, NJ: Humanities Press.

Chattopadhyay, Suhrid Sankar. 2010, April 10–23. 'End of a Revolution'. *Frontline* 27 (8).

Duncan, Graeme. 1973. *Marx and Mill: Two Views of Social Conflict and Social Harmony*. Cambridge: Cambridge University Press.

Engels, Frederick. 1847. 'Excerpt' from *Principles of Communism*. In *Marx and Engels Selected Works*, Vol. I.

————. 1976a. *Anti-Duhring*. Peking: Foreign Languages Press.

————. 1976b. *Revolution and Counter-revolution in Germany in MECW*, Vol. 1. Moscow: Progress Publishers.

Felson, R. B. 2009. 'Violence, Crime, and Violent Crime'. *International Journal of Conflict and Violence*, 3 (1): 23–39.

Galtung, Johan. 1969. 'Violence, Peace, and Peace Research'. *Journal of Peace Research* 6 (3): 167–91.

Glasser, M. 1998. 'On Violence: A Preliminary Communication'. *International Journal of Psycho-Analysis* 79 (5): 887–902.

Gupta. A. 2012. *Red Tape: Bureaucracy, Structural Violence, and Poverty in India*. Durham, NC: Duke University Press.

Henry, S. 2000. 'What is School Violence? An Integrated Definition'. *Annals of the American Academy of Political and Social Science*, 567 (Special Issue: January): 16–30.

Hiro, Dilip. 1976. *Inside India Today*. London: Routledge.

Iadicola, Peter and Anson Shupe. 1998. *Violence, Inequality, and Human Freedom*. New York, NY: General Hall Publishers.

Kujur, Rajat. 2008. *Naxal Movement in India: A Profile, Institute of Peace and Conflict Studies*. New Delhi: IPCS.

Marx. K. 1847. *The Poverty of Philosophy*. In *Marx and Engels: Collected Works*, Vol. 6.

————. 1852. *The Eighteenth Brumaire of Louis Bonaparte*. Accessed 9 July 2017. https://www.marxists.org/archive/marx/works/1852/18th-brumaire/ch01.htm

————. 1948, 29 June. 'The June Revolution'. *Neue Rheinische Zeitung*.

————. 2000 [1844]. *The Introduction to Contribution to the Critique of Hegel's Philosophy of Right*, Marx/Engels Internet Archive (marxists.org). Accessed 9 July 2017. https://www.marxists.org/archive/marx/works/1844/df-jahrbucher/law-abs.htm

Marx, Karl and Frederick Engels. 1844–45. *Marx and Engels: Collected Works*, Vol. 4. Lawrence & Wishart (Electric Book), p. 289.

————. 1848, June. 'The June Revolution'. *Neue Rheinische Zeitung*. Accessed 23 May 2017. http://www.marxists.org/archive/marx/works/1848/06/29a.htm

Mellersh, H. E. L. and Neville Williams. 1999. *Chronology of World History*, Vol. 2. Greenwood, Mississippi: ABC-CLIO.

NCRB. 2012. *Crime in India, Statistics 2012*. New Delhi: NCRB.

Paul, Wm. 1922, February. 'Force: The Midwife of Revolution'. *Labour Monthly* 2 (2).

Press Trust of India (PTI). 2010, 24 May. 'Naxalism biggest threat to internal security: Manmohan'. *The Hindu*. Accessed 13 July 2017. http://www.thehindu.com/news/national/Naxalism-biggest-threat-to-internal-security-Manmohan/article16302952.ece#!

Saha, Anoop. 2007, 14 September. 'The Myths of Salwa Judum'. Accessed 9 July 2017. Countercurrents.org

Zedong, Mao. 1938, 6 November. 'Problems of War and Strategy'. Vol. II of *Selected Works*.

Salvadori, Massimo. 1990. *Karl Kautsky and the Socialist Revolution, 1880–1938*. London: Verso.

Žižek, Slavoj. 2006. 'Robespierre or the "Divine Violence" of Terror'. Accessed 28 May 2014. http://www.lacan.com/zizrobes.htm

3

Kidnap as a Revolutionary Strategy: The Case of Sukma District Collector

G. Haragopal*

Chhattisgarh was back in the news after two months of the episode of abduction of Alex Paul Menon, the district collector of newly created Sukma district by the Maoists. While last time it was the abduction that brought Bastar tribals, otherwise ignored, into a wider public debate in the media particularly the electronic, this time it was Basaguda massacre. At the time of abduction, there was a widespread mobilisation of public opinion against Maoist politics to put pressure on the state to go hard and harsh. On 29 June, literally after two months, the state armed forces went hard and killed 17 tribals in Bijapur district whom the fact-finding teams called innocent and the security forces including Chidambaram hard core Maoist guerrillas. The very same media which wanted the state to go hard found the state forces guilty of the brutal attack. The print media, particularly *The Hindu*, 'extensively and prominently reported the incident on 30th June and raised a question as to how that many persons killed in this action

* I am thankful to the Centre for the Study of Social Exclusion and Inclusive Policy, National Law School of India University particularly its Director, Professor S. Japhet and his colleagues for a congenial academic atmosphere for research work. I am equally thankful to Ms Shashikala whose professional competence; commitment coupled with patience in negotiating my handwriting helped me in completing this chapter. We are also grateful to Bastar tribals who intimately shared their unbelievable experiences. We owe an apology to them for not getting any relief from the Chhattisgarh government.

were civilians that included women and children'. How come Ipra Chottu, a child of 14 years, who was grazing animals was shot? It also reported pathetically that some have to be buried, but there were not many to dig all the graves and some bodies were to be burnt but they found it difficult to collect the wood.

The facts about this so-called 'encounter' started coming out when the villagers recounted the incident that how security forces fired at a peaceful gathering of villagers, killing 17 of them including five children aged 12–15 and sexually assaulted at least four teenage girls. They gathered to discuss the upcoming seed festival, which is held every year before sowing begins. The security forces opened fire on this unarmed gathering and several of the bodies had bullet wounds in the torso and the neck. That six policemen were injured is also a fact and the villagers had no clue but one of the villagers said that 'may be they accidentally shot each other'. It was further reported in the media that the forces camped in the villages dragged a 14-year-old girl who narrated the horrendous experience by saying that 'they threw me on the ground, beat me, kicked me, tore my clothes and kept threatening to rape me'. She said that three other girls were similarly molested. There was yet another ghastly incident recounted by Irpa Raju that 'my son Ramesh stepped out of the house for the toilet when he was shot by a policeman, Ramesh ran to the house shouting Ayo (Mother, Mother) but the force followed him and killed him in our house in front of my eyes' (Sethi 2012).

The police forces maintained that they were taken by surprise as five of their men were injured right away, and in firing several of the dead were 'probably' civilians. They also claimed that 'they exercised maximum restraint and fired in self-defence'. They complimented themselves when they said that 'we did not use any area weapons such as grenades or rocket launchers. If we really wanted to, we could have razed the entire village'. This tone speaks of the character and attitude of the law enforcing armed forces towards the citizens. The Home Minister P. Chidambaram determined to put down the Maoist movement praised the forces for their courage and skills. But the whole episode took an unexpected turn when the Chhattisgarh Congress contradicted Chidambaram and held that he was given wrong information. The Congress' fact-finding team described the encounter as 'completely fake' and called the victims innocent Adivasis. They said that children have died, school students have died and women have died. How they all can be Naxalites? This version was supported by the union minister of state for Agriculture, Chanandan Mahout. The security establishment expressed unhappiness with the quality of information passed on to the paramilitary forces and said that 'pure imagination is being passed off as intelligence'. E. N. Rammohan, a former director general of the BSF, found fault with the very approach of the central and state governments to the whole question of tribal development and the deprivation that these sections suffered (Rammohan 2012).

The incident took another turn when the Minister of Tribal Affairs Kishore Chandra Deo observed, 'If those killed were "Extremists" then why were most of them un-armed? No arms were recovered from them'. He added, 'the first principle of counter-insurgency was that you don't shoot unarmed and if one says that it was dark, it would not wash the action as night vision services were available'. He also said, 'you cannot fire at random in the dark, it is inexcusable'. To the argument that the Maoist use tribals as human shield, Mr Deo sharply reacted, 'the state government has not provided protection to the tribals against the extremists if the tribals are being forced to assemble at some place, must they pay with lives?' The minister also said, 'I have always had my reser-vations about the notorious Salwa Judum created by the Government' 'while Maoist problem had to be dealt but until the Government addressed the root of the problem, there would be no solution'. He further said, 'the biggest threat to tribals and forest dwellers in the country apart from the manner in which they were being systematically deprived of all sources of livelihood was the prospect of mining activity in the areas they lived in'. He stressed that 'the Forest Rights Act must be implemented fully before commencing mining; this was the first step to recognize the rights of tribal over their land and if you throw them out, they will be rendered homeless and stateless' (Gupta 2012).

Notwithstanding the serious observations by his own cabinet colleague and his own party's fact finding, Chidambaram maintained that encounter in Chhattisgarh was 'transparent' and 'upfront' but added that he was 'deeply sorry' for the killing of innocent persons. On the demand for enquiry, the home minister passed the buck and said, 'it was for the Chhattisgarh government to take a call on it as the operation was conducted under the state police'. Vijay Kumar, DG, CRPF neither was willing to reflect nor probe into the matter. On the contrary, he maintained, 'what options did we have? We would have been dying and you would be saying we are incompetent'. Another senior police officer Prakash Singh maintained that some collateral damage is unavoidable. And Raman Singh, the chief minister of Chhattisgarh, endorsed the view that the encounter is not fake.[1]

These responses only suggest that a central home minister incharge of law and order being himself a lawyer, the DGP, a responsible police officer and the chief minister of Chhattisgarh did not even speak the language that is in conformity with the constitutional rights, the rule of law and our tall claim that we are a democratic polity.

---

[1] Pratap, 'Sarkingooda Marana Kandanu Vyatirekinchandi', press release, 30 June 2012, Central Regional Bureau, CPI (Maoist).

In a 'press release',[2] the Maoist spokesperson Pratap noted that about a hundred villagers from three tribal habitats—Sankinguda, Kottaguda, Rajampeta—that form a part of Basaguda village, left these villages to the neighbouring state of Andhra Pradesh because of terror unleashed by Salwa Judum, returned back and met on 20 June to decide about allotment of land and to plan how to go about agricultural activities that suffered a serious setback in terms of loss of cattle and other agricultural tools. It was completely a meeting of the villagers. This meeting spot was surrounded by the police from all the sides firing on the group causing killing of 17 persons that included women and children. Eight were dead in firing and nine injured were cold-bloodedly killed by the police force. The women complained eight cases of rape. There were also some animals killed in firing causing further loss of cattle. The press release also maintained that the attack by the CRPF, Special Task Force (STF) and Koya Commandos was pre-planned and aimed at destroying the social base of the revolutionary struggle as these were the very villages which were earlier the victims of the attacks by the Salwa Judum. This is also the area from where the Sukma collector was abducted. The armed forces resorted to this attack as a part of retaliation. This is evident from series of attacks on cultivators and other unarmed people.

> There was a mass arrest of tribals from these areas. The police kept a continuous surveillance on these villages as they have directives from the highest political leaders of the country who are obsessed with imperialist driven growth model. The press release further observed that Basaguda attack is only a prelude to a higher design of declaring a full blooded war against its own people.[3]

[2] Dakshina Regional Committee, 'Dandakaranya', press release, 22 April 2012, CPI (Maoists).
[3] Ibid.

About the whole episode, the critical point is whether this encounter was a genuine mistake or is it a part of a grand design of Operation Green Hunt. According to B. D. Sharma, Operation Green Hunt was a strategy contrived by the white immigrants of wiping out the indigenous people when they occupied the United States. On similar line, it appears that the central government and state governments in India, driven by the growth obsession, are determined to systematically evict or erase the local tribal population either through terrorisation or fake encounters so as to facilitate entry of the Indian and multinational corporates to recklessly mine the rich mineral resources in tribal areas. The creation of notorious Salwa Judum, an unlawful armed mafia, pitted against the local tribals under the pretext of fighting the Maoists is further evidence of the sinister design. These illegal and anti-social forces were let loose on the tribals of Chhattisgarh. They were so unlawful and brutal that even the Supreme Court found it totally unacceptable and directed the government to disband this entire force. In response to the Supreme Court's judgment, instead of disbanding it, this force was incorporated into the formal police force. This changed the name and frame of Salwa Judum but its essential character remained the same.

The atrocities in this area came to our personal notice (mediators) in the course of mediation in the wake of abduction of Sukma collector. Before our meeting with the Maoist leadership materialised, on the way there were hundreds of tribals waiting for us and each one wanted to share his or her agony and anguish. Several tribals met us on the way and narrated their horrendous experiences with the security forces and more so with Salwa Judum. We could not hear the tragic story of each one of them as there was time constraint, but sample of atrocities as recounted by the tribals, gives us a feel of terror that Salwa Judum and the state unleashed on these tribals.

Yadar Bodidar said that his father who was on his way to Avapally Market to buy *chawal* (rice) was killed and his dead body was not found. Similar was the case of Mari Bandi who was killed when he went to Tirupan Gadu market. A woman from Tana Jagargunda village said that her daughter Palki was tortured and abused in filthy language. Emla Bandhi complained that her son who had three children was killed when he was tilling the land and his body was buried by the police and Salwa Judum. Sodi Baudh said that her son Sodi Masec who had two children was killed when he was going to the market and his dead body was not found. Bade Aite said that her son Badke Edma was thrown into fire with his hands and legs tied. Another woman Umga said that her husband Tomo Rosi was brutally killed and his dead body was found abandoned. Andal of Jarimil village said her husband Kudam Andal, who had four children, three sons and one daughter, was killed in 2006 and no trace of his dead body was found. Madkampenki's husband Kadmal was picked up from home when he was performing puja and beheaded. Madvi Bandi of Chimlipenta village was killed in firing and their hut was burnt. Kuram Gangi of Kumal Khad village complained that her husband Anda was killed in 2006 firing. Hemla Setee of Khullampad village said that her husband Hemla Chikkas was surrounded by the police and Salwa Judum from all the sides of the hut and they threw her husband into the fire set by Salwa Judum. Hemla Bima of Khullampad said that her son Guddi, who was going to his in-laws house to bring back his wife after the delivery, was taken to Jegurgunda police station and was shot in penta. There were deep wounds on his body when the dead body was handed over to the family. In addition to these atrocities, a large number of innocent tribals more than two thousands have been languishing in Chhattisgarh jails without any legal aid or assistance. It is an unending tragic story.

The above accounts present a picture of ruthless war against the tribals reminding the Operation Green Hunt in the United States four centuries back. This systematic destruction by Salwa Judum is patronised by the state. Maoists complain that it is a part of larger design to terrorise the people and make them run away from these villages so that the land could be handed over to multinational corporations (MNCs) for mining without facing any resistance from the local people. We as mediators informed this alarming situation to the chief minister in our meeting with him. In response, he started narrating how the Maoists killed the police personnel and other people in the name of informers almost justifying the violence. Of course, he said that a judicial enquiry has been ordered on these incidents but the tribals were not coming forward to depose before the judge. It is strange that while a large number of tribals were anxious to talk to the mediators, that not many of them were willing to meet the enquiring judicial officer is a sad reflection on our institutions which are not able to inspire the confidence of the common people, particularly the tribals.

This is almost the context of the abduction of the District Collector Alex Paul Menon. It is not necessarily a justification of abduction but an account of the circumstances under which such episodes occur. This is evident from the demands the Maoist party made for setting free the collector: one, stop Operation Green Hunt, combing operations and confine all the police forces to barracks; two, release thousands of innocent villagers languishing in Raipur and Dantewada jails by withdrawing the false cases foisted against them; three, release Kartam Joga, Vijay Godi, Sannu Madavi, Sudaru Kunjam, Lala Kunjam in addition to Rajesh Nayak Banjara of village Golugonda, Madvidula, Burkha detained in Dantewada and Jagdalpur jails. All these persons, the Maoist party claimed, are falsely implicated in the incident of an attack on the congress leader at Kuwakonda. They also wanted the following party members, along with two journalists P. K. Jha and Asit Kumar Sen, to be released: (a) Madkam Gopanna (Satyam Reddy), (b) Comrade Nirmalakka

(C. Vijayalaxmi), (c) Comrade Jaipal (Chandrasekhar Reddy), (d) Comrade Malati, (e) Comrade Meena Choudhary and (f) Comrade Padma.

They stated in their communication in an audio message that these demands have to be fulfilled by Raman Singh's government by 25th April as deadline. In the event of government not responding to these demands, the future of the district collector would be decided in the people's court.

The Maoist party appealed to the general public to keep a watch on the kind of response from the government and also urged Mrs Alex Paul Menon, and friends and relatives of Menon and IAS Officers Association to put pressure on the government for meeting their genuine demands. They expressed their concern about Mr Menon's health as it was critical and suggested that medicines should be sent through the mediators without any delay. For any negligence in this regard, they held that the government will have to bear the full responsibility for the consequences. As a part of this statement, they suggested the names of B. D. Sharma (Former SC, ST Commissioner), Prashant Bhushan (Advocate, Supreme Court) and Maneesh Kunjam (national president of Adivasi Mahasabha) as their mediators and stated that only these three mediators were welcome to Tadimetla and appealed to these three respected personalities to agree for mediation. Prashant Bhushan and Maneesh Kunjam expressed their inability to mediate on different grounds. B. D. Sharma was the one who readily agreed and they asked G. Haragopal to join B. D. Sharma and be a part of the mediation.

In yet another press release (on 26 April 2012),[4] the Maoist party's South Regional Committee Secretary Ganesh offered justification with a caption 'why they abducted the district collector'. In this statement, they

---

[4] Dakshin Regional Committee Dandakaranya, 'Collector Ko Hamne Kyaon Bandhak Banaye' (Why Did We Take the Collector as a Hostage?), press release, 26 April 2012, CPI (Maoists).

blamed the state that instead of responding to their demands, the central government had high level meeting to further reinforce the armed strength and intensify the surveillance by an unmanned aircraft. The government also simultaneously increased its campaign for release of the collector on grounds that he was pro-poor officer and that he was from a Dalit background. Several groups and individuals appealed that he be set free on humanitarian grounds. In the light of this pressure, the statement was meant to clarify to the general public the stand of the Maoist party.

The press release reiterates that as the appeal to the Maoist party focused on humanitarian grounds, the party asked why a similar appeal was not made when the Indian state unleashed brutal attacks during last six years on innocent tribal people.[5] During the tenure of Alex Paul Menon, a young boy Podium Mada was illegally detained for four days in police station, and there he was tortured, his private parts were burnt sprinkling petrol and he was killed in a barbaric manner, it was declared that he committed suicide hanging himself in the lock-up. On 11 February 2011, Podium Sanna of Polampally village was picked up from his home by the police and was killed. In October 2011, Soni Sori, the warden of girls' hostel was detained and she was not only raped but the police also pushed pebbles into her sensitive organs in the most inhuman way. These details came to light in the medical reports. Instead of holding the Superintendent of Police Ankit Garg responsible for these violations, he was awarded president's gold medal. All the district officers kept silent. The entire tribals of Sukma district were suffering brutal oppression of the police; Alex Paul Menon as district collector did not object to this unlawful, barbaric behaviour of the police and paramilitary forces. The party

---

[5] Dakshin Regional Committee, 'Dandakaranya', press release, 29 April 2012, CPI (Maoist).

asked a question: why no member of the society raised voice and asked Alex Paul Menon why was he tolerating and agreeing to these barbaric acts?

The statement also stressed on the eight years of governance of Raman Singh in the name of good governance. No problem of the people has ever been solved except forcefully implementing the so-called 'development' programmes at the behest of the World Bank in spite of opposition from the local tribals. The party raised the question that when anti-people development model was being enforced through brutal force causing enormous suffering to the tribals, why those who speak of humanitarianism remained mute spectators? When the corporate world and the MNCs are looting rich natural resources of Bastar, why the government officials turned themselves into mere agents of these market forces? This raises the question as to which side and for whose sake these officers were working. It is obvious, the party asserts, that these officers are facilitating looting and tolerating widespread corruption of Gali brothers, A. Raja, Kanimelli and Chidambaram. The party also drew the attention to officers such as Sri Laxmi and B. P. Acharya, IAS Officers from Andhra Pradesh, conniving with the corrupt political leaders. Raman Singh himself as incharge of coal mines was responsible for ₹1,200 crores embezzlement. They asked the question, 'should we believe that officers like Menon are innocent about these affairs'? In such a situation, when the very survival of tribal people was threatened, it is the birthright of them to oppose and resist this exploitation. The abduction of the district collector was a part of this resistance.

The statement maintains that the concern of the people about health of the collector is understandable, but why these concerns are absent in the case of hundreds of tribals who are also arrested and detained in the jails of Jagdalpur, Dantewada, Raipur, Rajnandgram? They are huddled into already crowded jails and being treated worse than cattle. This number runs into at least two thousands; in Dantewada Jail alone, there are seven hundred prisoners, while its capacity is only 150. In several jails, they neither get food nor space according to jail manual instructions. The conditions of women prisoners is much worse; they are not supplied even a piece of cloth during the monthly periods. They are falsely implicated in some case or the other and detained for years together without any trial. Several of them have become victims of physical and mental health disorders. They are not even allowed the normal *mulakhat* (meeting) entitled by the law. Many of them have no legal aid. The statement further adds, 'our beloved comrade Jaipal Dad (Chandrashekhar Reddy) who is implicated under Section 149 is over sixty years suffering from a chronic Hepatitis B disease'. This is only one example but there are several comrades whose health condition is a cause of anxiety. This approach of government, the Maoist party thinks, is intentional and they are treating the struggling people as their enemies. The question is why the members of so-called civil society, who are concerned about the health of Alex Paul Menon, do not show similar concern towards these prisoners? Why do not they pressurise the government to be humanitarian in its approach? Why they do not ask the government to stop Green Hunt and allow the tribals to live their own life peacefully?

The statement also added that the police establishment has been carrying a vicious campaign against the Maoists in newer forms. They are organising the rallies of students, traders and businessmen to protest against the abduction. But the same police lathi charged Anganwadi workers when they took a rally to press for their demands. They did not spare women participants and some of them fell unconscious. The police establishment which unleashed unprecedented violence and burnt three hundred houses of the Adivasis, and molested the women, would they allow rallies against such atrocities? They do not care even for the Supreme Court directive to vacate the school buildings and allow children to pursue their education. Collector Alex Paul Menon as incharge of district administration and law and order, why did he keep quite when unlawful activities go on right under his nose? These officers should take the responsibilities for all such activities. They cannot pretend innocence and yet claim that they are pro-poor officers. One can ask what his view on Operation Green Hunt is. When the central government convened the meeting of the district collectors of Maoist-affected districts, did he take a pro-poor stand and submitted a report on conditions of the poor?

The government does not allow any democratic activity outside to mobilise the public opinion. They cited the instance of a meeting in Charla of Khammam district of Andhra Pradesh opposing Green Hunt, it is not only that they were not allowed to hold the meeting but also were forcefully sent back. Why the civil society did not remember democratic values? In March 2010, the police and paramilitary forces attacked and burnt several villages destroying livelihood in the name of 'operation Vijay'. An innocent tribal Durga Dhruv of Toke village was beaten to death. In all such brutal operations, there is the consent and connivance of district collectors. Those who are talking of humanitarianism and democracy should care to go to the roots of the problem and ponder over on the basic values. It is only then they will be able to see the logic behind the collector's abduction. It is this mood of the movement that sets the backdrop for the two mediators to carry on the task of mediation.

The two Maoist chosen mediators (B. D. Sharma and G. Haragopal) had several rounds of talks not with the Chhattisgarh government directly but with its nominees— Mrs Nirmala Buch and S. K. Misra—former chief secretaries of Madhya Pradesh and Chhattisgarh states. This was in contrast with the approach of Andhra Pradesh and Odisha governments who agreed to the mediators chosen by the Maoists as government mediators too and reposed confidence in them. This move of Chhattisgarh was a clever Kautilyan move. The issues raised by the Maoists that have been elaborated in their press release were brought to the notice of the government nominees and wanted them to consider some of their legitimate demands which the state should address on its own, if it were committed to rule of law and constitutional values. The two officers took a rigid and inflexible stand as instructed by the Chhattisgarh government which in turn was receiving directives from the Central Home Ministry and perhaps the BJP and its Sangh Parivar. The plea that some of the demands like release of falsely implicated tribals and activists whose health condition was delicate did not or could not evoke any positive response. They went on sticking to the point that setting free the collector was a precondition for consider-ing any demand. The mood of the government was that of indifference and the anxiety that Odisha government or earlier Andhra Pradesh government displayed to get their officers released was largely missing. The options before the mediators were either to walk out of the talks or meet the Maoist party to brief them and ask for their response. The only promise that the government was willing to make was that it would constitute a high powered committee with a permanent status as a standing committee to look into all the issues once the collector is set free.

On the three major demands, the government representatives maintained that there was nothing like Operation Green Hunt therefore the question of stopping it does not arise; about combing operations and confining police and military forces to barracks it was already in effect. To the suggestion of the mediators that peace talks could be initiated suspending all the armed action from both the sides, they asked if such a suggestion is agreed to, what would be the Maoist party's reciprocal action. About release of the activists whose release the Maoist party demanded, they expressed helplessness as there was a PIL filed by a retired army officer in the Supreme Court with a prayer not to agree to any exchange of prisoners. Therefore, they held any steps in that direction would be sub judice. To the demand for release of the Adivasis, the response was that it is a time-consuming process involving case by case review, but this will be considered sympathetically once the collector comes out. However, they facilitated meeting of the mediators with the Maoist leaders in the forest. They did take care of all travel arrangements and provided safe passage. The meeting between the mediators and the Maoist party came through in the evening hours of 27 April 2012.[6]

The mediators in their four to five hours discussion with the Maoist party conveyed the pattern of state response. On the first issue of stopping armed actions from both the

---

[6] Note given by mediators to Maoists:

The point one about Operation Green Hunt, police patrolling, combing operation and police being confined to their barracks, the government maintains that there is no Operation Green Hunt. About the other state actions, we suggested as mediators that there should not be any armed actions from both the sides; the government would like the movement to specify how to operationalise this whole process.

Related to this is the larger question of constitutional provisions relating to Schedule V and Schedule VI, Forest Rights Act, PESA and Article 19. The conflict is essentially on the control of the resources in the tribal areas. We expressed our stand that the resources belong to the tribal community and that is the spirit of the constitution and other tribal rights. We also think that the way to solve the crisis is to address this large question, which, in our view, will bring lasting peace in the region. How to operationalise this process is something that the Maoist party can suggest the steps to be initiated. About the innocent villagers who are in the prisons of Dantewada and Raipur jails, the government desires to know, if the party can furnish the details of these prisoners. The cases will be reviewed by a necessary mechanism on a fast track mode with immediate effect. The process can start forthwith and release as many villagers as possible against whom false cases are foisted. The government assures that a sympathetic view will be taken in all such cases. The government also promises to review the cases of six comrades mentioned by the party and take steps within the legal framework, for their release.

sides, the Maoist said they would convey their response the next day after due consideration. To the PIL in the Supreme Court, they laughed and gave a graphic account of lawless behaviour of the state forces in Bastar and maintained that rulers remember the law only when they were in crisis and added that the situation would not have reached this stage, if only the rulers respected their own laws and constitutional scheme of things. They felt that these legal niceties were just a pretext and stressed their demand for release of their eight comrades who were implicated in false cases. About humanitarianism, their reaction was very sharp. They said that those who are talking of humanitarian approach should realise that several of these comrades qualify to be released by those humanitarian standards that are being talked of. They drew our attention and said how would those people justify their appeal that Alex Menon's wife was on family way when an eight-month pregnant woman Korsa Sanni who was arrested had delivered her baby in the jail? Why these sections were so indifferent to such inhuman actions of the government? About the proposed high powered committee, they talked of futility of such committees and pointed out the fate of several such committees which did nothing to give relief to the struggling masses. They at the end of our pleading and persuasion insisted that out of the eight leaders, release of at least four, would be their minimum condition for setting the collector free. In the event of the government not agreeing to the demand, the issue will be taken to peoples' court. They specifically asked mediators not to appeal for the release of the collector, nor fix any deadline, if no demand is conceded.

On 29 April, they did send a communication as promised, the caption of which was 'Abduction of the Collector is a part of intensification of the peoples struggle'. The communication stated that despite that collector has been under their position for about 13 days, and the mediators did all that they could, as they had five rounds of talks with the government representatives for the release of the Adivasis and their comrades, there was no positive response from the government. On the contrary, what was clear was that the government was adopting a systematic policy to unleash terror through Operation Green Hunt on the struggling masses of 78 districts, unabated for almost 33 months. The government is simultaneously mobilising public sympathy and support. This two-pronged strategy—armed action and mobilisation of sympathy—is a part of war strategy. The high powered committee that is announced by the Chhattisgarh government has been constituted under the clear instructions from the Ministry of Home Affairs on the advice of FBI of America. This approach, according to their note, is a part of the development model impelled by the forces of globalisation, privatisation and marketisation. Unless the district collectors fully grasp the dangers of this model, they will not have clarity of their own role in the system. The government is badly committed for transfer of rich natural resource to private and corporate houses in the name of development. Those who are opposed to this development are brutally attacked. They use terms such as civic action programme, good governance to carry on their looting without any resistance. They organise all the officers and police forces under unified command to contain the struggles to enable exploitative forces looting the resources. This is backed by the paramilitary forces of the central government. Unless this dangerous development is resisted, the very identity and survival of the tribals is in peril. In fact, it is this resistance that constitutes the essence of humanitarianism or humanitarian values at this point of time. There is no humanism other than this resistance and this is the utmost priority of the movement.

The statement also questioned the Chief Minister Raman Singh's stand that there is no Operation Green Hunt and asked what could be the justification for the presence of thousands of police and paramilitary forces in the rural areas? How does he explain the ruthless repression unleashed by the security forces in Abuz Mad in the name of 'Operation Haka'? How can he hide the inhuman and brutal attacks in Singanmadugu, Somili and Tadmetla where the huts were burnt and women were raped? In the same communication, they appealed to the intellectuals, democrats, humanists and media who are anxious about the abduction of collector and his release, to have similar concerns and standby the struggling masses.

The Maoist party also held that the outcome of the mediation is in the form of constituting a high powered committee under the chairpersonship of Mrs Nirmala Buch and the chief secretary and DGP as members and that they would take up the cases of prisoners on fast track mode has no credibility whatsoever. The committee, if it wants to take its task seriously, should be willing to go into the very causes of arrests and evidence for the offences that these prisoners are accused of. But such search for the causes is not possible with a senior police officer and chief secretary as members of the committee. How can such a committee do justice to the people? This committee was nowhere in the demands made by the party. This is nothing but deluding those who continue to be naïve and believe in the government's commitments to the constitutional values. If the rulers were sensitive to suffering and injustice to the people, why did they not constitute such a committee before the abduction took place? The chief minister who claims that constituting such a committee is a historic decision and the committee will set a role model, is the same chief minister who had not cared the Supreme Court's judgment and misled the highest court in the Salwa Judum judgment. It is only with greater clarity and critical assessment that it would be possible to strengthen the resistance. The party believes that it is only in opposing the neoliberal assault by imperialism, the identity and livelihood of the tribals would be protected.

The attitude and approach of the Chhattisgarh government and the Maoist party led to a stalemate and at one point it looked that the whole mediation would break down.

That was the time when the whole idea of high powered committee was reconsidered by the mediators in spite of party's well-argued opposition. B. D. Sharma personally knew the chief secretary and Nirmala Buch as they were his colleagues. The chief secretary repeatedly claimed that he was a disciple of Sharma. Mrs Nirmala Buch pleaded that we repose full confidence in her and promised that she would be tough with the government and see that agreement is enforced. That was the stage when a meeting was arranged between the mediators and the chief minister. The chief minister promised that the agreement would be fully respected and implemented. The whole process that got reduced to a simple faith in those officers, could be a misplaced faith. The mediators, in spite of perceptional difference, felt that breaking the mediation process would leave the whole issue unresolved and detention of the collector would be unduly prolonged. The mediators thought that reposing confidence in the high powered committee, notwithstanding the critical assessment of the Maoist party, was the option open in those given circumstances. The mediators insisted on an agreement between the government representatives and the mediators with the government as a direct party to the agreement.[7] The

---

[7] Note given by mediators to the Government of Chhattisgarh

1. About the committee, the Maoist party felt that the experience with earlier committees does not inspire any confidence. Once the problem is over, the government just does not care for such committees. To inspire confidence, at least a few innocent tribal prisoners should be released.

2. The second demand which is most important is, 'release of at least six following persons who were acquitted in a number of cases or those who were arrested after they were acquitted by the courts'. They are: (a) Gopanna, he was acquitted in all cases except one or two; (b) Meena, there are two cases but she is in the prison from 2008; (c) Padma, she was acquitted in all cases but arrested after the release; (d) Jaipal, in the prison from 2007, literally no case and he is more than 60 years old and suffering from Hepatitis B; (e) Korses

principal secretary law of the Chhattisgarh government
N. K. Aswal became a signatory on behalf of the government.

Once the mediators expressed their willingness to
appeal, the agreement was drafted by the government so
cleverly with such a craft that an outsider will get a feeling
that the mediators gave in to the tactics of the government[8]
(see the agreement in the notes). Frankly, the government
hardly gave any firm commitment. The representatives
of the government were not willing to incorporate any
suggestions from the mediators. We expressed our deep
dissatisfaction with the way it was drafted. The government representatives, particularly Mrs Nirmala Buch,
went on maintaining that the government for various legal
and technical reasons cannot commit much on paper, but

Ammi in prison from 2008, she had delivery in the prison and
(f) Madkam Hinge in prison from 2008, there are no serious cases.

About PIL in the Supreme Court, they held that it is the government
which managed it. Since the state forces resorted to so much of
lawlessness, invoking a finer provision of such a law is ridiculous.

When we shared our concern about the collector, they asked why so
much of concern, when the government itself is not bothered.

[8] The agreement between the Government of Chhattisgarh and the
mediators:

1. The mediators were concerned with the safe return of the district
   collector and as a goodwill gesture would appeal to the Maoist party
   to ensure safe return of collector within 48 hours.
2. The state government had agreed to set up a high powered committee
   to be the standing committee to regularly review all cases of persons
   in respect of whom investigation and prosecution is pending. This
   includes Maoist related cases. It was agreed as the prisoners are in
   distress in view of the long time taken in investigation/prosecution
   for various reasons and great inconvenience caused to their families.
3. The high powered committee will be chaired by Mrs Nirmala Buch
   and shall have the chief secretary, the Government of Chhattisgarh
   and director general of police (DGP) of the state as members.
4. This committee will review the lists of cases received by the
   mediators in respect of tribals of Bastar and surrounding areas shall
   be given priority. The committee will give its recommendations to
   the state government which will consider these cases with a sense
   of urgency.

the spirit of mutual understanding will prevail and most of the Maoist demands will favourably be reviewed. The understanding was that the cases of a large number of tribals in Raipur and Dantewada jails would be reviewed on fast track mode and maximum number of tribals would get relief. About the six Maoist party members, the committee will take a very sympathetic view and initiate all the steps in the direction of their release. This was viewed as a 'secret deal' by our overenthusiastic media.

It is at this stage the mediators appealed to the Maoist party to set the collector free in 48 hours, despite their advice not to appeal and set a deadline. After the appeal, the Maoist party in a telephonic conversation did say that it would have been better if we had not appealed, but chose to respect our appeal. They only asked for the extension of time, instead of 48 hours, they suggested 72 hours. They also asked us to go to the forest to accompany the collector and hand over him safely to his family.

As we reached the forest facilitated by the government, the second rung leadership was waiting for us. That they were not happy with our appeal was very evident. The mediators had to argue at a great length to convince the reasonableness of the appeal and conditions in which the appeal had to be made.[9] They still did not look fully

---

[9] Appeal to the Maoists by the mediators:

The mediators nominated by the Maoist party, have had discussions with Mrs Nirmala Buch and Mr S. K. Misra after their meeting with the Maoist party. The government assures on the following points:

1. The government will constitute a high powered committee under the chairpersonship of Mrs Nirmal Buch with chief secretary and DGP of Chhattisgarh as members. This committee will review the cases of all prisoners who have been languishing in Chhattisgarh jails including the cases demanded by the Maoists party. The committee will review the cases periodically to expedite the disposal of maximum number of cases especially related to tribals.
2. Relief will be provided in all cases where there is proof of Human Rights Violations.

convinced. Their inconvenience with the appeal was that the abduction did not give any relief to the tribals and what would be their explanation to their social and political supporters was their dilemma. In a confrontation between the powerful and an adamant state and an armed resistance, the limitations of the mediators—human and circumstantial—became the limitation of the movement.

The collector Alex Paul Menon was handed over to the mediators in late hours of 3 May. As the whole process was time consuming, the restless media which was waiting for this exciting moment let loose its imagination and started spinning 'fiction' around the event. As the mediators chose to address press conference where a note 'our concerns' was released, the media was with full of stories. Two questions that were hurled at the mediators were, how much of money changed the hands and what was the secret deal between the Maoists and Chhattisgarh government? Taken aback by this unexpected third-degree interrogation, mediators retaliated back saying that corporate media hunting for profit, which never debated the suffering of Bastar tribals, has no moral right to question the credentials of the mediators. Surprisingly, 'our concerns' that were distributed widely in the press conference did not find even a mention in the print or electronic media.[10]

Under the given circumstances, we as mediators feel that this was the agreement that could be worked out. We appealed to the Maoist party Southern Regional Committee, Dandakaranya to consider this proposal favourably and ensure safe return of the Collector Alex Paul Menon, whose spouse is in the family way. The concern for human life will promote higher human values.

[10] Press release by the mediators' 'Our Concerns':
We all are extremely happy that Mr Alex Paul Menon, collector of Sukma is back with the people and is joining his family. We are confident that he will stand by the poor, defend their natural rights and earn a place in the hearts of the vulnerable sections of our society. We also thank the Communist party of India (Maoist), south Bastar for the trust they have reposed in us and hope that

It is a sad reflection on the media which promotes and propagates distorted stories about the tribal struggles have no appreciation of peaceful end of an abduction story.

The response to the abduction of Sukma district collector by Chhattisgarh government was in sharp contrast to the responses of governments of Andhra Pradesh and Odisha. In Andhra Pradesh, when seven IAS officers were kidnapped, popularly known as Gurtedu kidnap, in 1987 with a demand for release of their seven comrades,

---

meaningful deliberations will continue. We appreciate the gesture of Chhattisgarh government for agreeing to our mediation.

The mediation process, notwithstanding its limitations, does mark the beginning of a transformative process that would pave the way for peace and development in the state. In our view, it is also marked with the beginning of an era where the draconian terms such as Operation Green Hunt, combing operations and violations of human rights of the simplest people on the earth, about whom we are so proud, will be erased from the wonderful enchanting world of Bastar. We will be reverting to the regime of self-governance of the community on whom colonial laws were imposed ironically after Independence. We will bid goodbye to the era of eminent domain of the State in favour of traditional commands of the community. In this frame, the rich resources will be under the control of the community and not the state. Prior consent of the community before undertaking any enterprise shall be strictly enforced. Community ownership of industrial enterprises, as recommended by the Bhuria Committee, shall be effectively implemented. Entrepreneurs of industrial enterprise, if any, will be junior partners of the community and not its masters.

The so-called development of all descriptions has invariably led to displacement of the tribal people uprooting them from their livelihood, resources and habitat. Influx of outsiders commanding vantage positions has resulted in large-scale land alienation, deprivation and distress. The constitutional protection of the people under article 19(5), which has provided protective shield to the tribal people in the north-east has remained dysfunctional in the extensive tribal territories of Central India. This must be operationalised forthwith so that simple tribal people can develop according to their own genius.

In our view, it is this approach, which will be the real mark of progress and development and will bring back lasting peace in this extensive region. This is our personal concern as also that of the Maoist party.

the government not only agreed for the release but acted with an unusual sense of urgency. There was literally an exchange of the officers and the leaders of the People's War. In another case of kidnap, known as the Koyyur Kidnap where an IAS officer, local MLA and five district officers were kidnapped, the Government of Andhra Pradesh sought the mediation of civil liberties leaders who took almost three weeks to get the hostages released and the demand of people's war to release one of their leaders was met, although after a week that the hostages were released. This kidnap led to a serious public debate and the People's War decided not to resort to this form of resistance though it appears they kept the option open. There was hardly any kidnap after the Koyyur Kidnap (Haragopal 2012).

This form of resistance unexpectedly came back with Malkangiri Kidnap in Odisha in 2011 after a gap of almost two decades. The pattern was different, this time it included 14 demands mostly relating to the tribals. That the Maoist party should demand from the state some

---

We may also refer at this stage to the Excise Policy 1974 whose seeds had been sown by me (Dr B. D. Sharma) as collector of Bastar in 1969. Commercial vending of liquor was abolished in 1974 with power to the Gram Sabhas for effective control there on. The results were fabulous. It remained in effect till about 1985. Today, neither the Union not the concerned states are aware about that policy, let alone the question of controlling the same. It is being pursued for earning revenue, wages of sin, with no questions asked. The 1974 policy must be revived effectively. This intervention against this policy remained unattended for more than a year now.

Lastly, we may refer to the situation in Abujmarh that has been kept outside the purview of revenue and forest policy since 1933. I (Dr B. D. Sharma) as collector of Bastar reinforced the policy in 1968—toured extensively in this 'unknown hill'. There are serious intrusions in this territory for about two decades. This intrusion is in violation of the hoary traditions and also the spirit of UN Declaration on the rights of the indigenous people. I (Dr B. D. Sharma) drew the attention of the governor of Chhattisgarh to protect especially the area of Abujmarh, but with no response.

relief for the tribals marks a shift in its approach. The Odisha government came out with a prompt response to most of the demands in principle and showed considerable anxiety to get the collector released. Once the collector was released, the government started dragging its feet. In fact, on two issues: release of Maoist activists and Adivasis, and question of tribal land, they agreed to constitute two committees to address the problems. However, outcomes have been totally disappointing and they hardly respected their commitments and the meetings of the committees that were agreed to were not even convened. This response smacks of contingency approach and lacks conviction in a democratic belief that such an approach should inspire public confidence. This casualness is a reflection on a state lacking public accountability and a part of 'unbroken history of broken promises'.

In the case of abduction of the Sukma district collector, the response of Chhattisgarh government brings out the hardening of the state and its increasing belief in the use of force than democratic dialogue and peaceful resolution of issues. They carried a nominal dialogue through their trusted nominee who was more rigid than the government itself. The response of the government to even genuine demands like release of innocent tribals and falsely implicated leaders was lukewarm. There was no anxiety to get the officer released. The entire episode, of course, raised several questions about lawful and democratic functioning of the state, bureaucracy and civil society. The questions raised by the Maoist party in the course of mediation will have to be debated and answered by responsible democratic sections of the society.

The so-called civil society and the middle classes believe that there is no place for abduction and violence in a democracy, yes in a democracy they have no place. But if we analyse the Chhattisgarh episode and the ruthless, lawless behaviour of the state armed forces and atrocities inflicted by an unlawful state promoted force like Salwa Judum, how are we to interpret Indian democracy? Those political scientists who have been extensively focusing on institutions, electoral politics, shifting power balances will have to grapple the phenomenon of how democratic systems negotiate a crisis, and how it responds to the struggles for survival and sustenance of excluded sections. Such an approach gives insight into the dynamics of substantive democracy. It is increasingly evident that the state is determined to deal with the problems through militarisation and brutalisation. In the process, democratic means like mediation is reduced to a mockery with far reaching implications and consequences.

The indifference to the detention of thousands of innocent tribals in the jails being interpreted by media and political analysts as democratic determination of the chief minister and a model for other states does not auger well to the future of Indian democracy. The central questions, why there are politics of resistance, why people have to take to arms, will have to be looked into. There is no point in summarily dismissing the resistance as undesirable, undemocratic and characterising it as the 'greatest national security threat'. A democratic society is one which arrives at conclusions through causation and what Amartya Sen calls public reasoning. The public debate in India, thanks to irresponsible print and more so the electronic media, is more opinionated than rationally arrived at. The way Maoist movement is so characterised, as if everything around is right in the existing social and economic order.

One of the problems, of course, with the Maoist movement is their public pronouncements of protracted armed struggle, overthrow of the Indian state as if that is only the preoccupation of the movement. The peace talks in Andhra Pradesh where they demanded self-reliance, democratic rights, land reforms, tribal rights, separate Telangana and in the case of Malkangiri Kidnap, and in Chhattisgarh they came out with a charter of demands mostly relating to tribals. This may be tactically to expose the hollowness

of the Indian state and subvert its legitimacy, but secur-
ing relief and belief in mediation to resolve the issues also
suggest the immediate concerns and democratic expectations. In fact, central issue for the outside world to be
debated is not the violence of the Maoists but its support
structure. It is time that we ask why the entire tribal belt
in India supports the movement and what are the basic
issues to be addressed? In fact, to dub the entire tribal
struggles as Maoist instigated is distortion of widespread
tribal unrest, a result of the growth-driven development
model. As mediators, we did convey our anguish at the
loss of life of two constables at the time of kidnap and also
suggested to reconsider abduction as a form of resistance.
As members of civil society, it is necessary, we initiate
a meaningful debate with the movement to economise
violence and enlarge the democratic space.

The kidnap of Sukma district collector and the issues
that came up in their pronouncements and communication
was the model of development which in the name of
growth surrendered rich natural resources to corporates
and multinationals for pittance in return. Instead of
using the mineral resources to strengthen manufacturing
sector, gifting the raw material to powerful forces like
the old monarchs or colonial power does not speak of
strengthening the economy nor deepening of democracy.
This also raises the question of the very position of the
nation state. In the course of mediation, the mediators
raised this question with the chief minister that how
come a BJP-ruled government with backing of RSS who
claim monopoly of nationalism and patriotism sell away
raw materials to foreign economic powers? This reckless
mining has been evicting the tribal communities through
the infamous Operation Green Hunt, and the government
has shown some inclination to even deploy the Indian
army to fight against its own people. Is it not that the
very character and original function of the nation state to
protect the capital and natural resources within a territory
backed by sovereign power of the people gets subverted?

It has become more an agent to facilitate the movement of global capital negating the very purpose of nation state.

Indian state is caught up between its increasing loyalty to global capital and people's resistance. The forms of resistance like abduction or undue violence may be a challenge to a democratic society, but the society should realize that Indian state has been promoting and patronising unlawful reckless violence of Salwa Judum kind of forces. There is rise of huge mafia which threatens the system from within. This mafia has killed several right to information (RTI) activists who are unarmed and fighting within the democratic legal framework. There has to be serious analysis of purposeless mafia violence and Maoist violence which is politically disposed. The mediation during the kidnaps and issues that came up is an evidence of its concerns. In all the cases of abduction, the moral pressure of mediators did work.

Indian state increasingly believes in use of force to tackle the politically resolvable questions. Rise of Narendra Modi, who is responsible for a massacre of helpless minorities, is becoming the hope of so-called democratic politics. The global capital and Indian corporates feel the need for a ruthless leader for reckless development, they want a Suharto. The growth obsession and Gujarat being projected as the model state, forgetting enormous brutal violence it witnessed, is to impose such a model on whole of India. If people's resistance movements—peaceful and militant—are not viewed in their proper context, we are giving in, either knowingly or unknowingly, to the rise of a fascist state.

References

Haragopal, G. 2012. 'Maoist Movement and the Indian State: Mediating Peace'. *Socio-Legal Review*, 8 (1): 113–144.

Gupta, Smita. 2012, 4 July. 'Home Ministry ill-informed on Bijapur killings, says Deo'. *The Hindu*. Accessed 17 July 2017. http://www.thehindu.com/

news/national/other-states/home-ministry-illinformed-on-bijapur-killings-says-deo/article3599436.ece

Rammohan, E. N. 2012, 16 July. 'Unleash the good force: Implement land ceiling acts and enforce fifth and ninth schedule'. *Outlook Magazine*. Accessed 17 July 2017. https://www.outlookindia.com/magazine/story/unleash-the-good-force/281554

Sethi, Aman. 2012, 1 July. 'Villagers bury their dead as Maoists & forces trade charges'. *The Hindu*. Accessed 17 July 2017. http://www.thehindu.com/news/national/other-states/villagers-bury-their-dead-as-maoists-forces-trade-charges/article3589185.ece

PART II

PART II

4

The Ambiguities of Revolutionary Violence

Neera Chandhoke

Introduction

Let me as a prelude to the argument below, speak briefly of the three distinguishing feature of revolutionary violence. First, the proponents of revolutionary violence believe that in deeply unequal societies such as India, the grip of three-fold injustice–social discrimination, extreme deprivation and lack of 'voice'—upon the lives of people—is intractable and can be broken only through acts of that involve coercion. Second, the Maoists renounce political obligation to the state, but they do not renege on moral obligation to the rest of the citizens. They seek to replace a state that has displayed remarkable and a somewhat stunning incapacity to provide justice to its citizens, with one that will be responsive to precisely those people who have been abandoned on the sidewalks, or consigned to the ditches of the pathway treaded by history. Third, revolutionary violence manifested as guerrilla war is less about the use of instruments of force and destruction, and more about the political mobilisation of, in particular, the constituency on whose behalf the group has picked up arms, and in general society. The objective of revolutionary violence is to transform the politics of voicelessness into the politics of voice. For those of us who prefer politics in the progressive mode, revolutionary violence proves a far better bet for the recovery of agency through the repossession of voice, than other forms of political violence.

Even so a great deal of ambiguity proscribes clear and unconditional endorsement of this particular mode of politics. We simply cannot turn a blind eye to the multiple pitfalls that disfigure the preferred route to political Utopia in the revolutionary imaginaries of the Maoists. Etched starkly onto the political horizon, in blazing alphabets of mayhem and gore, are the costs of violence unleashed by the state, as well as by the Maoists. So many lives lost, so many innocent people killed, so much arson, so much destruction of public property, so much turmoil and so much insecurity. The condition of people living in regions that the Maoists have made their base is nothing short of the Hobbesian state of nature—'nasty, brutish and short'.

The Paradox of Revolutionary Violence

Let us frontally confront the paradox of revolutionary violence. As responsible citizens of the Republic of India, we recognise the sheer stubbornness of particularly vicious forms of injustice. Prima facie, there seems to be no way out of this spiral of injustice, suffering and state-sponsored violence, except revolutionary violence. The paradox is that this mode of politics need not always add up to political wisdom or marked by prudence. It is bad politics to wave away losses of human lives, and destruction of habitations as collateral damage, and focus on the goal instead. It is also completely unethical. For we cannot, ever, be confident that the objective for which the guerrillas have picked up arms will ever be attained. None of us, not even a prescient and exceptionally gifted fortune teller can predict with certainty that the route of violence will lead to the desired goal, and nowhere else. Despatches from history tell us that contingency is the name of the game.

I am, note, not bringing into the argument the consideration that violence is morally bad. Certainly, violence is morally bad, but multiple injustices under which some of our own people quake are also morally bad. The issue is different. Even if we justify revolutionary violence with reference to the immediate context, this cannot be the end of the story. We cannot exempt revolutionary violence from political judgements on the basis of the here and now, and ignore the wider dimensions of the issue. As a form of politics, revolutionary violence impacts our collective existence. Our collective lives are shaped by the political context we live and work in, in association with others, and our choices are enabled or circumscribed by this context. We cannot possibly be indifferent to acts of the state as well as of non-state actors that impress this context with their brand of politics.

Moreover, as members of a political community, we hold obligations to our fellow citizens. If they have come to harm, we need to engage with the state that has seriously lapsed on its responsibility to citizens. At the same time, we also need to engage with the Maoists who have picked up arms on behalf of those who have been harmed. There is a need to politically evaluate the efficacy of revolutionary violence as a means of achieving given objectives. In any case, are we not bound to adjudicate this avatar of politics much in the way we evaluate other forms of politics from collective action, to political parties, to the high politics of the state? Why not? Political practices, especially those that carry great costs, cannot be their own defendant, judge and jury. They have to be judged on some criterion. Concerned observers and analysts have to be Janus-faced, with one face turned towards the state and its policies and the other towards political practices in society.

On balance, we can and do evaluate politics and political practices from different vantage points, the ends a specific practice espouses, its tactics, its conventions and its procedures of mobilisation. If as democrats we are committed to equality, we should be assessing political practices by reference to the following question. Does a particular mode of politics enable vulnerable people to 'stand up', speak back to a history that is not of their making and thereby acquire agency? In a society stamped by inequality, oppression and injustice, democratic politics is about facilitating and catalysing the transition from subject to agent.

Therefore, I suggest that instead of resorting to empty and sanctimonious arguments on the immorality of violence, we should proceed to investigate revolutionary violence from its own parameters, its principles and its conventions and not from a moral standpoint outside the practices of violence. And then we can see whether the main presupposition that of giving the marginalised agency is borne out by the strategy of the Maoists in India.

Maoism: Reclaiming Selfhood

In deeply hierarchical and unjust societies such as India, does Maoism as praxis enable people who are triply disadvantaged to recover agency and make their own histories? Of course, the history that ordinary people make, might not be the history they wanted to make in the first instance, or they might make these histories badly. But that is not the main issue, the issue is whether people have voice. Do they need to resort to violence to do so, or support those who wield AK-47s?

Sumanta Bannerjee, who styles himself as a one-time Maoist, suggests that the objective of the earlier Naxalite movement was not only to assure access to basic material goods but also to secure justice and equal treatment for the landless labourer and the tribal. The Naxalites, he suggests, gave back dignity to the downtrodden peasantry, which had been socially discriminated against and exploited for centuries. In a world where the upper class landlords treated the 'doubly disadvantaged' as untouchables, denied them civic rights and had no compunction in abducting and raping their women, Naxalite politics inspired precisely these people to assert themselves as equal human beings. Revolutionary violence enabled them to resist humiliating codes of conduct imposed by the upper castes. He cites the voice of an old Bauri (depressed class) peasant in a village in Burdwan district who said in 1969 that Naxalbari had authorised him to walk with his head held high. He no longer had to make way for the upper castes when they crossed his path (Bannerjee 2012, 54).

In a similar vein, George Kunnath, who has carried out considerable field work in Bihar, seems to suggest that violence, involving very often the killing of notorious landlords and moneylenders, occupation and redistribution of their land, imposition of fines and summary executions, might well be necessary precondition of the recovery of self-respect (2012).

These arguments echo the arguments made in the famous work *The Wretched of the Earth* authored by Frantz Fanon during the Algerian struggle for independence (1985a). Till today, it is seen as a classic that dwells not only on the production and reproduction of violence under colonialism but also on the violence of the post-colonial elite and resultant loss of hope.

In this much acclaimed work, Fanon brings out in fine detail the subtleties and the power of violence, as well as its waywardness. He wrote elegantly and powerfully of the crippling effects of settler colonialism on the collective psyche of the colonised. The reach of violence, he theorised, is widespread, timeless and enduring. The footprint of the cloven hoof of violence is practically ineradicable. It is perhaps not surprising that the post-colonial elite cannot, but be cast in the mould of the same violence it had led the struggle against. The colours of violence do not wash out quite so easily.

But violence, theorises Fanon, is double edged, both lethal and liberating at the same time. The violence of settler colonialism hammers the colonised into submission. Logically, the only way 'natives' can speak back to a history that has enslaved their minds and bodies is to use the weapon of the coloniser against him. This may even be advantageous because violence enables the 'native' to shrug off intimidating inferiority complexes produced by colonialism. Violence rescues them from inertia, restores their self-respect and enables men to recover 'manhood' translated as agency.

> At the level of individuals, violence is a cleansing force. It frees the native from his inferiority complex and from his despair and inaction; it makes him fearless and restores his self-respect. Even if the armed struggle has been symbolic, and the nation is demobilised through a rapid movement of decolonisation, the people have the time to see that the liberation has been the business of each and all and that the leader has no special merit. (Fanon 1985a, 74)

Even the reactive form of violence adopted by the colonised is advantageous. Violence develops consciousness of a common cause, of a national destiny and of a collective history (1985a, 74).

The theme of violence as liberation was highlighted in the 'Preface' to *The Wretched of the Earth* written by Jean Paul Sartre.

> When the peasants lay hands on a gun, the old myths fade, and one by one the taboos are overturned; a fighter's weapon is his humanity. For in the first phase of the revolt killing is a necessity; killing a European is killing two birds with one stone, eliminating in one go, oppressor and the oppressed; leaving one man dead and the other man free, for the first time the survivor feels a national soil under his feet. (Fanon 1985b, 19)

Fanon too is clear about the advantages that violence delivers into the hands of the colonised, notably recovery of the self.

Reclaiming Selfhood

The passionate advocacy of violence as a tool of emancipation is, however, only one part of the story Fanon told the world. The paralysing influence of colonialism can be broken only through the use of violence. This is incontrovertible. Spontaneous violence has its uses, but it can be self-defeating, it can subvert liberation. You do not carry on a war, he wrote, nor suffer brutal repression, nor look on while all other members of your family are wiped out in order to make hatred triumph. But

> [r]acialism and hatred and resentment—legitimate desire for revenge—cannot sustain a war of liberation. Those lightning flashes of consciousness which fling the body into stormy paths or which throw it into an almost pathological trance where the face of the other beckons me on to giddiness, where my blood calls for the blood of the other, where by sheer inertia my death calls for the death of the other—that intense emotion of the first few hours falls to pieces if it is left to feed on its own substance. (Fanon 1985a, 111)

Not only do hatred and bloodlust peter out within a short span of time, 'hatred alone cannot draw up a programme'.

At this point in the argument, Fanon warns against excessive or sole reliance on violence. This course of action, he suggests, is hardly prudent, politically speaking. Unless those who wield violence are clear about the purpose of what they are doing, they tend to capitulate to the blandishments of the settler. The objectives of the struggle ought not to be chosen without discrimination Fanon tells us, for people might begin to question the prolongation of the war the moment the enemy offers concessions. So seductive is the need to be recognised as a human being that the 'native' can easily cave in (1985a, 112–13). The headiness of the gun is replaced by another sort of headiness that of being recognised as a human being by the very people who had denied to the Algerians humanity. People engaged in liberating themselves from brutal colonialism must not imagine that the fight is won by these small concessions; their demands must not become modest. The revolution will certainly collapse and the recovery of agency through violence will prove short-lived, placated easily by meaningless sops.

Hatred for Fanon is not a political agenda; it can never be an agenda, just one temporary and dispensable milestone on the route to liberation. The users of violence have to be constantly patrolled; the use of violence has to be moderated and educated by the leaders. The activist and the leader must take control. 'Once again, things must be explained to them; the people must see where they are going, and how they are going to get there'. Politics has to control violence otherwise the entire project of liberation can go haywire. In order to prevent this, in order to politicise people into the intricacies of the issue at hand, the war has to continue, but not as a project of violence but of that as politics.

The task of bringing the people to political maturity demands certain preconditions. For one, the political organisation should be thoroughly structured and the leaders should exhibit a high degree of political excellence. The task of party vanguard is not easy; it has to educate people to take stock of a situation, enlighten consciousness, and advance knowledge of history and society (Fanon 1985a, 114). Fanon argues that revolutionary elements, which form the embryonic political organisation of the rebellion, have to establish a mutual current of enlightenment and enrichment with the people. It is only then that in each fighting group, and in every village, people who have begun to:

> splinter upon the reefs of misunderstanding [can] be shown their bearings by these political pilots.... Such a taking stock of the situation at this precise moment of the struggle is decisive, for it allows the people to pass from total, undiscriminating nationalism to social and economic awareness. (Fanon 1985a, 115)

Hatred alone cannot draw up a programme, wrote Fanon, cautioning us against excessive reliance on violence as the architect of history. Spontaneous and passionate outbursts of violence will disintegrate if the users of violence do not graduate to a different level of political consciousness. A transformative agenda can be created only when people seek horizons hitherto undreamt of, beyond violence. If nationalism 'is not enriched and deepened by a very rapid transformation into a consciousness of social and political needs ... it leads up a blind alley', writes Fanon in the chapter on 'The Pitfalls of National Consciousness' (1985a, 165). In the concluding paragraph of the chapter on 'Spontaneity: Its Strengths and Weaknesses', Fanon pens this politically significant sentence, '[v]iolence alone, violence committed by the people, *violence organised and educated by its leaders*, makes it possible for the masses to understand social truths and gives the key to them' (1985a, 118; italics added).

Though Fanon has been conceptualised as the theorist of an unreflective and muscular violence as a means of recovering agency, his theory, we see, is much more nuanced. Colonial violence stripped the colonised of self-respect. They wilted before the sheer brutality of colonialism. In the specific context of dehumanisation and disempowerment, Fanon sees violence as the only way out. The arrogance of the settler cannot be broken by any other means; the agency of the colonised cannot be recaptured in any other way. But violence, warns Fanon, has to be viewed instrumentally, as a mode of recovering agency, as a mode of connecting to others and as a mode of constituting a collective. Violence confers power on its users, but power in the abstract can turn out to be a mirage, an illusion. For these reasons and more, violence for Fanon is not a political programme; its use has to be constantly patrolled, controlled and educated by the leaders. Politics have to control violence otherwise the entire project of liberation will collapse. The proper aim of liberation is to destroy the circle of violence and counter-violence, to destroy the exploitation of existing elites as well as the potential project of exploitation by future elites and to fashion another sort of politics. The psychic and physical costs of perpetrating uncontrolled violence are far too high.

Fanon, always the psychiatrist, understands and appreciates that for the colonised and the subjugated, violence might appear to be the only way in which they can regain selfhood. When there is no archive outside the one fashioned by the violence of the ruling elites, whether colonial or post-colonial, it is easy for people to engage in violence as a resolution to what they perceive as a problem. But rather than being a solution to problems, unrestrained violence is a problem in itself. In suggesting that violence needs to be channelled and restrained by another form of politics, Fanon tells us that though violence is a form of politics that might cleanse, there is also a politics outside violence. The politics of violence cannot be allowed to transform itself into a permanent mode of violent politics. Fanon says that the advocacy of violence is purely contextual.

We have to learn from Fanon when we set out to evaluate revolutionary violence in India. It is true that picking up the gun to confront the agents of the state and upper castes for whom suppression and exploitation of the so-called lower castes and tribals is an unquestioned creed, and for whom the marginalisation of these groups is neither here nor there, appears justified. When the upper castes show no compassion, no solidarity, no pity, no charity, let alone consciousness of human rights, when they lack vision of what it means to be human, what does one expect the oppressed to do, except try to reshape society? Yet the benefits of violence are limited.

The Politics of People's War

Specific to the Maoist theory of guerrilla war is the notion of a people's war. The decisive factor in armed struggle, Mao had theorised, is not weapons, but people who are convinced of the rightness of a cause. 'Without a political goal, guerrilla warfare must fail, as it must, if its political objectives do not coincide with the aspirations of the people and their sympathy, co-operation and assistance cannot be gained. The essence of guerrilla warfare is thus revolutionary in character' (Tse-tung 1937). Guerrilla operations are not an independent form of warfare; they are one step in the total war, one aspect of the revolutionary struggle.

In India, in the 1980s, cadres of People's War Group were hounded out of the state of Andhra Pradesh by state-sponsored irregular forces called the Greyhounds. Escaping from the security forces in Andhra Pradesh, the cadres entered the Dandakaranya forest region and began to organise the villagers to claim rights over land, resources and forest produce. In the process, they garnered support from the tribals. They established front organisations and the membership of these organisations, such as the peasant–worker front Dandakaranya Adivasi Kisan Majdoor Sangh, and the women's front Krantikari Adivasi Mahila Sangathan swelled considerably.

It is not as if the people among whom the Maoists came to work, and on whose behalf they picked up the gun, lacked political consciousness. Peasant and tribal rebellions have been an integral part of the history and folklore of the Central India. What the Maoists have done is to integrate memories of, and revolt against, oppression into a broader vision that is ideologically informed and historically grounded. This is an essential part of political mobilisation. Yet when it comes to the question of whether the Maoists have followed the script laid down by theories and the history of people's war, we run into a raging controversy. The jury is still out on this question. On balance, even sympathisers of the Maoists are forced to accept that the struggle is more military than political for reasons that are not difficult to fathom.

Normally, guerrillas set out to cultivate popular support through political education and through transmission of a political vision means of visual representation. An unconventional peoples' war cannot be run on coercion alone. At the minimum, cadres of the party have to excite a certain amount of popular sympathy for the cause and for war. In regions in Central and eastern India, the Maoists began to disseminate ideology and a vision of a future that will be unshackled from the bonds of caste and class, through village meetings, community groups, theatre performances, speeches, public meetings and lectures in schools. In pursuit of a just order, they fought for higher wages, redistributed land and charted out agrarian strategies.

Armed cadres can, of course, coerce local populations into supporting them and their ideology. They have guns, the villagers do not. But if the objective of revolutionary war is to liberate people whose lives have been since birth yoked to threefold disadvantage, and if the intention is to create a new society based on redistribution of material resources and recognition of equal worth, this strategy will necessarily prove not only counter-productive but also subversive of the basic tenets of revolutionary war.

Yet scholars and activists who have done field work in Maoist areas tell us that in Bastar, Jharkhand and parts of Andhra Pradesh, the Maoists employ tremendous coercion to being the constituency to heel. Kangaroo courts sentence suspected informers, landowners, moneylenders, errant revenue officials, delinquent party members, school teachers and government officials to brutal punishment and certain death by slitting of throats. Can this be accounted for as collateral damage or as the costs people have to pay for revolutions? Moreover, the reported participation of the Maoists in corruption, whether pricing of tendu leaves, or taking a cut from the contractors or imposing taxes on infrastructure projects, has deeply compromised their political dream of building an alternative to the system that exists. Alpha Shah's argument that the Maoists run protection rackets in Jharkhand has dented the image of our flaming revolutionaries to quite an extent (2006).

From the perspective of peoples' war, the indiscriminate use of coercion to herd people to the constituency of Maoism runs up a number of problems. First, it catapults an issue that many are familiar with, and many are unfamiliar with; that people who do the fighting are not the people who have been subjected to triple injustice, even if the latter join the party, to the centre of the political stage. We simply do not know whether the tribals and the Scheduled Castes in the Red Corridor have been persuaded, coaxed or coerced into sharing the goals of the party, or indeed whether they prefer immediate solutions to pressing problems rather than the long-term objective of seizing state power. It is debatable whether villagers line up behind cadres of the party out of fear, or whether they are genuine converts to the ideology of the party. Do strategies of political mobilisation, rather than that of force gather popular support? Reports from the field suggest that the latter is more prevalent. Ironically, suggests Bela Bhatia, who has carried out field work in Bihar and Andhra Pradesh, a movement that promises liberation can actually land up making people feel less free. It is also problematic that members of the mass front pay the price for actions taken by the underground party. These actions, again ironically, are taken on behalf of the people but without their knowledge or consent. The use of violence has taken a heavy toll, she concludes (2006, 3181–82).

Second, we can hardly overlook the political context of democracy in which the Maoists have launched armed struggle. No village in times of competitive democracy and an even more competitive market economy can remain a political tabula rasa or a neutral site into which an armed group can march and proceed to persuade, influence and rouse people to action. It is doubtful whether any social collective in history has ever been without tensions and rivalries, but competitive electoral democracy creates its own schisms. Resultantly each village is earmarked by complex pecking orders, competing structures of loyalty to 'this' leader or 'that' political party, feuds large and small, with each group wishing to score points off another and modes of profit through informal economies. Guerrillas might use villagers instrumentally to secure shelter, food and information. Villagers can also use a man with a gun instrumentally; this might help them to settle disputes. These complexities make the task of sorting out the issue whether this is a people's war; a war conceived and executed by elites, or a war that serves the interest of some group or the other, a difficult one.

Third, if the use of coercion to garner and retain support inhibits the task of political mobilisation, the task is further truncated by tremendous coercion deployed by the state. In response to the guerrilla war launched by the Maoists, the Indian state has marshalled formidable military arsenals, mounted a military onslaught on the region termed the 'Red Corridor' and surrounded guerrilla zones. Counter-insurgency doctrines learnt from the Vietnam War, and assimilated by experts, have given the security forces an added advantage strategy wise. The military offensive launched by the Indian state against the Maoists has forced the guerrilla militia to concentrate its energy on rear guard action and protect fields of operation. That this strategy has come at the expense of the political component of the peoples' war doctrine is manifest. The ultimate objective of launching a people's war to overturn existing forms of power, and to create a people's democracy, has been pre-empted if not aborted by the onslaught of the security forces.

For both time and space for intense, sustained and prolonged political mobilisation is denied to the Maoists. When the energies of the armed wings of the party are focused on defending their regions of engagement, opportunities for unremitting political mobilisation through dissemination of ideology, and the harnessing of energies to a cause cannot, but, be scarce. The Maoists, as Bernard D'Mello, a keen observer of party strategy, points out, have not succeeded in turning any of the guerrilla zones into base areas where they can establish a miniature state based on self-reliant economic development and land to the tiller (D'Mello 2010). If that is so, the one factor that makes radical armed struggle acceptable, notably that cadres introduce people into alternative ways of doing things whether production or regulation of social relations, and the belief that these alternative ways enhance agency, is greatly subverted.

Fourth, if the Maoists seem to have underestimated the military power of the Indian state, they also seem to have underestimated the legitimacy that Indian democracy, howsoever flawed be that democracy, commands even among people who continue to be triply disadvantaged. Sumanta Bannerjee suggests that in India, a parliamentary republic, despite large-scale corruption and criminality, still enjoys democratic legitimacy among wide sections of the people, and major contending social groups find democracy useful for their own ends. 'The system apparently has not yet exhausted all its potentialities of exploiting the hopes and aspirations of the Indian poor and underprivileged sections' (2006, 3159). The sophisticated bourgeois Indian state, skilled in evoking and harnessing loyalties to its own cause, is even more skilled in neutralising challenges and upping the ante.

Since 2011, in areas that have been cleared of Maoism, the 'clear, hold and develop' strategy uses the 'magic mantra' of development to win back tribal populations. After decades of neglect, the government has now concentrated on building infrastructure, particularly landmine-proof roller-compacted concrete roads in Maoist zones, under the protection of combat forces of the Central Reserve Police Force. The parallel with Fidel Castro, who built modern highways in the Sierra Maestra region of Cuba to reward inhabitants for their support, but also to ensure that guerrilla onslaughts would not be repeated, cannot be ignored. The history of guerrilla war gives us an idea of the geography of remote and difficult terrains. Modern means of communication and information technology have neutralised the potential of guerrilla war to fight armies that are technologically superior in many ways.

We, of course, cannot say that nothing has been done by the Maoists. Whereas the long term goal of the Maoists is takeover of state power, the immediate objective is to carry out land reform, construct irrigation projects to protect the villagers from drought, protect peasants against moneylenders, fight atrocities on the basis of caste and struggle against mining corporates intent on displacing villagers from land. Analysts and field reports tell us that in pockets of the Dantewada region, land has been transferred to the tiller, aid has been extended to poor farmers, cooperatives have been set up, measures to obtain just prices for agricultural commodities and minor forest produce have been put in place, modern knowledge about agriculture has been disseminated, better quality seeds have been gathered from elsewhere distributed and voluntary labour to construct tanks with canal systems has been deployed (D'Mello 2010, 17). The Maoists have filled in a fissure created by decades of neglect by the Indian state. Will this go a long way in building up popular support for the cause? Do measures that have been initiated by the Maoists provide the sort of alternative structures that were put in place in liberated zones in Vietnam, China and Guinea Bissau, alternative both to feudal structures of exploitation and the many injustices of capitalism that is?

Nirmalangshu Mukherjee has made an interesting point in this context. Even if wages in the region have increased because of the bargains the Maoists have finalised with the contractors, he suggests, these are far less than the minimum wages paid in other parts of the country, for example, Kerala (2010, 17). The system that has been established by the Maoists appears as but a pale resemblance of development projects in other parts of the country that have been initiated by the same state they wish to overthrow and see as illegitimate. The anthropologist Nandini Sundar has drawn on interviews she conducted as part of a citizen's initiative visit in the forests of Bastar in May 2006 to make roughly the same point. According to her, the Maoists claim to include 60 lakh people in the organisational sweep of their Dandakaranya guerrilla zone. Here they have established mass organisations called sangams and carried out development work. For instance, they have set up 135 people's clinics, educational facilities and a large number of irrigation works. Sundar, however, concludes that these efforts are not a patch on what the government could have done for the villagers, if only it had the will to do so, for example, undertaken development, taken up women's issues and promoted the Gondi language and literature (2006, 3189–90).

Far from providing alternative modes of social and economic relationships, the Maoist development agenda seems to have become a mirror image of the former. Nirmalangshu Mukherjee accepts that the Maoists have trained tribals in agricultural techniques and taught them to construct harvesting structures such as ponds and wells. None of these strategies, he suggests, sounds anything more than routine. Compared to the development models established in the rest of the country, these strategies of agricultural development are at best routine and primitive. Thirty years of occupation of a backward region has neither resulted in the establishment of alternative development models, nor in the construction of schools and hospitals that might have lessened illiteracy and ill health. The inhabitants of these regions continue to be severely malnourished, and high levels of infant mortality and illiteracy mark the area. The cadres of the party could have formed democratically constituted cooperatives to administer livelihoods in tribal controlled panchayats, collected and delivered tendu leaves and eliminated contractors (Sundar 2006, 18). But they chose to go the way of mainstream development.

What is it, then, that the Maoists have accomplished even as they have let loose violence in pursuit of a radically new society, and even as this violence has catalysed extreme violence by the state? John Harriss holds that the Maoists have tapped into and to some extent, at least, have articulated the long-standing grievances of the Dalits and landless peasants against high caste landowners, and the grievances of the tribal people against the state for what is has done, notably displacement and sanctioning of repressive policies as well as what it has not done in the provision of basic necessities (2012, 41).

Indisputably the Maoists have dramatically fore-grounded the interests of the poorest of the poor, an agenda which had been washed off the success story that India has written for itself, a success story that has now run out of steam. Yet the use of violence to accomplish this act of focalising ill-being is a sad commentary not only on the ability of the Indian state to provide for the citizens but also on the political worldview of the Maoists. Does our democratic government come alive to the needs of the triply oppressed only when they take recourse to violence or back those who employ violence? Has Maoist violence become the harbinger of a world that is not significantly different from what exists in other parts of the country?

Above all, political mobilisation to support the people's war has turned into a contest between existing loyalties to power holders and evoking loyalties to a cause weighted in favour of the poorest and the most exploited. It is not clear which way the tide will turn because though the state is coercive, the Maoists have also displayed a remarkable capacity to be coercive. If the Maoists struggle for social and economic justice, the Indian state is also the dispenser of largesse. It is for the villagers to decide which way they want to go. But if they have to decide which way they want to go, or which path will lead to the recovery of agency, the context in which they do so has to be free of violence both of the state and of the Maoists. No one can make choices in a context shaped by one sort of violence or another coming from different sources. This is simply not conducive to the recovery of agency. Both the democratic state and our revolutionaries deny to people who have been stripped of agency the appropriate political context in which they can choose how they want to make their own history. Are then these people condemned to living a life that is bleak, and living in a circumstances that bode ill for any possibility of a dramatic transition from subject to agent?

We have to ask this question with some regret. Are the Maoists fighting a people's war at great cost to themselves and to their constituency only to implement the agenda of mainstream parties? Tilak Gupta has put the point across well, to tell the truth, he writes, there is not much of a difference between the Maoist programme and that of communist parties functioning within the system of parliamentary democracy. The correspondence between clauses relating to land reforms, fair wages for labour, recognition of the right to work as a fundamental right, improvement of farming methods, removal of gender discrimination in matters of wages and ownership of land and promotion of peasant cooperatives is striking. It is true that no political party has followed the cause of the rural poor with so much zeal. The Maoists have tried to fill this vacuum. But they are more eager to propagate the path of armed revolution than their revolutionary aims (2006, 3172–73). The diminution of the Maoist agenda has become painfully apparent. There is cause for unease with the promise of acquiring agency through revolutionary violence.

The main problem, it seems to me, is another one. Given the context of a democracy that is considered legitimate by many, and given the military might of the Indian state, the space and time for political mobilisation of the constituency of the Maoists has shrunk dramatically. Without the political in the concept of political violence, we are left with violence. Fanon had warned us that though anger, rage and revenge lead to violence, these sentiments are not enough to liberate people. Spontaneous and passionate outbursts of violence will disintegrate if the users of violence do not graduate to a different level of political consciousness. A transformative agenda can be created only when people seek horizons hitherto undreamt of, beyond the reach of violence. Otherwise the elite that comes to power will do little, except reproduce the violence of the previous order.

The problem is that without politics in command, violence goes berserk. It can best be likened to a quagmire that relentlessly sucks people into its murky depths. From here there is no escape. When violence holds individuals and groups in thrall, moral disintegration follows. For we cannot control violence, violence controls us. Fanon had told us long ago that when the colonial finger writes the alphabet of power in blood and gore, the script is ineffaceable and the imprint it leaves on the body politic, indelible. Violence leaves stigmata much like the murder of Duncan left blood on Lady Macbeth's hands: 'What, will these hands ne'er be clean?' How can, then, a new society free of oppression and exploitation be created? All we will have on our hands is a bloodstained history, not a political history that can show the way out of the highly exploitative society that we have on our hands today.

Conclusion

If revolutionary violence is about politics more than violence, then Maoism has to be judged in terms of whether it has managed to (a) go beyond Gramscian common sense and introduce people to critical perspectives on, and engagement with Indian society; (b) set in place alternative institutions and practices that introduce beleaguered communities to the wider goal of the armed struggle, an alternative society, economy and politics; and (c) enabled ordinary people to realise agency. Political mobilisation serves to catalyse political consciousness and encourage people to stand up and be counted as actors in their own right. This is the basic criterion on which we judge the efficacy of political practices.

It is indisputable that the project of Maoism is geared towards all these objectives. Yet the political and the military context proscribes sustained political mobilisation of people caught up in the trap of triple injustice. Politically, the Indian state despite the many injustices it perpetrates is seen as legitimate in the eyes of the citizens, largely because it is democratic. The village is thus not a neutral site, receptive to political mobilisation in the radical mode. The village is apt to be divided and fragmented between those who back the state and those who back the Maoist agenda. The outbreak of armed struggle has compelled the Indian state to introduce and accelerate development initiatives in zones of conflict. The Indian state has also launched a major military onslaught against Maoist strongholds. Caught between the Scylla of massive military operations and the Charybdis of state-led development initiatives, the Maoists are denied both time and space in which they can engage in sustained mobilisation and establish institutions that code a radically different perspective.

Whereas a people's war is more about politics than coercion, and more about political visions mediating the course of armed struggle, things seem to be different in the case of Maoism. The use of violence against class enemies and against the state not only leads to loss of lives but also to fear. We do not know whether people line up behind the Maoists out of fear or out of conviction. Whether agency can be realised in an environment where the guerrilla forces are engaged in a rear guard action against the might of the Indian state, and when the constituency is terrorised by the same weapons used to fight the state, the political agenda is put by the wayside. This is incontrovertible. No politics that focuses on telling people what they are owed by society can succeed when the environment is stamped by violence. Moreover, whatever alternative institutions have been built by the Maoists, observers tell us that these are mirror images of dominant development agendas. In sum, the Maoist agenda is diminished because it has unfolded in a context very different to the colonial context in which guerrilla wars proved successful. Revolutionary violence without revolutionary politics further truncates the agenda. And the case for justifying revolutionary violence because it enables agency is deeply compromised.

Political violence without political mobilisation, for all seeming heroism and dare devilry, is a lazy way of doing politics. It is executed by a handful of cadres, and it eschews transformation of either the body politic or of its members. Violence as spectacle reduces people into an audience or bystanders. In the process, nothing changes, perhaps nothing ever could, not even the recovery of agency.

In sum, we have to be aware of the indeterminacy and the unpredictability of this avatar of politics, and the incapacity of human beings to control violence, or rather the relentless impulse of violence to control those who handle it for definable ends. Any study of revolutionary violence has, therefore, to track the dilemmas, the quandaries and the political predicaments that stalk the practice of revolutionary violence.

References

Bannerjee, Sumanta. 2006, 22 July. 'Beyond Naxalbari'. *Economic and Political Weekly* XLI (29): 3159–63.
———. 2012. 'Reflections of a One-Time Maoist Activist'. In *More than Maoism: Politics, Policies and Insurgencies in South Asia*, edited by Robin Jeffrey, Ronojoy Sen and Pratima Singh, 47–68. New Delhi: Manohar.
Bhatia, Bela. 2006, 22 July. 'On Armed Resistance'. *Economic and Political Weekly* XLI (29): 3179–82.
D'Mello, Bernard. 2010, 21 March. 'Spring Thunder Anew, Neo-Robber Baron Capitalism vs "New Democracy" in India'. Accessed 19 March 2012. http://monthlyreview.org/commentary/spring-thunder-anew
Fanon, Frantz. 1985a. *The Wretched of the Earth*. Translated by Constance Farrington. Middlesex: Penguin Books.

Fanon, Frantz. 1985b. 'Preface' by Jean Paul Sartre. *The Wretched of the Earth*, 7–26. Middlesex: Penguin Books.

Gupta, Tilak D. 2006. 'Maoism in India: Ideology, Programme and Armed Struggle'. *Economic and Political Weekly* XLI (29): 3172–76.

Harriss, John. 2012. 'What Is Going on in India's "Red Corridor"? Questions About India's Maoist Insurgency'. In *More Than Maoism: Politics, Policies and Insurgencies in South Asia,* edited by Robin Jeffrey, Ronojoy Sen and Pratima Singh, 25–46. New Delhi: Manohar.

Kunnath, George. 2012. 'Smouldering Dalit Fires in Bihar'. In *Window into a Revolution: Ethnographies of Maoism in India and Nepal*, edited by Alpha Shah and Judith Pettigrew, 89–112. New Delhi: Social Science Press and Orient Blackswan.

Mukherjee, Nirmalangshu. 2010, 19 June. 'Arms Over the People: What Have the Maoists Achieved in Dandakaranya?' *Economic and Political Weekly* 45 (25): 16–20.

Shah, Alpha. 2006. 'Markets of Protection. The "Terrorist" Maoist Movement and the State in Jharkhand India'. *Critique of Anthropology* 26 (3): 297–314.

Sundar, Nandini. 2006, 22 July. 'Bastar, Maoism and Salwa Judum'. *Economic and Political Weekly* XLI (29): 3187–92.

Tse-tung, Mao. 1937. *What Is Guerrilla Warfare?* Accessed 11 March 2013. www.marxists.org.org/reference/archive/mao/works/1937/guerrilla-warfare/ch01.htm

5

The Crisis of Maoist Theory of Agrarian Relations and Strategy of Revolution in India

Sumanta Banerjee

The armed revolutionary stream of the Indian Communist movement has got bogged down in a quagmire, and its Maoist phase is coming to an end. The roots of the crisis are embedded in three problematic domains—political, economic and organisational. The first is the Maoist political strategy and tactics that have been adopted by the Indian Communist revolutionaries. The second is the transformation that is taking place in the present Indian rural economy which is rendering much of their theory of agrarian relations and strategy and tactics following from it, obsolete and irrelevant in vast areas. The third is the organisational dilemma within the Communist Party of India (Maoist; CPI [Maoist]), around the tactics of prioritisation of militarism over mass mobilisation, which quite often violates human rights and alienates them from the common citizens.

The Political Strategy: Achievements and Failures

Let us take up the first problem—the adoption of Mao's programme of agrarian revolution in India by the Naxalite leaders in the late 1960-early 1970 period. Charu Majumdar and others adopted lock stock and barrel, the strategy and tactics of the New Democratic

Revolution that was formulated by Mao in China in a totally different historical context in the 1930–40 period. The Indian Maoists wanted to replicate a Maoist-type guerrilla-based agrarian revolution in India, forgetting that the contemporary Indian situation was far removed from the Chinese scenario. India was held together by a centralised political system, unlike the China of Mao's days, which was fragmented along territories controlled by local Chinese warlords, areas ruled by the Kuomintang and those occupied by the Japanese. It was in this historical situation in China during that period that Mao took advantage of the absence of a centralised state power and developed his strategy of an agrarian revolution through the tactics of guerrilla warfare and creation of liberated zones, where land reforms and other socialist programmes could be carried out, thus the communist government in Yenan emerged.

In a different situation in India in the 1960–70 period, the Naxalites did indeed carve out patches of temporary liberated zones in the tribal poor-dominated Srikakulam in Andhra Pradesh, which was hailed by Charu Majumdar as the 'Yenan of India'. But the Indian Yenan—unlike Mao's Yenan—was soon destroyed by the Indian state's security forces. A more sophisticated bourgeois ruling class than the Chinese Kuomintang, the Congress-led government in India adopted a carrot and stick policy. It crushed the rebellion of the Naxalite tribals in Andhra Pradesh's Srikakulam and followed it by ameliorative measures in 1972, like setting up the Girijan Co-operative Corporation which advanced loans to the tribal farmers for agricultural improvement. In West Bengal's Naxalbari itself, from where the Maoist movement started in 1967, the support base of the movement was neutralised by the introduction of land reforms by the Left Front government in the late 1970s which benefited to some extent the poor peasantry which had earlier opted for an armed struggle under the Naxalite leadership to bring about such benefits.

The erosion of the original Maoist bases in Naxalbari and Srikakulam raises an important question. Were the peasant supporters of the Maoist programme at that time ideologically committed to the political goal of overthrowing the Indian state and replacing it with a socialist system, or were they more concerned with their immediate economic needs—ownership of their little plots which was being threatened by encroachers, minimum wages for agricultural labourers, among other demands? Once these demands were met by an accommodating administration within the structure of the Indian state, the erstwhile peasant supporters of the Maoist movement in Naxalbari and Srikakulam in the 1960–70 period withdrew into their cocoons of an assured sustainable existence.

But after the setback in Naxalbari and Srikakulam, the Maoists were able to regain their space in the Indian political scenario during the decades spanning 1990 and 2010. They expanded their influence and controlled a large terrain stretching from Bihar, Jharkhand and Odisha in the east through Chhattisgarh and bordering parts of Maharashtra in the centre and the west and Andhra Pradesh in the south. Here they picked up the threads from Srikakulam of the 1970s and mobilised the rural poor around those old issues of land reforms that were not yet addressed to by the state in these areas. They drove out the local feudal oppressors and commercial exploiters and introduced alternative mechanisms of governance that ensured equitable distribution of resources and social justice through popular participation. Their achievements were acknowledged even by a government-appointed team in 2008. Its report which was submitted to the Planning Commission in April 2008, describes (in Chapter 3) how over several years the Maoists organised their base in these inaccessible and neglected forest and hilly areas, whose inhabitants (mainly tribals) had been denied their basic rights like minimum wages (for tobacco leaf pickers in Andhra Pradesh, for instance) and had been exposed to violence by feudal landlords, private contractors and forest guards and police. In these base areas, the Maoists carried out land reforms, established schools and provided health facilities, thus acting as a sort of surrogate government.[1] Writers such as Arundhati Roy and Jan Myrdal, journalists and social activists like Gautam Navlakha and film makers like Soumitra Dastidar who visited these areas during the last decade have recorded the achievements as well as failures of the Maoist leaders and their followers in these zones under their occupation (Myrdal 2012; Navlakha 2012; Roy 2010).[2]

This Maoist-controlled territory—described as the Red Corridor by the media—is besieged from all sides by the Indian state's armed forces. Regular raids and overrunning of the guerrilla bases by the security forces are shrinking the size of the 'Red Corridor' and reducing the effectiveness of the Maoist armed resistance.[3] A large number of senior leaders have either been killed or jailed, and some have even surrendered to the police. Their main spokesperson Cherukuri Rajkumar, known as Azad, was killed in a false encounter in Andhra Pradesh during 1 and 2 July 2010. This was at a time when Azad was coming out from the underground in response to an invitation for a dialogue with the Union Home Ministry of the Indian government, at the initiative of the well-known social

---

[1] Report of the Expert Group set up by the Government of India to examine Development Challenges in Extremist Affected Areas (April 2008).

[2] Soumitra Dastidar's documentary film covering more than a decade of the armed struggle in the Maoist belt is yet to be released. His book in Bengali recording his experiences, entitled *Maobadi Deray Ajana Kahini* (Unknown Stories from the Maoist Guerilla Zones), has been brought out by Offbeat Publication, Kolkata in 2012.

[3] The aggressive nature of this military encirclement and its consequences on the villagers of the Red Corridor have been vividly described by Nandini Sundar in her latest book *The Burning Forest* (2016).

activist Swami Agnivesh. His killing by the police casts doubts on the sincerity of the invitation for dialogue that Home Minister P. Chidambaram extended to the Maoists at that time. Was it intended to trap them and eliminate their leaders?

The Maoist guerrillas are putting up a stiff resistance against the state's offensive on their bases. They explode land mines or ambush vehicles passing through their territory. But such tactics are a double-edged sword. They can be effective in eliminating and terrorising their enemies—the security forces. But by their indiscriminative nature, they can also hurt the common people who may be killed during such operations. This is exactly what had been happening in Chhattisgarh and outlying areas during the last several years, when several innocent people like those travelling by public transport or ambulance cars had lost their lives in this war of crossfire between the Maoists and the state. This is often acknowledged as a dilemma by the Maoist leaders themselves, but despite promises to avoid such happenings, they have failed to stop their cadres from resorting to such acts.

The Indian State's Strategy and Tactics

When analysing the crisis faced by the Maoist movement, therefore, we have to consider both the extrinsic and intrinsic factors. The extrinsic factor is the Indian state's military offensive against the Maoists. The Maoist bases pose a threat to the Indian state, by their armed opposition to its neoliberal model of development and by providing their local people with an alternative model of decentralisation and equitable distribution of local resources. Incidentally, these bases also happen to be located in a stretch which has rich mineral resources. The Indian state, dependent on multinational investors who want to extract and utilise these minerals, has to suppress voices of the local people who protest against such extraction of their indigenous resources by external powers. It cannot afford to allow vast swathes which contain these mineral resources to be occupied by the Maoists who have set up parallel centres of power there and are demanding that the indigenous tribal population should have a voice in policies regarding the use of mineral resources. The stakes of both the Maoists and the Indian state are thus quite high in this mutual contest. It is no wonder, therefore, that the offensive launched by the state against the Maoists in the second decade of the twenty-first century has been on a much higher scale than that witnessed in the 1960–70 period.

The Indian state is following a twofold strategy to destroy the Maoist movement—first by capturing and killing its cadres, and second by removing its ideologues from the leadership. The arrest of Kobad Ghandi (a well-known intellectual in the CPI [Maoist]) party) and the killing of Azad in Andhra Pradesh, and later of Kishenji in West Bengal, have dealt a severe blow to the Maoist movement. Bereft of their political leaders—who have either been killed, or arrested, or forced to surrender—the well-armed Maoist cadres are now reduced to roving gangs of marauders and extortionists. The emphasis on militarism to the exclusion of ideological teaching has driven some of its cadres to anti-social activities like extortions. It has repelled some of its leaders who were ideologically committed to the cause but are now surrendering to the police. The most notable example is that of G. V. K. Prasad (known as Gudsa Usendi), a long-time spokesperson of the party's Dandakaranya Special Zonal Committee, who along with his live-in companion Santoshi Markam, surrendered on 8 January 2014. Explaining the reasons for leaving CPI (Maoist), he said that the party leadership had ignored his oft-repeated objections to acts such as the destruction of school buildings and indiscriminate killing of the Adivasis in the name of destroying informer network. He added, however, that his health problems were also behind his decision to surrender (*Indian Express* 2014).

Limitations of the Maoist Political Strategy and Military Tactics

These developments lead us to examine the intrinsic factors within the Maoist movement that have led to some extent to their present crisis. What went wrong? Both the political strategy and the military tactics following from it were flawed from the beginning. As for the political strategy based on the Chinese revolutionary paradigm, what could have been valid for China in the 1920–40 period, was not universally applicable in India with its diversified agrarian society and economy that was fractured by sociocultural values and practices, driven by caste and tribal loyalties. Despite their individual courage and self-sacrifice, the Indian Maoist leaders had remained crippled by a limited understanding of these complexities of the vast heterogeneous Indian society.

Unable to formulate a multi-pronged strategy for these various layers of our society, the Maoists concentrated mainly on the most exploited layer—the tribal poor in the inaccessible forest and hill areas of the Dandakaranya region of Central India and Jharkhand in the east. Here they found a fertile soil for experimenting with their programme. These people fit into the Maoist class category of poor peasants. They suffered from extreme forms of economic and social exploitation by landlords, as well as displacement from their lands by multinational industrial houses—the two enemies who could be described as 'semi-feudal' and 'semi-colonial' in Maoist theoretical terms.

Another factor that the Maoists found to their advantage was the militant tradition of peasant jacqueries that marked the history of these tribal populations from the

British colonial period. The Maoists could revive this spirit among them in their attempts to mobilise them against their oppressors, by recalling the heroic deeds of their past heroes such as Sidhu, Kanu and Birsa Munda. Thus, during all these decades, the Maoist political strategy of an agrarian revolution through guerrilla struggles had remained restricted to and been tested only in the confines of a tribal society in inaccessible forest and hill areas. Although successful within these areas, the CPI (Maoist) has not been able to build up a similar armed resistance against feudal oppression in the plains areas of North India. Yet, the Dalit agricultural labourers who are daily terrorised by upper caste landlords and traders in vast stretches here, fit into the traditional Maoist category of 'poor peasants'. Is the Maoist set of strategy and tactics, therefore, fit only for a particular favourable terrain?

Maoist Movement as a Catalytic Agent

Despite their control over a limited stretch only, the Maoists' articulation of the demands of the rural poor has sent loud echoes across the country, which often force the Indian state to pay heed to those demands. The Maoist movement can be described as playing the role— unwittingly though—of a positive catalytic agent for the betterment of rural society in post-colonial India. Since its first manifestation in the 1967 Naxalbari uprising, and following its development during the next decades, under its pressure a recalcitrant Indian state had been compelled to enact a number of legislative reforms relating to forest rights of the tribals, minimum wages for agricultural labourers, provision of rural employment, among other similar ameliorative measures.

The Maoist leadership may quite rightly dismiss these measures as the Indian state's double-faced conspiracy to woo the rural poor with promises of jobs and land reforms on the one hand, and to simultaneously deprive them of those facilities through the same state-patronised mechanisms of bureaucratic obstruction and corruption on the other. We know how public funds meant for government-sponsored rural employment projects, public distribution schemes, health and medical facilities among others, have been siphoned off to the private coffers of the axis of local politicians and traders, road contractors and building mafia, thus defeating the objectives of these legal measures. But despite such distortions—which corrupt the implementation of almost every egalitarian law in our society—these legal weapons have become useful for organised civil society groups in certain parts of the country to approach the judiciary which pressurises the state to ensure jobs under the national rural employment programme, regular payment to those employed and entitlement of forest dwellers to their produce among other demands.

At the political level, the Maoist movement has been able to sensitise sections of our people to the character of the Indian state—which acts only under popular pressure, and that also when it takes the form of violent resistance against the intolerable violence of the state. The Indian state believes in pushing the envelope of repression of popular discontent till the point of compulsion where it has to concede to the demands of the people. But, if we leave aside these indirect beneficial spin-offs from the Maoist movement (e.g., legislative measures), we have to ask whether the basic Maoist strategy and tactics of capturing state power is applicable to the vast stretches of the rural plains (as well as the urban metropolises) of India, where the inhabitants cope with different types of problems emanating from various layers of the socio-economic system?

Changing Contours of India's Agrarian Economy

This brings us to the next problem that the Maoists have to face—the changing pattern of economy in the present Indian rural sector, which is the main site of the Maoist revolution. The changes challenge the traditional Maoist theory of agrarian relations.

Recent findings suggest that the rural economy is undergoing radical changes—transforming the nature of landholding, changing the character of the agricultural classes and giving birth to a footloose working class from amongst the poor peasantry who are forced to work in non-farming sectors as contractual labourers.[4] From the available evidence, it appears that the current trends in the Indian countryside do not conform to the conventional Maoist theoretical analysis of a rural society along a four-class categorisation of landlords, rich peasants, middle peasants and poor peasants. These strict class divisions are being blurred by the intrusion of global neoliberal industrial interests in the rural economy.

These powerful interests are disrupting the old economic feudal order and dividing the rural population along different lines. After the abolition of the traditional zamindari system in post-Independence India, the rural socio-economic power structure was ruled by a class of big farmer-turned landlords (known as *jotedars* who were identified as the main class enemies by the Maoists). But today that rural power structure has been taken over by a variety of vested interests ranging from progenies of old landlords who have diversified into non-agricultural occupations such as trading, services, etc., to extraneous

---

[4] For an extremely well-documented and theoretical analysis of these changes, I would like to draw the attention of all to Basu and Das (2013) and Harriss (2013).

forces such as industrial houses, building contractors, road construction agencies, owners of passenger buses and trucks to carry freight, among others. They offer employment opportunities to the unemployed rural poor, which to some extent, have loosened their dependence on—as well as freed themselves from exploitation by—the *jotedars*. This has weakened their traditional semi-feudal ties. These rural poor have developed stakes in the present economy according to their respective occupations.

We thus find a new generation of Indian rural population, whose demands and requirements are different from those that used to be nurtured by their counterparts in China in the 1920–30 period, when Mao formulated his programme. It is, therefore, difficult for the Maoists today to mobilise these diverse segments of the rural poor into one homogeneous class of exploited peasants with the single target of the 'semi-feudal' system as their enemy.

A multi-layered system of semi-capitalist relations that is simultaneously marked by exploitation and concession is developing in the Indian countryside. Exploitation (outside the factory system) is taking different forms—usurpation of agricultural land and forest areas by industrial and mining corporations; recruitment of landless peasants ousted from these areas as contractual labour in construction projects and trafficking of their women to the red light areas of cities. Concession is being meted out by these same forces of exploitation, through state-sponsored programmes like rural employment schemes as safety nets to counter the ill-effects of unemployment brought about by their industrial policies.

Their concession also takes ominous forms—like buying off sections of the exploited poor by recruiting them as paid agents for violent suppression of popular dissent. The most notorious example is the formation of the state-sponsored armed vigilante group of Salwa Judum from among the tribal poor of Chhattisgarh, or the recruitment of unemployed tribal youth in the police force in Jangalmahal of West Bengal to counter Maoist influence among the tribals—thus sowing seeds of division within the tribal communities.

In the face of this triangular challenge of exploitation, repression and concession by the state and its agents, the Indian Communist revolutionaries are yet to shape a multi-levelled strategy that dovetails with the needs and compulsions of these various layers of the agrarian poor who inhabit the multifaceted complex that criss-crosses vast stretches of the Indian countryside. As pointed out earlier, the Maoists have remained confined only to the most backward tribal belt which till now has not been exposed to the effects of the fast-changing pace of agrarian economy that is occurring in other parts of India. But they cannot hold on for long to their precariously protected zone in the face of the state-sponsored and corporate sector-dictated drive for commercialisation of the forest and mineral resources of this territory. This drive is marked by the same cunning combination of exploitation and concession—reinforced by militarist repression. While the Indian state at the military level is encircling the Maoist territory with its security forces, at the commercial level its corporate sector partners permit their contractors to come to deal with the Maoist guerrilla squads to allow their profitable operations like mining, in exchange of 'protection money'. The revelations made by one such contractor (Dharmendra Chopra), who was arrested for negotiating deals with the Maoists on behalf of business houses and politicians (*Indian Express* 2014), expose the duplicity of the present generation of the Maoists operating in the interior Bastar region. Although the Maoist central leadership, in its programme adopted in 2004, pledged to resist displacement of the tribals and forest dwellers due to mining and industrial projects, the Maoist guerrilla squads today are apparently allowing the agents of these same projects to operate in their areas in exchange of protection money.

In fact, a report of the CPI (Maoist) Bihar Jharkhand Special Area Committee has acknowledged this surreptitious alliance between its members and 'the huge battery of contractors and middle-men in the rural areas', who 'maintain links with organizers (comrades at zone and even higher levels), appease them'. The report states: 'That relation with such type of contractors have been maintained by party organizers is a matter of concern' and then adds:

> Some of our comrades use such contractors not only for various work, but also the most secret work of the Party.... Among cadres ill-feeling arise as they take sides between the contractors; different contractors even take recommendation letters of their 'protector' party comrades to Block development Officials and engineers in order to win the competition for contracts.... (Navlakha 2014, 165–66)

Maoist Organisational Crisis: Lalgarh Tragedy

This leads us to the third problematic in Indian Maoist praxis that I mentioned at the beginning—the organisational structure, which was shaped by the compulsions to resist feudal exploitation and state repression. The Maoists emphasised the tactics of armed warfare as the main form of resistance, to the exclusion of mass movements, against such exploitation and repression. The primary agents of the warfare were to be village-based guerrilla squads (mainly recruited from the poor peasantry and led by the party's local leaders) which were expected to graduate later into people's liberation army. These squads and their local leaders were allowed by the central leadership a certain degree of autonomy to adopt policies to suit the conditions of their respective areas of operation in order to meet the party's objective of 'area-wise seizure of power'. But over the last few years, such autonomy allowed to local Maoist leaders and their guerrilla squads had paved the way for reckless actions and opportunistic alliances between the Maoists and regional political powers.

The most illuminating example of this is the sequence of events in Lalgarh in West Bengal from 2008 to 2012. On 2 November 2008, the Maoists launched a bomb attack on a convoy of the then CPI (Marxist) state Chief Minister Buddhadeb Bhattacharya—in a knee-jerk reaction to his anti-Maoist stance—without taking into account the impact of such an attack on the local villagers. Although the attack failed, it provoked Bhattacharya's Left Front government to unleash a reign of terror on Lalgarh. The villagers in response formed the People's Committee Against Police Atrocities (PCAPA). They were able to prevent for quite some time the security forces from invading their homes by digging up roads and setting up barricades. During this brief period, the Maoists and the PCPA collaborated in running health centres, schools and working on other developmental projects in these villages.

But this grass roots nature of the Lalgarh uprising was soon to be stymied by the intervention of the Trinamool Congress leader Mamata Banerjee (who was then the railways minister in the United Progressive Alliance [UPA] government at the centre). Eager to dislodge the Left Front from her home turf in West Bengal, she began to woo the Maoist leaders and cadres in Lalgarh. The Maoists fell for her. They organised a rally in her support on 9 August 2010 in Lalgarh. The CPI (Maoist) central leader Koteshwar Rao (who was deputed by the party's central leadership to take charge of West Bengal)—famously known as Kishenji—while lauding Mamata Banerjee in television interviews, even went to the extent of supporting her as the future chief minister of West Bengal. This was despite her notoriety as a dyed-in-the wool anti-Communist politician. Kishenji apparently suffered from the naïve belief that if brought to power in West Bengal, she would release his party comrades who had been imprisoned by the CPI (M)-led Left Front government. Following Kishenji's decision to support her, Maoist armed squads killed the cadres of the ruling CPI (Marxist) and other opponents, cleared the villages by forcing out their followers and paved the way for the electoral victory of the Mamata Banerjee-led Trinamool Congress. In an ironical twist to this ugly tale of deal between the Maoist leaders and the Trinamool Congress, Koteshwar Rao himself had to pay the price for his folly. Mamata Banerjee, after winning the elections and being installed as the chief minister of West Bengal, no longer needed Kishenji. In November 2011, she allowed the security forces to kill him in a false encounter.[5]

As in Lalgarh, elsewhere also in Chhattisgarh, Jharkhand, Bihar, the Maoists are steadily losing their bases. Due to absence of guidance from the central leadership (many among whom have either been killed or arrested), and the gradual erosion of ideological commitment among its cadres, the latter out of the sheer need for survival, have either surrendered to the police, or degenerated into bands of extortionists.

Need for a Post-Maoist Strategy

In view of the changes described above, instead of stubbornly sticking to a mood of denial, the Indian Maoist leadership should take the bull by the horns by recognising the crisis that it faces.

At the immediate level of operations, it has to revamp its entire organisational structure—by purging its guerrilla squads of mercenaries and extortionists. But at a more fundamental level, it has also to re-interrogate its strategy. It has to break out from the time warp in which it remains trapped. It is a time warp where its leadership imagines a

---

[5] For an exhaustive account of the Lalgarh movement, and a critical analysis of the role of the CPI (Maoist) in it, see Roy (2012, 2013).

situation where Mao's strategy of revolution that succeeded in particular historical conditions in China way back in the twentieth century will become a reality in twenty-first century India. Indian Communist revolutionaries should realise that they are fighting quite a different war (and on a different turf) than what was fought by their Chinese comrades from the 1920s till the 1940s in China. They will have to forge a new strategy to cope with the neoliberal capitalist features that mark the Indian rural economy and larger society today—which we have tried to analyse earlier.

Besides, in the new political arena today, along with the four old major contradictions that have been identified by the CPI (Maoist) in its programme (e.g., between imperialism and the Indian people; feudalism and the broad masses; capital and labour; and among the ruling classes), another contradiction is emerging—that between religious fanaticism and secular and democratic values. The former (mainly represented by Hindutva-oriented organisations like the BJP and its militant outfits like the Bajrang Dal) poses a threat to the Maoist ideology of secularism and egalitarianism.

At its ninth Congress in 2007, the CPI (Maoist) recognised this threat by adopting a resolution 'Against Hindu Fascism', where it pledged to 'do its best to defend the sections of the population targeted by the Hindu fascists' and added that it was 'willing to unite in a broad front with all the genuine democratic forces which would be willing to fight back the Hindu fascist offensive....' Following this, in August 2008, a Maoist guerrilla squad killed a Vishwa Hindu Parishad leader Swami Lakshmanananda Saraswati in Orissa, who had acquired notoriety for forcibly converting local Christians into Hinduism. But when following the assassination, the Sangh Parivar goons massacred neighbouring Christian villagers of Kandhamal (thus communalising the assassination by blaming it on Christians) on 9 September 2008, the Maoist guerrilla squads were nowhere in the scene to resist these goons and protect the villagers. As evident from this incident, and the un-resisted onrush of the Hindu fascist forces in other parts of India in the years that followed, the CPI (Maoist) has miserably failed to gear up its armed machinery to fight the violent challenge posed by the better organised armed gangs of the RSS, Bajrang Dal, Vishwa Hindu Parishad and Shiv Sena among other Hindu communal outfits.

The present leaders of the Maoist movement, therefore, need to move beyond exclusivist class-based politics. While empathising with the grievances of wider sections (like religious minorities and the Dalits—who, whether rich or poor, are threatened by the Hindu religious communal and casteist forces), they will have to formulate suitable tactics to 'defend the sections of the population targeted by Hindu fascists'. They should also recognise the importance of the new forms of popular protest against the neoliberal economy—ranging from non-violent mass agitations like the Narmada Bachao movement against big dams, to sporadic explosions of violence by villagers resisting their displacement by multinational industrial projects like POSCO in Odisha or popular demonstrations against special economic zones or nuclear plants. There is a need for a post-Maoist political strategy that can include these popular concerns and link up with these social movements. This can help the hitherto isolated Communist revolutionaries to become a part of the mainstream of popular resistance, dialectically interact with various movements and both influence and learn from them, to be able to move further towards their well-meaning goal of setting up a people's democratic state.

References

Basu, Deepankar and Debarshi Das. 2013, July. 'Maoist Movement in India: Some Political Economy Considerations'. *Journal of Agrarian Change* 13 (3).
Harriss, John. 2013, July. 'Does "Landlordism" Still Matter? Reflections on Agrarian Change in India'. *Journal of Agrarian Change* 13 (3).

Myrdal, Jan. 2012. *Red Star over India*. Calcutta: Setu Prakashani.

Navlakha, Gautam. 2012. *Days and Nights in the Heartland of Rebellion*. New Delhi: Penguin Books.

———. 2014. *War and Politics: Understanding Revolutionary Warfare*. Kolkata: Setu Prakashani.

Roy, Arundhati. 2010, May 29. 'Walking with the Comrades'. *Outlook*.

Roy, Biswajit, ed. 2012. *War and Peace in Junglemahal*. Kolkata: Setu Prakashani. Kolkata.

———, ed. and trans. 2013. *Letters from Lalgargh: The Complete Collection of Letters from the Peoples' Committee against Police Atrocities*. Kolkata: Setu Prakashani.

The Indian Express. 2014, 24 January.

6

Revisiting the Question of Violence: Maoist Movement in Andhra Pradesh*

K. Balagopal

Birpur, near the Godavari river in the northern corner of Karimnagar district, is the native village of Muppalla Lakshmana Rao, better known as Ganapathi, the general secretary of the central committee of the Communist Party of India (Maoist; CPI [Maoist]). Before a road-building mania took over the state in the regime of Chandrababu Naidu, it was a village difficult to access. Today it is accessible by a blacktop road from the temple town of Dharmapuri on the incompletely laid out National Highway 16 from Nizamabad in Telangana to Jagdalpur in Chhattisgarh. As you approach Birpur from Dharmapuri, you see at the entrance of the village a fresh white memorial with two pigeons atop, evidently intended to symbolise peace. The white colour of the memorial and the pigeons on top are in contrast to the hundreds of red memorials with the hammer and sickle on top that are strewn all over Telangana. It was built recently by the police to signify what the police gleefully regard as their decisive achievement in gaining an upper hand over the Maoists in their major stronghold, the Godavari river basin of northern Telangana. That it was built in the village of the top Maoist leader and inaugurated by the most unlikely symbol of peace, the superintendent of police, Karimnagar, is a juvenile gesture that could have

---

* This chapter has been published previously as 'Maoist Movement in Andhra Pradesh' in 2006 in *Economic and Political Weekly* 41 (29): 3183–87.

easily seemed merely tasteless in a different context, but in fact symbolises a disquieting fact: the politically juvenile attitude of successive governments in Andhra Pradesh towards the Naxalites. Peace per se would be desired by many people in the area. But very few are gleeful that the Maoists have been pushed back as never before. May be they are unrealistic but the ordinary people in their majority would want that the Maoists should be around, guns and all, but there should be peace in the sense of a life free of fear from this side or that. At the height of the six-month farce of talks between the Maoists and the Government of Andhra Pradesh in the second half of 2004, a common apprehension heard in most of the long-term strongholds of the Naxalites was that the talks was a good thing and it was hoped that some reduction of violence would result from it, but 'they won't leave us and go away, will they'?

The fact is that in much of this area the first time the common people experienced anything resembling justice was when the Naxalite movement spread there and taught people not to take injustice lying down. Unlike the rest of the state where the Naxalites spread through the armed squads, in northern Telangana there was a clear period in the late 1970s and early 1980s of the last century when it was the mass organisations, mainly the agricultural labourers associations and the student and youth fronts that were the instrument for the spread of Maoism as an ideology and a political practice. The phase was soon to pass and the people would start depending on the armed squads for justice but the sense of attainability of justice was a fundamental change. In very plain terms, the oppressors of local society, whether upper caste landlords or insensitive public officials, started dreading the wrath, initially of the awakened masses, and later of the well-armed squads composed of cadre born and brought up in poor families of the very same villages. Today the old landlords are no longer there but new local elites have come up and there is this fear that if the Naxalites go away, 'the poor cannot survive'. It is a matter of choice whether one sees this as revolution in the mould of Robin Hood, or merely as one instance in the saga of a Maoist long march, which is not to be freezed into a representative moment.

State Repression

From the very beginning, the attitude of the governments in Andhra Pradesh was one of extreme hostility. Police camps were set up in villages and the poor were tortured most inhumanly. It was always an explicitly political assault. The policemen incharge of the areas never made secret of the fact that they were not merely 'maintaining law and order' as the expression goes. They had the political task of protecting the landlords and the medieval mould of society, and they were executing the task. The underground Naxalite activists were no doubt armed, but their violence in those days was by and large selective and in any case not much in extent. On the other hand, it is said by everyone who knows—including police officers at retirement—that the fight of the Naxalites in those days was against what is generally referred to as feudal domination, and the economic oppression of the poor, and in this they were remarkably successful. Abolition of '*begar*' (bonded labour) and payment of something close to minimum wages, too, impeccably constitutional tasks, were performed by the Naxalites. The fight for land was not so successful since the police would not allow the land left behind by runaway landlords to be cultivated by the poor. Such land by and large remains fallow to this day, but it is not a very significant matter either way because as a proportion of the total cultivable area of the districts, or the land needed by the landless, it is slight in extent.

More would be added to such fallow land in the days to come when cultivation of land would be forcibly stopped by the Naxalites, not to take over the unconscionable acres of landlords, but as a measure of punishment imposed on any landed person for having harmed their cause, but even so the 'land struggle' in the plains areas was not an achievement of any moment. The encouragement given to the tribals in the forests to cut down the reserve forests and cultivate the land was far and away the most successful land struggle of the Naxalites, and not any struggle against landlords. Its extent in the five districts of Adilabad, Warangal, Khammam, East Godavari and Visakhapatnam has been plaintively estimated by the government as upwards of four lakh acres, counting together the achievement of all the Naxalite parties. However, after about the first decade and a half, the Naxalite parties came round to the view that beyond a point such a land struggle is harmful to the forest dwellers themselves and have since the mid-1990s imposed quite a successful ban on the cutting of forests. It is tempting to speculate what would have been the result if the government had appreciated this phase of the Naxalite struggle for what it was and responded by means other than repression. Forgetting class interests and all that, and accepting the arguments made at face value, one would perforce describe as one-sided the argument that it would have legitimised the use of violence for social/political ends, which is unacceptable in a democracy.

A blanket condonation of the use of violence by a group that lives by its own norms, which are enforceable only by itself is no doubt unacceptable in any society, even when it is declared to be for the good of the oppressed, but the contrary argument that a positive response from the government would perhaps have delegitimised the argument for revolutionary violence was never considered. That was no doubt not an innocent lapse, and the rulers had their reasons for that. The upshot was heavy repression on the Naxalite movement, in particular, the rural poor who were part of the movement or its social base. Extremes of torture and incarceration in unlawful police custody, destruction of houses and despoliation of drinking water wells and fields and framing of severe criminal cases en masse were the norm. And 'encounter' killings began from where they left off the day the internal emergency was lifted. It would again be interesting to speculate what would have been the result if the Maoists had decided not to hit back but concentrate on exposing the anti-poor bias of the government and extend their mass activity to a point that would have given their aspiration for state power a solid mass base. It would no doubt have been painful, but the alternative has not been any less painful.

Maoists Hit Back

As it happened, the Maoists hit back. The first killing of a policeman took place in June 1985 at Dharmapuri in Karimnagar district. And then a sub-inspector of police was killed at Kazipet in Warangal district on 2 September that year. That was followed the next day by plain-clothes policemen going in a procession behind the sub-inspector's dead body killing Ramanadham, a senior civil rights activist, in his clinic. 'Encounters' increased and decapitation of the limbs of police informers followed. The police acquired better weapons and the Maoists followed suit. Sizeable paramilitary forces were sent to the state in the mid-1990s but the terror they created was such that they were soon sent back. Not, however, before they had a taste of the Naxalites' newly acquired proficiency in blowing up police vehicles at will. Almost from the mid-1980s, brutal special police forces meant for eliminating Naxalites came into being and were allowed to operate totally incognito, the most successful being the greyhounds, which is a well-trained anti-guerrilla force that lives and operates as the Naxalites' armed squads do and is bound by no known law, including the Constitution of India.

The armed squads soon became the focal point of the activity of the Maoists, barring the two short periods when they were allowed freedom to conduct their political activity, both significantly in the immediate aftermath of the Congress party coming to power after prolonged Telugu Desam rule, leading to credible speculation about some pre-election agreement between the Congress and the Maoists (known till two years ago as the Communist Party of India [Maoist-Leninist; Peoples War]; CPI [ML]). Soon the Maoists declared the whole of northern Telangana and the Eastern Ghats hills to the north of the Godavari river, guerrilla zones, followed later by a similar proclamation for the Nallamala forests in the Krishna basin to the south. With this, the changed context of the movement was formalised. The immediate economic and social problems of the masses took a back seat and the battle for supremacy with the state became the central instance of the struggle. This brought its own imperatives, which were no longer immediately congruent with the needs of the masses who continued to be the base of the Maoists. So much so that while the youth in the areas of their activity look upon them as militant heroes even when they do not approve of them, it is the elderly who talk of them with affection. It is the parents' generation that remembers the days when *begar* used to be demanded by the landlord and a pittance paid for wage labour. Many of the youth frankly say that they may be valiant fighters, but what have they done for us except to bring the police to our villages? The state has its difficulties dealing with mass movements but it has tested strategies for dealing with armed struggles. It creates informers and agents for itself from the very masses the insurgency claims to represent. That is not difficult with the money and resources of power available with the state. This is a trap the militants fall into. They kill or otherwise injure those agents and informers and thereby antagonise more of their own mass base, in turn enabling the state to have more agents and informers.

Without exception, all militant movements have killed more people of their own social base than their purported enemy classes. This may be taken as one of the invariant laws of the sociology of armed insurgencies. The very fact that this is true of the Naxalites, the most politically sensitive of all insurgents, is proof enough. And this is true even without the impatience that comes with being armed, which results in more violence against dissenters among your own people. It is not as if they no longer addressed themselves to the social and economic problems of the poor. They did and they continue to do, but notwithstanding their claim that the village committees (often semi-secret) established by them deal with these problems, though not in the open as in the past, the overwhelming reality, except in totally isolated villages—and totally isolated areas such as the Abujmarh hills of Bastar—where such committees can actually function, is that it is the armed squads that deal with the problems. And they too often deal with them in a rough and ready manner made easy by the fact that there is no possibility of any opposition to them in society, so long as the police are taken care of.

The people for their part have come to look up to the squads as a substitute for their own struggle for justice. This has, on the one hand, created more enemies—victims of revolutionary arbitrariness—than they need have made, and, on the other, corrupted the masses into receivers of justice rather than fighters for it. You only have to report to the militants and get them to put up posters with appropriate demands and threats, and you will get what you want, provided that in the meanwhile the police have not made it impossible for the militants to come to your area to hear your pleas and put up posters. Then, of course, you wait till the militants turn the tables on the police. But even where such issues are addressed, the central place in the practice of the Maoists has been taken up by the guerrilla struggle against the state, aimed at weakening its hold to a point where the area can be considered a liberated zone.

This requires a range of acts of violence, which have no direct relation to the immediate realisation of any rights for the masses, though the resulting repression invariably hits at the masses. The Maoists have developed considerable expertise of a military character, which is admired even by policemen in private, even as their political development has stagnated. The state has met this with even more brutal violence, which has bred further violence from the Maoists. For at least about a decade now, each year has seen between 300 and 400 deaths in this gruesome game. The ability of the state to obtain information on an extensive scale, thanks partly to its resources, partly to the demise of values at all levels in society, including the lower most, and partly to the large number of enemies created by the Maoists around themselves in the course of their battle with the state, the state's ability for the same reasons to inject covert operatives into the Maoist ranks, and the very successful forays of the greyhounds deep into the forests, has resulted in its establishing a clear upper hand in this killing game for the present.

Retaining Support of the Next Generation

But the difficulties faced by the Maoists do not end here. To discuss the rest of them requires attention to considerations that Marxism at its best would find difficult to deal with, given the lack of any attention to an understanding of the human subject of history other than the practically useless profundity that 'it makes itself while making history'. And Maoism is not Marxism at its best, at any rate for this purpose. The strategy of providing armed support to the aspirations of the masses succeeds at the first round without much difficulty, once willing cadre are found, in areas historically subjected to extremes of deprivation and oppression and neglected by governance. But the very success means that a new generation is created, which is freed from the severe disabilities its parents suffered from and is able to see and seize opportunities in the existing polity and, therefore, may not be as hospitable to armed struggle as its parents. The state too learns and makes some efforts to draw the area from out of neglect and into what is usually described as 'the mainstream' even as it suppresses the struggle by brute force. The eagerness to join a life-and-death struggle is usually diluted to some extent as a consequence. If, at that stage, instead of toning down the armed component of struggle the radicals proceed to fight the state over the heads of the masses, the masses can withdraw further and even become resentful.

After the first immense success of the Maoists among the Gonds of Adilabad district in the late 1970s and early 1980s, from the next generation that came of age in the 1990s, one often heard the honest query: Are the Adivasis the guinea pigs of revolution? The temptation to which the Maoists have too often succumbed, namely to condemn all such doubt as arising from the 'petty-bourgeois tendencies' of a new elite only makes matters worse. In this sense, the real challenge for the Maoists is not whether they can militarily get the better of the greyhounds, who have a clear upper hand at present, but whether they can retain active support from one generation to the next while retaining their Maoist strategy, or even by recasting it to suit the changes in the needs and aspirations of the new generation in the changed social context created by their very activity and the state's response to it. Till now, there is no sign of any thinking along these lines. Often the first thing that happens to people who find political awakening from a state of dormancy is to turn to a search for their own social identity, whether caste, tribe or gender. This has led to many ex-Naxalites becoming Ambedkarites, or at least sympathisers of Ambedkarism, since any way the overwhelming majority of them are from the outcastes or backward castes of the Hindu society. This does not necessarily mean that they have lost interest in revolution as the communists understand it. But the Maoists have too often reacted with a lack of sympathy to this phenomenon. So much so that while their cadre, and leaders too, except a handful at the very top, are from the Dalit, Adivasi or backward communities, unlike the Parliamentary Left which continues to be a bastion of upper castes, and while they have in the last few years inducted women into their armed squads on a scale that will soon probably put to shame the eternally unfilled promise of one-third reservation in the legislatures, they remain not only theoretically but practically too, hostile to any expression of identity politics, seen invariably as opportunistic deviance. Instead the Maoist response to stagnation after the first round has been to transfer attention to a new area amenable to initiation of their kind of politics—and there are many such areas, thanks to the utter neglect of vast regions by governance in the last 50 years, and the current philosophy of governance which is a philosophy of non-governance—and do the same thing again. Other Marxist–Leninist groups have often criticised the Maoists for this hop, skip and jump mode of revolution but they have never taken the criticism seriously, probably regarding their conduct as part of the strategy of guerrilla struggle. Leaving aside the political rights and wrongs of it, the practical consequence has been a rapid spread to new areas such as the area surrounding the Nallamala and other contiguous forests in southern coastal Andhra and Rayalaseema. This spread has been mainly through the guerrilla activity of armed squads, not preceded by anything comparable with the mass activity that illuminated and remedied much of the social and economic oppression people suffered from in the Godavari basin districts of northern Telangana. But the spread has not been as smooth and successful as in northern Telangana.

Whatever Maoist theory may say, the guerrilla phase of struggle involves establishing armed dominion over society, often described by the police with exaggeration as a parallel government. Such dominion is easier to establish in areas whose social culture is characterised by a certain quiescence than in factious areas. The northern Telangana districts, of all the areas of the state, do exhibit that characteristic whereas the south, especially the region surrounding the Nallamala forests, is the most factious area. Armed activity of any kind, with even the best of intentions, can degenerate easily into factious violence. The fate of the Maoists in Anantapur in Rayalaseema is a classic instance of this. More vitally, armed dominion in factious areas calls up private vengeance which the state will not hesitate to encourage. The 'Nallamala Cobras' who have committed three murders of democratic activists in the last nine months and silenced much of democratic activity in the southern districts constitute brutal proof of this. We know that each mode of life is found attractive by persons of certain character traits and in turn encourages certain traits in those who partake of it. It is a species of conceit that refuses to see that this applies to political strategies too. To speak of negative traits alone, just as the Sarvodaya philosophy attracts a lot of hypocrisy and the parliamentary strategy of the Communist Party of India and the Communist Party of India (Marxist) a lot of opportunism, strategies of militancy attract unruly types who straddle the border line between rebellion and mere rowdyism. These types can, and have, caused considerable harm to the Maoists and have constituted easy subjects for the state's tactics of shaping covert operatives inside their ranks. Once outside the party they have fit equally well the role of 'renegades' as they are called in Kashmir. The conduct of the Maoists who leave little room for appeal for persons whom they brand enemies of the people has in turn created cadre for the vengeful renegades, and the resulting gangs that call themselves cobras and tigers of various kinds have played a major role in immobilising the very substantial overground support activity the Naxalite movement had.

Decimation of Organic Leaders

This is as far as the story of Maoist revolution has come in Andhra Pradesh. Since there is little sign of any rethinking on either side, one has no basis for expressing much hope about the future. What makes it a tragedy is that the lives of lakhs of people belonging to the lowest orders of society in terms of community as well as class are involved in it. Many dimensions of the tragedy are known or amenable to imagination but there is one which is not usually commented on. This is that many if not all of the lives that are being lost at the hands of the police in this process are lives that the oppressed can ill afford to lose. They are the organic leaders of the class, who have adopted a political path of their choice. It is not all among the powerless classes that can dare challenge the system and be ready to pay for it. It is not every day that the oppressed produce such elements from amongst themselves. The rights or wrongs of their choice have no bearing on the tragedy of the decimation of this organic leadership. They chose to be Maoists, but they could have chosen to be something else, and whichever the choice, they would have added to the strength of the oppressed. The daily loss of such persons is a sacrifice the oppressed cannot be called upon to put up with indefinitely.

Definition of Organisation

PART III

7

Coming to Be 'Maoist': Surviving Tropes, Shifting Meanings

Chitralekha

I was twelve. ... They used to come to the village to hold meetings. They would call us and talk about Chandrashekhar Azad, Khudiram Bose, Marx, Lenin ... they said let's fight for the poor, make a new world order. I had no second thoughts. What could be better than a krantikari (revolutionary)? Agriculture was not for me ... and what good is it to be a teacher or a doctor?
    —Rinkuji, area commander, Maoist Communist
            Centre (MCC), personal interview, 2003

Left extremism in India has been amongst the most extensively researched subjects of political and academic interest, inspiring study through its various phases and shifts. The available literature ranges from landmark works in the early years of the movement (Banerjee 1984; Mohanty 1977; Ray 1988), studies in central Bihar in the 1990s (Bhatia 1998; 2005), attention towards continuities between the informal economy of the state and the political economy of Maoism (Mukherji 2010; Prasad 2010; Shah 2006; also see Shah 2013 on agrarian transitions, Maoist strategy and mobilisation) as well as discussions around the now increasingly complex questions of violence and counter-violence, democracy, justice and development in the Maoist areas (Balagopal 2006; Gudavarthy 2013; Guha 2007; Mohanty 2009; Navlakha 2006; Sundar 2006, 2016). In addition, we now also have available several documents in the public sphere that draw attention to ideological positions of the Maoist leadership (Azad 2006; Ganapathi 2010; Ghandy 2008).

In an intellectual and political atmosphere often charged with (sharply divided) positions, this chapter reflects on an ethnographic work with Maoists in Jharkhand and Bihar that brings into the discourse voices of those in the armed movement, not its highest leaders or ideologues but its unknown and virtually unheard of foot soldiers (Chitralekha 2010). Over several months in 2003 and across seven districts in Jharkhand and Bihar, I gathered histories of the armed cadre of the Maoist Communist Centre of India (MCCI) and People's War (PW), travelling with their *dastas* (armed squads) or living with their families in remote villages.[1] I met Rinkuji, a 16-year-old area commander with the MCC (whose memories I start this chapter with), in Mahuadanr, a small, remote village in Latehar, Jharkhand, set in the midst of mountainous, heavily forested terrain, with no electricity, limited water resources, no public healthcare, secondary or high school. In the course of my stay there, and before my own meetings with him, I encountered different aspects of the mosaic of 'reasons' that had drawn a 12-year-old to the MCC: his younger brother's feelings that he joined the 'party' *shaukiya* (of his own wish) because he enjoyed being with them; his childhood friend's memories of how he had taken the party's help to get someone beaten up (and had to join); an elderly relative's pointing out that 'for young boys here, there was nothing else to do'. Rinku's family owned a large pukka house, 30 acres of land and rare amenities like a self-owned well; his father had a permanent job as a teacher in the city, and his three brothers and one sister were all school going. They were Rajputs, the dominant caste in the village.

My unsuccessful attempts to relate those reasons and Rinku's own memories with meanings ascribed often to association with Naxal parties in academic discourse (and in the wider public sphere) were amongst the early links to the recognition of 'drifters' as a significant ideal–typical

---

[1] MCC was renamed MCCI after merger with the Revolutionary Communist Centre of India (Maoist) in 2003.

category of participation in the movement. This can also be located in histories of those who joined in the late 1980s and early 1990s but now dominates the contemporary phase of the Maoist movement, straddling a dispersed caste, class and gender profile. If Rinku joined from a landed family, was upper caste and male, many drifters were also Dalit or Adivasi, female and poor. While the chapter is by no means an attempt to universalise the relationship with the Maoist cause, its findings do suggest that some of the most critical things young people seek from the movement today stretch across caste, class and even gender divides. I argue here that entry into the *dastas* for many not just acts as a means of access to the public sphere but they also serve as sites for construction of individual identities along pathways not always predictable by the imperatives of the collective. Quite different from dominant discourses on Naxalite politics and goals that emanate from or revolve around narratives of the Maoist leadership or ideologues, narratives of guerrillas, including those from the most oppressed classes, often ruminated with urgency, not so much on the formal struggle for the equalisation of group identity or resources, as on a deeply individual quest for recognition and self-actualisation. Within this context, the following sections engage with certain tropes that have for several decades been traditionally associated with the Naxalite movement, exploring through this reading of narratives of armed cadre meanings ascribed by participants to their practice, and in relation, the troubled and shifting relationship of the movement with caste and izzat, livelihood, occupational choices and 'success', violence, death and martyrdom.

Revisiting Izzat

The struggle to regain izzat or human dignity has in many ways been the pivotal element of Naxalite mobilisation in

Bihar and Jharkhand—experienced, posited and remembered as fight for equal social status and honour centred in
caste identities. While the CPI (ML) groups theorised the
class aspect as primary and caste as secondary, derivative
or superstructural (PUDR 1998, 4–5), popular political
speech in central Bihar in the period of mobilisation
tended to express the conflict in primarily caste terms,
placing caste at the centre and property relations or class
in a derivative or secondary position. What the organisation theorised then as agrarian struggle was for many of
its participants most fundamentally a struggle for izzat.
While the historical overlap between the caste and class
dimensions has been undeniable in central Bihar, the two
are nevertheless not identical. Not all of those who fight for
izzat, whose denial springs primarily from caste, though
also secondarily from economic disability, need be poor or
interested in *gair mazarua* (village commons) land, though
many in fact are. Conversely, not all the landless or poor
are from the lowest castes and therefore involved in a
fight for dignity that their caste status has denied them,
though once again most are. Apart from the lack of total
physical overlap, the predominance of izzat in the popular
discourse in central Bihar at the time points towards the
fact that the nature of economic and caste deprivations
while entangled are qualitatively different and perceived
and experienced differently.

Narratives of cadre who joined the movement in its
heydays—in the 1980s and early 1990s—mostly those of
Dalit, landless peasants in central Bihar, carry overrid-
ing vivid memories of zamindari oppression—a deeply
remembered experience of social and economic subjugation
at the hands of the landed, dominant castes in the village.
Anil joined the MCC in the first flush of the movement in
Bake Bajar in Gaya in the early 1980s. He was 25 then
and vividly recalls the day he took part in his first 'action'
against the archetypal cruel landlord as a thrilling, heady
experience. 'The landlord was overconfident that no one

will be able to harm him. ... Because his crime was that he had humiliated our women, we castrated him. ...' His participation in that remembered evening of blood and brutality was premised on neither any personal enmity nor dreams for himself but to put an end both materially and symbolically to the humiliation his people had endured over the years. 'Since I came to my senses, this is what I saw. ... If I am a poor man, you don't allow me to reap my crops, you misbehave with my family, with female members'. Party Unity (PU) cadre Pranav Vidyarthi too had led the struggle to acquire and redistribute *gair mazarua* and ceiling surplus lands in and around his own village. Paying the price for his political practice in dehumanising conditions in Aurangabad jail, he too had no regrets. The years of bloodshed had for him a core and local purpose, which he recounted fervently, '*Aisan gaon banavan jai / Jahan sapno me julmi jamindar na rahe / Sabke bharpet mele khana, aur rahe ke thekana / Koi koi ke kuboliya bolen har na rahe. ...*' (Let us make a village/where even in your dreams there is no cruel landlord/where everyone has enough to eat, and a roof over his head/where no man can talk down to another man.)

While Anil and Vidyarthi were deeply committed cadre, Vijay, Dalit zonal committee member of the MCC who also joined the movement in its heydays in Aurangabad, had gone on to amass considerable personal wealth with the party and was finally 'betrayed' by his own peers in the party. Arrested and 'broken' under severe torture in police custody, the Latehar jail superintendent recalled that when he was brought in, both his legs had fractures and it took months of treatment before he could walk again. When I met Vijay in jail, he reminisced that MCC had been his first (and only) chance at 'success'.

> When I was small, the zamindar's men would give me roti (bread) and salt and tell me, this is it, now eat it up fast. ... By the time I was in the 9th class I had realized that nothing would become of me like this. ... I completed my matriculation ... everyone has

dreams of becoming a doctor, engineer … don't you? But in these areas, nobody lets you do anything even if you want to.

The matter of izzat, or its perceived deprivation, was again recounted somewhat differently in narratives of MCC cadre who participated in the brutal massacre of upper castes in Dalelchak Baghaura in Aurangabad district of Bihar in the late 1980s; an entire village of Rajput women and children were beheaded here by MCC cadre on a rudely improvised chopping block. Convicted on the testimony of a sole survivor (a four-year-old child) who witnessed the carnage that night, Suraj Yadav was serving a life sentence in Gaya central jail at the time of my fieldwork. Thirty-six years old and now a postgraduate with an additional degree in law (LLB), he reiterated that the '*ghatna*' (event) occurred as it was a matter of '*izzat*'; the Rajputs had to be taught a lesson, and they (the Yadavs) merely did what had been done to them over the years. In conversations with other members of Yadav's (visibly affluent, landed) family, several other imperatives emerged, including those of pending disputes between two sets of rich farmers (one of whom was Yadav's family), confusing attempts to locate the killings within the meanings traditionally ascribed to the seeking of izzat. Nevertheless, the scale of the killings, the brutality with which they were executed and the absence of regret in Yadav's and his family members' recall of the events of the day are also—as in the bitter recall of Vijay's memories—still markers of the repertoire of collective memory and historically remembered angst of oppression or discrimination that are related to the specific way in which izzat was then framed: as honour and perhaps as recognition sought to be wrested from the (vilified and long hated) other castes.

Much had changed, however, by the time of my fieldwork in Jharkhand and Bihar soon after the turn of the millennium. Wage struggles and Naxalite mobilisation pivoted around the idea of izzat over decades of struggle had yielded by now visible gains; the dignity of the poor and the landless was not as easily played around with as was earlier (Bhatia 1997, 58; Mukul 1999, 3465–70; Wilson 1999, 343). Caste wars as well as the internal conflict and confusion of the 1990s was also by now more or less a thing of the past. The PU had merged with the CPI (ML) PW, and the CPI (ML) Liberation had almost disbanded its armed guerrilla operations to enter electoral politics. MCC and PW in Bihar and Jharkhand had grown significantly in strength and spread, and since 2001 shared manpower, resources and skills. Some of the areas of my fieldwork (in 2003) were in fact already manned by joint *dastas* of the two groups. In 2004, this working alliance between the (by now renamed) MCCI and the PW was consolidated by a formal merger into a single entity, the Communist Party of India (Maoist). By the time of my fieldwork, Jharkhand was already the epicentre of the strongest (till then) consolidation of Naxalite strength and activity, and the conflict in the region had deviated quite radically from the original Naxalite agenda. From a movement once deriving local allegiance around issues of land redistribution, fairer wages and human dignity, it was often framed by cadre across areas of my fieldwork (in both Jharkhand and Bihar) as an 'international struggle' pitched now almost completely against the police and state apparatus. Recurring battles with security forces and sharply heightened surveillance on Maoist activity further marginalised already weakening mass front activities. As opposed to memories of cadre who had joined the movement in central Bihar, it was difficult to locate the Naxalite 'enemy' in discourses of armed cadre I met in Jharkhand, conceptualised variously as (still) exploitative zamindar, brutish police, corrupt contractor, partisan state and so on (Chitralekha 2012; see Shah 2013 on the historical specificity to this realignment in the hills and forests of Jharkhand).

Within this context of flux and deep changes in the movement, this section locates manifestations of identities of cadre (from across various castes and communities) being re-negotiated in multiple ways. Caste consciousness, certainly not absent in contemporary times, rested uneasily amongst these changing, often dislocated identities, especially amongst the young in the movement. Based on my own extended fieldwork in the region, I suggest that izzat, the pivotal idea for mobilisation to join the movement in the past, has assumed different meanings for contemporary practitioners of Maoism. In this transformed context, while the reason young people—not all poor or underprivileged—join still perhaps has more to do with izzat than *zameen* (land) or roti, izzat now is not so much about the respect or honour demanded from the enemy or the hated other as about the recognition sought from peers, amongst one's own community in locations which have not been able to provide too many other avenues of differentiation or fulfilment. It does not help that these political 'choices' are mostly made at an average age of 12–15 years, an age where young people, in their own recall, found guns and the power that came of holding them undeniably attractive.

Manishji,[2] 22-year-old deputy commander of an MCCI *dasta* I met with in the early hours of the morning in Kotila village (Hariharganj, Palamu), recalled that he joined at 14. He said he had had 'no problems of his own' but was influenced by *'partywallahs* who used to come and go' in his village in Hazaribagh district. Rinku's home village, Mahuadanr, was also in many ways prototypical of the kind of life conditions within which young people from even ostensibly 'prosperous' families became 'Maoist'. His neighbour Brijesh who joined the PW was also of the Rajput caste, with lineage going back to the erstwhile raja (king)

---

[2] My meeting with Manishji and his *dasta* was not an appointed one. Fraught more than usual by problems of pre-judgement, performativity and imminent disruption, many specificities of his history (caste, for instance) were not gathered. On questions of pre-judgement in fieldwork, see Chitralekha (2017).

of the region. The family had 25 acres of land but (despite the grand lineage) was barely able to make ends meet. Low rainfall, poor irrigation and inability to pay for wage labour had over the years reduced most of their fields to wastelands. Rice procured from their rain-fed fields barely lasted a few months, and dwindling income had taken its toll on basic nutrition and healthcare among other things. At the time of my fieldwork, PW cadre Brijesh's mother and her two youngest sons (aged 10 and 11) had been, for instance, suffering from untreated malarial fever for many months. His mother said they had been facing penury and humiliation at every front, and Brijesh's decision, or sacrifice as she saw it, in fact, changed everyone's stance towards them.

In the late 1980s, two of Brijesh's own uncles were tortured and hacked to death by the PU (later merged with PW in Jharkhand) in full sight of immediate family members. But in current circumstances, Brijesh's grandfather does not think it strange that his own grandson Brijesh had joined those who were his family's bitter opponents not so long ago. 'The school here is only till the eighth, and the quality of education is very poor. The boys have nothing else to do. Naturally, they get excited by the *aavo-bhaav* (demeanor) of the Naxalites'. If committed cadre like Vidyarthi and Anil joined Naxal parties with the hope to transform not just their own but others' lives riddled by caste humiliation and extreme deprivation, Rinku or Brijesh did not see a future for themselves. Joining the MCC or the PW, on the other hand, brought instant rewards, social and economic. For Rinku, the transition from life as a village bully to life as a guerrilla was not easy, but area commander after four years with the MCCI, he does not think he has got a bad deal. 'We communists get a lot of izzat from the people. ... Anyway it's not as if all of us will get jobs now if we leave the party'.

Rinku's story was not unusual but indicative of the shifting logic of association with Maoist groups, where

joining MCCI or PW was often an outcome of real or perceived failure of other avenues of occupation, achievement,
'success' or 'profitable enterprise'. Most of those I encountered were at least matriculate; several were students or
unemployed when they joined front organisations but went
on to become hard core armed cadre. Suresh, 25 years old
when we met, from the Kahar caste, was a pure science
graduate and at the time of my fieldwork one of the five
members of the Bihar Jharkhand State Youth Committee
of PW. 'I had different dreams. Soon after college, I took
the help of the MLA (member of legislative assembly) and
started a loan banking company. ... Collections were good,
but the Bihar government banned it in 1994'. Pandeyji, a
Bhumihar youth from Panki (village) in Palamu, postgraduate in history, had also been looking much like Suresh
to 'make something' out of his life when he met the party.

> I was drifting around after Matric—doing nothing for a while.
> Those days, big (MCC) names like Vinod Yadav Vidrohi, Jugal
> Pal, Gopalda, Gautam Paswan used to come to our area.... In one
> meeting, they asked me to speak ... said you must contribute ...
> we are not forward virodhis, we are against oppressors ... they
> said would help me study further.

Romeshji, commander of sub-zonal rank, had completed
his intermediate from Lohardaga. After several failed
attempts to secure employment with the Bihar Police (he
could not put together the required bribe money), he left
for Delhi and after a few years of hard labour finally got a
'prestigious job' as a 'machine operator' in Wazirpur, the
industrial belt of the capital city. The factory, however,
closed down some years later; he returned to his village,
got involved with the Adivasi revival organisation *Oraon
Sarna Samiti*, national political party Congress (I) and
finally with (then) MCC. 'I didn't think so much. I felt if
I help them they will help me.' His education and diverse
experience was valued in the party, and he made it
through the ranks relatively quick. Hesitant about what

the 'international struggle' aims to change ('I don't study anymore, how can I know?'), Romeshji is nevertheless loyal and takes pride—much in the manner of a successful professional—in his role in the party. 'Don't you realize there is politics even in MCC? I have struggled very hard to reach this level. I can lose it all with one mistake.'

Death, Martyrdom and Acceptable Risk

What does death mean for a Naxalite? Are the torn, bullet-ridden and blood-splattered bodies of young people—frequently splayed on regional news cover pages, occasionally on national television screens—evidence of the Maoists' willingness to give up life for political ideas?

Death itself has been the subject of rich anthropological scholarship, yet work on its political aspects is still recent. Early scholarship in this domain includes Taussig's examination of colonialism in South America, its creation of the 'space of death' (Taussig 1987), the corpse as origin of taboos, and in relation, power that accrues to the modern state—'great machine of death and war' (Taussig 1997). Around the same time, Agamben's *Homo Sacer* (1988) contended that what characterises modern politics is not that life becomes object of the calculations of state power but that the exception becomes the rule: bare life gradually coincides with the political realm. Besides anthropological interest in flows between state power, politics and the symbolic capital (and cultural apparatuses) of death (see particularly Robben 2000; Verdery 1999), early influential attempts to theorise death for politics included its interpretation as psychological learning (Binmore 1994; Hoffer 1951) and the dominant security perspective to 'terrorism studies' (Pape 2003; Primoratz 1990; Sprinzak 2000; Weinberg 1991). In many ways, it was 9/11 (or the terrorism of the spectacle aka Baudrillard) that, however, brought human mortality decisively into the discursive realm of the political.

The aftermath of the September 11 suicide bombings in the United States saw not just a spate of writings in American and European newspapers on martyrdom (jihad), it inspired substantial academic work, mostly coalescing around its comprehension as pathology of contemporary Islam (Juergensmeyer 2003; Strenski 2003). The violence itself was seen as nihilist, in that the Islamic militant was assumed to 'seek' a decisive encounter with death, evoking horror in the deliberative use of his or her own body as weapon. Euben was amongst the earliest in this milieu to draw attention to the chasm between scholarly reflections on the premises of politics and the proliferation of rhetorical gestures and practices in which death, martyrdom and the remaking of politics are uneasily yet decisively conjoined. Martyrdom in this context, she points out, is abstracted from the ethico-political contexts through which it is defined and made to signify a general eruption of the irrational, archaic and pathological; she deliberates instead on jihad and shahada as political action seen as necessary to the founding of a just political community on earth (Euben 2002, 5–6). In engagement with these arguments, Asad reflects that the absolute right to defend oneself by force becomes, in the context of industrial capitalism, the freedom to use violence globally: the suicide bomber belongs, in an important sense, to a modern Western tradition of armed conflict wherein to save the nation (or to found its state) in confrontation with a dangerous enemy, it may be necessary to act without being bound by ordinary moral constraints (Asad 2007, 62–63).

Far removed as 9/11 and the context of suicide bombings may seem to be from the Naxalites in Bihar and Jharkhand, none of all this is too distant from the acridity of contemporary public, deeply mediatised discourses on Naxalite practice in India. The Maoist unlike the suicide bomber is in the main (recognised even in popular speech) as 'willing' to—as opposed to 'intending' to—die; neverthe-less, in recent years, the Maoist's readiness to die (more appropriate—be killed) is seen as closely entangled with the intention to take as many lives as possible. My interest in this chapter, however, is not with detailing of popular perception of Maoist violence/death or utility of that death to the cause or to the functioning of the organisa-tion (see Suykens 2010, however, for a careful analysis of the ideological basis and functionality of martyrdom for the Maoist movement) but instead to attempt an under-standing, however tentative or frail, of what such (violent) death may mean to the Naxalite soldier. What meaning/s does 'martyrdom' hold for those intended to be its likely recipients? How is the possibility of imminent death, in so far as it can be confronted, leave aside told, described by young people in the movement today? Acknowledging the important distinction that must be made between seeking motives for and the circumstances of death (see Asad on how motives themselves [in the context of suicide bombing] are rarely lucid, invested with emotions and may not be clear even to the actor [Asad 2007, 64]), my attempt here is a limited one. The intention in this section is to document meanings ascribed to (prospective) death, in so far as the actor of violence 'knows' or can name his practice—and wishes to tell it. In this effort, I have been often limited but also sometimes enriched by the absence of verbal articu-lation (with in lieu, the speaking poignancy of silence) in this ethnographic engagement (for detailing of the wider historical/sociopolitical context that renders such death as a critical tool of class struggle, see Chitralekha 2012).

I have previously attempted to place narratives of armed cadre I met with over several districts in Jharkhand and Bihar within the ideal–typical categories of committed, opportunists and drifters framed to clarify (shifting) Naxalite practice and relationship to cause (Chitralekha 2010). Across contexts of my fieldwork, I found neither caste nor class background and not even life experience had a determining relationship with ideological commitment. Even from amongst the poor, only a bare few had joined and engaged in violence 'for' the cause but many more associated as drifters (even committed cadre sometimes 'joined' for reasons not very different from those that drew the drifters in). I argue that the committed are not created by Left (or other) extremist organisations but 'tapped', so to say, by them in time: cadre like Vidyarthi or Anil were 'found' by the movement (Chitralekha 2010, 327–28). This innate sincerity or commitment to cause, despite being located in the probable nature of a predisposition or bent of mind, is, however, as far from being located in caste/class/religious locations as from psychological theories of assumed predisposition to violence or death (Fromm 1977; Hoffer 1951). It also complicates Shah's conceptual separation of the motivation of the ideological renouncer (upper caste Maoist leadership) versus Adivasi rank and file (see Shah 2014). In continuity, the committed Naxalite also cannot be identified by the 'willingness' to die; even the opportunist factors in this probability into his calculations as he negotiates what he wants out of the movement and its affected parties (the state, the poor, etc.): the unpredictable and likely imminence of violent death is implicit in the very nature of Naxalite work. Yet significantly, it is only the rare few committed cadre who see (the possibility of) death as honourable loss or willing sacrifice in pursuit of a cherished cause.

Jopan Manjhi of village Gangapur in the Dhanbad district of Jharkhand remembers that he started 'working for' MCC when he was 10. Initially in awe of the *'partywallahs'* who supported his family in a (land) dispute with relatives, he recalls he was drawn to the *'samajik'* (socialistic) vision of Marx and Lenin, and a few years later, he left home with them for good. By the time of his capture and arrest in 1996 (he was 21 then), he had risen to the rank of senior commander incharge of two districts in Jharkhand. Despite sustained interrogation and inhuman torture,

Manjhi (his compatriots said) never 'talked' to the police, and at the time of my fieldwork, he was amongst the rare few that the party was still actively trying to get back into its fold. The years of torture and struggle, he said, had only strengthened his resolve. 'I like to endure. ... I enjoy this struggle. ... I want to do it the hard way'. Different from his comrades, most of whom too had reconciled with (the possibility of) death, Manjhi seemed to voluntarily and eagerly almost embrace pain, sacrifice and the possibility of death for a larger cause: 'I am a highly respected cadre. If something happens to me, they will make me a martyr'. For Manjhi too, death is then justified by hope of (having contributed to the creation of) a just world; however, 'immortality' is sought in the symbolic, more nebulous and somewhat paradoxical terms of retrospective honour and recognition in 'the world left behind'. Martyrdom in this context is not an otherworldly reward but constitutes the elevation of an ordinary cadre into an idealised hero 'within the party'. In the highly mediatised post 9/11 discourses, martyrdom or shahada has often been sought to be understood or rationalised by rewards prospectively associated with political death: for the suicide bomber who dies fighting, in this (popular, televised, digitised) imagination, the death of the physical body is, paradoxically, sought to be compensated by promise of 'this-worldly rewards' such as *houris, jannat* or the pleasures of heaven (see Engineer 2010, however, for the Koranic meaning of *hur*).[3]

---

[3] The Koranic meaning of *'hur'* has reference to morally pure men and women who will be companions of those who enter paradise (*jannah*). Engineer, whose take is that the popular belief on *'houris'* (beautiful, virginal women) is used by vested interests to recruit young people to die in the 'cause of Islam', quotes from the Qur'an (56: 22–26) to clarify how the discourse on *hur* (*houris* in popular parlance) has, in fact, no reference to sex or lust, but rather richness of soul and moral purity (2010).

Manjhi's reading of martyrdom is placed in a secular framework quite different from that of religious sacrifice; his imagining of immortality can hardly be comprehended in terms of the vast body of work surrounding the human quest for continuity through death of the physical body or its actualisation in forms of religious symbolisation (Becker 1973; Lifton and Olsen 1974; Malinowski 1954 [1925]). I was in some moments reminded of Hoffer's timeless perspective on dying and killing as ceremonial performance, or make-believe, that masks the grim reality of death for actors in armies: when the individual (cadre) faces torture or annihilation, his only source of strength is in not being himself but part of something mighty, glorious and indestructible (Hoffer 1951, 65–67). Performativity, while an aspect of Manjhi's (as anyone's) ontological survival, nevertheless does not exhaust the range of complicated meanings he ascribes to his practice and possible death. With the party since he was 10, his association with the cause was hardly chosen, but he trusts the MCC leadership and holds on doggedly to his faith in the Maoist agenda, keeping what he says is his 'mission' alive through painstaking reading in jail of (by now torn and dog-eared) texts provided by the party about the political history of 'successful' communist regimes. Deeply trusted by the party, he is an insider; if unexposed to the world outside the party, he is aware of that vulnerability and shies away from facing contradictions in the worldview or practices of MCC, seeing it as treason, recognising that such deconstruction could tear away legitimacy from work that he had not just killed and risked his life for, and outside which he knew no other, and knowing that within the choices he had had, he contributed (Jopan's self-aware, reflexive consciousness of his own vulnerability is quite different from Hoffer's 'true believer's' unwillingness to qualify the certitude and righteousness of his holy cause [Hoffer 1951, 84]). Vidyarthi, whose body by the time I met him was already evidently frail, wasted away by decades in jail, had no regrets about a youth lost in struggle, only jubilation that he could contribute to huge changes in land ownership in his village. Anil believed it is because people like him risked their lives that others (of his caste) in his village are asked to today 'sit side by side' with the upper castes and not on the ground. Mahato said he had never feared death and (even though troubled by changes in the functioning of the party) would return to contribute. Manjhi, too, believes his death would not have been in vain. 'It is not as if we have done nothing. ... Wherever we are active, it is those districts that have seen development'.

Manjhi (or Vidyarthi or Mahato) was deeply committed to the cause, pursuit of which also imparted meaning to his own life, making it worthwhile to have lived—and when necessary, died; but for most in the party, life (and its death) is not 'for' the Naxalite cause. What is it then for? Why do those who join as children stay on with the party, often long after the first flush of life change has faded and lost its charm? Can (the probability of early) death be discounted without ideology? In a journey—or perhaps, adventure—embarked on in a bid to improve one's life chances, can the possibility of an end to life itself be calculated for as acceptable risk? What is the relationship of killing without ado, or trauma or regret—to dealing with one's own death? Manishji had explained (in the watchful presence of both his commander and *dasta* comrades) how he had no troubles of his own but joined 'this line' to 'help his poorer brothers'; the party's enemies, he said, were zamindars, but he was uncomfortable when asked about the party's work in Kotila, where there were none. Deputy commander of an evidently important *dasta* at 22 (unlike the well-worn and recycled arms of most I met, Manishji carried with evident pride a gleaming machine gun), his parting words, as he left in the darkness of night to continue miles of trek in hard terrain, were a jaunty, smiling *'zindagi rahi, to fir milenge'* (see you again if I am alive). Sixteen-year-old Rinku too says dismissively that he may be shot down one day but it does not matter.

> If we die, what is the problem? But if we leave the party, the police will certainly hold us under POTA (Prevention of Terrorism Act) ... so what dreams. ... My dreams have been fulfilled. ... I will never bow my head to the police. ... I would prefer to die in an encounter.

Rinku's young cousin Brijesh, who had joined PW (and in whose home I lived in Mahuadanr), came home abruptly one night in the course of my stay and cross-questioned me about the purpose of my visit, but despite my efforts did not speak much himself. Brijesh left in the early hours of the next morning, citing important work; I was informed of a landmine blast in the adjoining Saranda forest later that day which PW had claimed responsibility for.

Trawick's work in an LTTE village in eastern Sri Lanka (2007) draws our attention to the ludic aspects that pose challenges to the understanding of violence (with its expected effects of fear and horror, and sorrow and grief). Showing how categories of war and play become interchangeable in the lives of young LTTE cadre, Trawick writes that the LTTE Tigers represented the battles they fought as 'child's play', 'fully intense, concentrated, and serious, but also elevated above the mundane world, and fun' (2007, 13). For the Naxalites, too, and definitely those who joined so young, (the tryst with) violence was perhaps indeed encountered as play; in this adventure, even death may have been seen (and dismissed) as acceptable risk. Throughout my ethnography, there are repetitive records of nonchalance or of pleasure (including in the experience of a new vesting of power); Manishji's elan and bravado and Rinku's flippancy are only some amongst them (see Chitralekha 2010). If it started as play, it does not continue as that, but I have fewer oral records of that shifting experience, of exhaustion, fear, longings for escape or of terror—including of death that is eventually as intimately

faced as dealt out in the past; more frequently evasions
and silences speak of what could not be asked, leave aside
acknowledged or told (see Das's reflections on the reality
of killing and being killed, which is openly spoken about,
known and yet never fully comprehended [2008]).

Through the period of my fieldwork in Jharkhand and
Bihar, local regional papers would often carry photographs,
sometimes on the front page, of the Naxalite 'terrorist'
eliminated in encounter in a neighbouring village or an
adjoining district. Mostly, I would see these papers at
the local chai and samosa shop or sometimes when it was
brought into the homes of those I lived with. That imagery
and its accompanying text, as in Verdery's reminiscence
of Levi-Strauss's words on the properties of corpses that
make them 'good to think' as symbols (Verdery 1999),
spoke of the finally overpowering might of the state,
of Naxalite bodies killed like vermin, of de-infestation
(a random perusal of a month's news feed around the
keyword 'Naxalite' in Indian nation press would easily
throw up the word 'infested' several times); the picture
though would be of a young boy, mostly painfully thin, now
bloodied and his body splayed out, rarely claimed in death
(accepting the body of a 'terrorist' would mean trouble for
other members of the family, also often associated with
the party in many ways). Brijesh's grandfather believed
he joined PW as he enjoyed the power and privileges, but
his mother towards the end of my stay in Mahuadanr
(and when we were alone) would often say, 'What is he
getting for this. … /Because of him his father and brother
could open a motorcycle shop/We could get his sister
married' or (after cooking a meal of *dal–chawal* [watery
lentils and rice]), 'Who is giving these boys good food to
eat. … They only get stale leftovers from homes'. Did she
worry about the real risk of early death of her teenage
son? Had she seen those pictures in newspapers? I could
not ask. She did not tell. If grief itself is a product of
culture (Scheper-Hughes 1992), there are contexts where

its acknowledgement is not a choice; if for Brijesh, death was an acceptable risk to take in the future to improve life chances now, she too had been complicit in that bid.

The Question of Violence

Azad, the official spokesperson of the CPI (Maoist), wrote eloquently about the need to see Maoist violence within the context of an oppressive system: 'Dalits have to face humiliation and abuse on a daily basis.... One cannot appreciate the need for revolutionary violence unless one understands the fascist nature of the state, the cruelty of the state's forces, tortures and fake encounters' (Azad 2006, 4380–82; Azad was killed in 2010 in an encounter with police forces).

Azad's plea for the need to understand the structural causes of violence resonates in the narratives of many who had joined the movement in the agrarian plains of central Bihar: Anil whose participation in the brutal castration of the zamindar was made possible by collective memory of humiliation and grief, Harihar Paswan who was beaten up by upper castes for wearing new clothes, Vijay who was tossed a piece of bread and so on. In all of these cases, violence was deeply mediated and performed through entrenched—and long suffered—structures of caste inequality, becoming in many ways as Arendt saw it also 'the only way to set the scales of justice right again'; in these conditions, to be cured of rage and violence would mean dehumanisation or emasculation (Arendt 1969, 64). But barring those of few committed cadre, in most narratives, the recalled joy in use of violence is more difficult, not easily contextualised or encompassed by ideas of accumulated rage or defence against long victimisation, less still as ideologically justified means towards fulfilment of a cause. Across social psychological categories of participation in the movement and time–space coordinates (in the sense of including those who may have joined in the 1980s or early 1990s), there was hardly any recall of anxiety or doubt about the use of violence as legitimate means to realise ideological or other goals; for most, the opportunity to possess and use arms was, in fact, eagerly anticipated. If for committed cadre like Anil or Vidyarthi, knifing the zamindar was not just practice leading to freedom from oppression but also simultaneously a direct and physical symbol of newly won power and strength, even Sadanand Mahato, who had not suffered or experienced zamindari, reminisced that killing (the enemy) was a privilege in the line of duty. He recalled entering the armed cadre 'with gusto'. 'I was so happy the first time I got a gun. I didn't take long to learn. I asked questions. ... They said nothing has ever changed without guns. Many people died .... We took it in our stride as part of the struggle'. Jopan Manjhi, much younger than Mahato when first handed a gun, says, 'I have never felt confused about what I am doing, not even the first time I had to kill'. No stranger to violence even as a child, Manjhi joined the party without too many complicated thoughts. Whatever few inhibitions he may have had were dissolved in the long years of training that went into making him a 'hard core', and by the time of my fieldwork, he had killed more times than he could remember: '*Bahuto ko cheh inch chota kiya* (we beheaded many)'.

Killing for those who joined the party in more contemporary times was bereft of the triumph and vindication that described the practice of cadre who had participated in the violent reprisal against then deeply entrenched zamindari. Also, the modalities of killing itself had changed for the younger generation of cadre who had joined closer to the time of my own fieldwork in Jharkhand and Bihar. From the direct and physically tactile method of the 1980s and 1990s (as when a peasant cadre would slit the throat of a landlord), the usual practice in Jharkhand by the time of my fieldwork (as now in Chhattisgarh, West Bengal etc.) was 'killing from a distance'—by shooting at the enemy or triggering a bomb, for instance. The post-millennium generation of the Naxalites (Navjyoti, Brijesh, Rinku etc.) had, in fact, seen far greater dependence on methods of attack such as landmines and other explosives, which did not involve direct combat. Yet paradoxically, even for them, remembered over the years, it was the arms and the guns that were recounted as amongst the best perks of a hard life. Killing was either adventure or non-event but mostly unmarked by trauma or regret. Manish, unselfconsciously proud of a gleaming, closely strapped machine gun, admits, for instance, that he 'liked holding a gun at fourteen and even now'. Even Pandey, neither happy with MCC's organisational culture nor the hardship involved in the job, had fond memories of his acquaintance with arms in the party, 'They gave me arms training. ... I enjoyed it ... but when you can cut open a man with a knife, why waste a bullet. ... It used to cost sixty rupees a piece even in 1995'.

How is Manish's or Pandey's transition from 'ordinary' youth to a nouveau but enthusiastic practitioner of violence to be understood? The (violent) practice of the committed may be seen as located in ideological commitment, and those of the oppressed as pursuit of freedom from subjugation. For mercenaries or opportunists, violence was mostly a non-event, expediently used as part of personal means–ends calculations. But what of young people who 'drift' into the party almost as an occupational choice in a context bereft of real choices? If they take up arms neither for politics nor for material gains (and were not coerced either), where does the readiness, even eagerness to participate in violence derive from? In both Bihar and Jharkhand, I did not encounter discomfort or unease around the use of violence itself; the practice of violence as means to realise ends had mostly already been rendered usual 'prior' to joining Naxalite groups. Narratives of drifters (as most other cadre) pointed towards a high degree of early acclimatisation to violence, of its routinisation as a way of life for respondents across contexts. Several drifters, most opportunists and even a few of the committed, in fact, had had prior familiarity with use of firearms—often through exposure and training within the family circle—even before joining the party. As Mohan, whom MCC cadre expelled on grounds of corruption, put it, evidently amused when I tried finding out more about aspects of his acclimatisation to arms and violence after joining the armed cadre: 'In *Kalyug* (ongoing and morally most depraved state of civilisation in Hinduism), one already knows how to operate a gun.'

What is of note perhaps is that not only is violence already normal or is not reflected on or evokes few, if any, ethical dilemmas but rather how its practice is now inspired by or associated with independently resonant and culturally valued symbolic attributes. If, as in Roy's account of women activists who joined the Naxalbari movement in Bengal in the late 1960s, the leaving behind of the everyday or the taken for granted was in yearning for a heroic life, where by going 'underground' to lead fugitive lives, women too led exalted lives of courage and adventure (Roy 2007); now close to half a century later, joining the movement for most is still in quest of 'heroism', only somewhat differently envisaged. For most of those I met, often, even before joining the party, possession of the means to violence, ownership of arms or (perceived or manifested) capability to be the actor of violence was desirable as indicative of strength and power, as were values of tolerance or non-violence already indicative of weakness or insufficiency. I find Fromm's conceptualisation of 'social character' useful to locate that prior culture of violence in regions of Maoist influence (and perhaps across more dispersed scapes in India as elsewhere, but it is not the subject of this chapter). Fromm suggests that the process of transforming general psychic energy into specific psycho-social energy is mediated by the 'social character' of particular spaces; the means by which social character is formed are essentially cultural (1977, 339). Fromm, of course, wrote in the context of the holocaust, and the idea of social character is certainly easier to relate in a context of ethnic antagonisms (I have argued elsewhere for its importance in understanding the work of mobilisation of the Dalit youth in Ahmedabad or the Bhils in Sabarkantha, or for that matter, the murderous mobs that attacked Muslims in Ahmedabad in 2002; see Chitralekha 2012). Nevertheless, while there are evident limitations to the lengths to which Fromm's ideas can be relevant to understanding the historical and contemporary complexities of Maoist practice, it calls attention to the need for richer analysis of the underlying processes of larger political and cultural changes (including erosion of the region's rich history of Gandhian–socialist movements). These may link to ongoing structures of social–psychological change that assist understanding of not just the prior normalisation of violence in the region today but also the semiotic re-rendering of its meanings altogether, of the encountering of pleasure in being the possessor of means to violence and its associations or linkages with recognition and esteem.

Conclusion

A significant part of the shared text between histories of cadre such as Rinku or Brijesh or Pandeyji can perhaps even here be traced to the impact of 'education' and 'development', both of which, no matter how uneven or inadequate, promised livelihoods and futures that were never realised, leaving in their wake restless populations that were easily tapped by rebel movements. Studies in Nepal have documented how the Maoist spread is also an unintended consequence of the state's neoliberal policies, wherein membership in a Maoist party can, in a sense, be seen as rejection by rural youth of that which they were excluded from (Shah and Pettigrew 2009, 240). Despite evident differences in their gendered locations, there were also significant resonances between the complex, entangled contexts and hopes that brought unlikely soldiers such as Rinku or Brijesh to kill for Naxal parties, and those of the few women cadre I could meet and spend time with.

I met Navjyoti in Navada, a remote Santhal hamlet in the western Tundi ravines bordering Dhanbad and Giridih districts of Jharkhand, where she had spent her childhood and met with the MCC. Out on bail after the National Human Rights Commission (NHRC) intervened against her prolonged third-degree torture in police custody (her condition was acknowledged as serious after maggots appeared in her wounds), she spoke finally, not about the party or about Maoism but about herself and the kind of forces that drew her into the party. The youngest of three sisters, she reminisced she had thought she may become a 'leader'. '*Ham soche achha hai, kuch seekh rahe hai ... leader bhi ban sakte hai*' (I thought it is good, I am learning something ... I may even become a leader). Those who had known her before she left with the MCC, including a school teacher associated with the National Literacy Mission (Sakshartha Vahini), remembered how she became close to the '*partywallahs*'. 'She had a good voice and was useful for the Nari Mukti Sangh (front organisation). She got a lot of attention from them'. This teacher believed that Navjyoti had a different 'bent of mind' from other girls (including her own sisters), and it was the party's recognition of her sense of self-worth that led her to them. Despite the brutalising experience of incarceration, torture and near-complete closure of options, the stubborn wish to overcome her life conditions had survived. As I was to leave Navada, she said, 'If I have the support of more women like you, I can do a lot even now. ... If you have come so far to meet me, I too can come to Delhi with you'.

Nisha, area commander of a couple of villages in Khelari (Ranchi district), had completed high school in Sunduru, Lohardaga, before joining the party. She recalls walking 6 km every day to attend school in an adjoining village, then again attending 'coaching' after school—sometimes without lunch. Her family did not have too much land, but there was, as she put it, 'enough to eat'. Once she joined the armed cadre, she went through a period of intensive training. She said,

> I found it hard to learn the firing positions ... sitting, standing positions ... fire straight at the target. At first, I felt uneasy ... how to eat, how to sleep, how to bathe. One day I got *makkai* (corn) fodder to eat. I refused but Kuldeep *bhaiya* (MCC's sub zonal commander in the region—with whose consent she spoke to me) said, 'Learn to eat whatever you get'.

When we met on the far outskirts of a village in Khelari, Nisha was a 'confirmed'—and evidently influential—cadre of the party. 'Now I have a uniform, a gun. ... People have even published about me in the press. ... They must have seen me in *jan adalats* (court sessions held by Naxal parties) or other meetings'. Nisha acknowledges linkages between economic and status deprivation and women's association with Naxalite *dastas*, admitting many women in the party, including in her own *dasta*, joined when all doors closed for them. 'They are very poor. ... Some have no parents. They come because the party is a different society ... brotherhood, equal rights'. She demands that her own position, however, as a respected full-time cadre of the party be recognised as different from that average. 'The other girls here are very jealous of me. The sub zonal (commander) gives me a lot of importance'. Much like Pandey or Rinku, she recalls with evident pride how (even before she actually joined) she was especially recognised by the commander: 'I was even asked to give talks in various meetings'. Open to building conjugal ties within the party ('If seniors [in the party] say marry, I will'), it was nevertheless not a matter of importance for her, though many women, she points out derisively, did, in fact, join MCCI only to find mates. 'Sometimes soon after they get married, women leave Nari Mukti Sangh. Doesn't it prove they came here only to marry in the first place?'

Nisha's overt pleasure in being photographed by journalists and in seeing her pictures that appeared in newspapers is not dissimilar to the documentation of the insurgency in Nepal in a fast-changing context wherein images of rural youth that were previously either invisible or presented as backward in media terms became front-page material as 'gun-toting young women were as likely to be featured as beauty queens' (Shah and Pettigrew 2009). Her motives and aspirations—much as those of other 'drifters'—have to be acknowledged perhaps as more than 'private issues' on the periphery of a social movement—as urgent indicators, in fact, of a shifting politics of recognition. If the first steps towards equal participation are taken when actors are given resources to interact with others as peers, for those like her, this came in the form of possession of arms. If we are to hear voices such as those of Rinku or Navjyoti or Nisha, we may not be able to assume that young 'Maoists' want different things than our own children do. The youth joining the MCCI in Jharkhand may far too often have been motivated by aspirations not very different from those that get other young people inside an Ivy League University, a coveted law firm or a Fortune 500 company. It is another matter that the scape of choices for them is often restricted to a question of membership of 'which' armed group.

References

Agamben G. 1998. *Homo Sacer: Sovereign Power and Bare Life*. Stanford, CA: Stanford University Press.
Arendt, Hannah. 1969. *On Violence*. London: Allen Lane.

Asad, Talal. 2007. *On Suicide Bombing*. New York, NY: Columbia University Press.

Azad. 2006, 14–20 October. 'Maoists in India: A Rejoinder'. *Economic and Political Weekly* 41 (41): 4379–83.

Balagopal, K. 2006, 3 June. 'Chhattisgarh: Physiognomy of Violence'. *Economic and Political Weekly* 41 (22): 2183–86.

Banerjee, Sumanta. 1984. *India's Simmering Revolution: The Naxalite Uprising*. London: Zed Press.

Becker, Ernest. 1973. *The Denial of Death*. New York: The Free Press.

Bhatia, Bela. 1997, February. 'Anatomy of a Massacre'. *Seminar*, 450: 53–58.

———. 1998. 'The Naxalite Movement in Central Bihar'. Accessed 2 August 2014. http://www.civilresistance.info/challenge/naxa

———. 2005, April. 'The Naxalite Movement in Central Bihar'. *Economic and Political Weekly* 9: 1536–49.

Binmore, Ken. 1994. *Playing Fair*. Cambridge, MA: MIT Press.

Chitralekha. 2010, October. 'Committed, Opportunists and Drifters: Revisiting the Naxalite Narrative in Jharkhand and Bihar'. *Contributions to Indian Sociology* 44: 299–329.

———. 2012. *Ordinary People, Extraordinary Violence: Naxalites and Hindu Extremists in India*. New Delhi: Routledge.

———. 2017. 'Why Does the Subject Speak? Prejudgement in Fieldwork with Naxalites and Hindu Rioters'. *Journal of Royal Anthropological Institute* 23: 155–74.

Das, Veena. 2008. 'Violence, Gender, and Subjectivity'. *Annual Review of Anthropology* 37: 283–99.

Engineer, Asghar A. 2010, 16 July. 'The Concept of Martyrdom'. *Dawn*. Accessed 11 July 2017. https://www.dawn.com/news/547348/the-concept-of-martyrdom

Euben, Roxanne L. 2002, February. 'Killing (for) Politics, Jihad, Martyrdom, and Political Action'. *Political Theory* 30 (1): 4–35.

Fromm, Erich. 1977. *The Anatomy of Human Destructiveness*. Great Britain: Penguin Books.

Ganapathi. 2010, 12 February. 'Interview with General Secretary, CPI (Maoist) by Jan Myrdal and Gautam Navlakha'. Accessed 29 June 2015. http://sanhati.com/articles/2138/

Ghandy, Kobad. 2008, 23 September. 'Interview with Suvojit Bagchi'. *BBC South Asia*. Accessed 11 July 2017. http://news.bbc.co.uk/2/hi/south_asia/8270583.stm

Gudavarthy, Ajay. 2013, 16 February. 'Democracy Against Maoism, Maoism Against Itself'. *Economic and Political Weekly* 48 (7): 69–76.

Guha, Ramachandra. 2007, 11–17 August. 'Adivasis, Naxalites and Indian Democracy'. *Economic and Political Weekly* 42 (32): 3305–12.

Hoffer, Eric. 1951. *The True Believer: Thoughts on the Nature of Mass Movements*. New York, NY and Evanston, IL: Harper and Row Publishers Inc.

Juergensmeyer, Mark. 2003. *Terror in the Mind of God: The Global Rise of Religious Violence*. Berkeley, CA, Los Angeles, CA and London: University of California Press.

Lifton, Robert Jay and Eric Olson. 1974. *Living and Dying*. London: Wildwood House.

Malinowski, Bronislaw. 1954 [1925]. Magic, Science and Religion. Garden City, NY: Doubleday & Company.

Mohanty, Manorajan. 1977. *Revolutionary Violence: A Study of the Maoist Movement in India*. New Delhi: Sterling.

———. 2009, 5 December. 'Dialogue in Democracy: Challenges for Government-Maoist Talks'. *Mainstream* 47 (51).

Mukherji, Nirmalangshu. 2010, 19 June. 'Arms over the People. What Have the Maoists Achieved in Dandakaranya?' *Economic and Political Weekly* 45 (25): 16–20.

Mukul. 1999, 4 December. 'The Untouchable Present: Everyday Life of Musahars in North Bihar'. *Economic and Political Weekly* 34 (49): 3465–70.

Navlakha, Gautam. 2006, 3–9 June. 'Maoists in India'. *Economic and Political Weekly* 41 (22): 2186–89.

Pape, Robert A. 2003. 'The Strategic Logic of Suicide Terrorism'. *American Political Science Review* 27 (3): 1–19.

Prasad, Archana. 2010, March–April. 'The Political Economy of "Maoist Violence" in Chhattisgarh'. *Social Scientist* 38 (3/4): 3–24.

Primoratz, Igor. 1990. 'What is Terrorism?' *Journal of Applied Philosophy* 7 (2): 129–38.

PUDR. 1998. *After Bathe, Civil Rights Situation in Central Bihar After the Lakshmanpur Bathe Massacre*. New Delhi: People Union for Democratic Rights.

Ray, Rabindra. 1988. *The Naxalites and their Ideology*. New Delhi: Oxford University Press.

Robben, Antonius C. G. M. 2000. 'State Terror in the Netherworld: Disappearance and Reburial in Argentina'. In *Death Squad: The Anthropology of State Terror*, edited by Jeffrey A. Sluka, 91–113. Philadelphia, PA: University of Pennsylvania Press.

Roy, Srila. 2007, July. 'The Everyday Life of the Revolution: Gender, Violence and Memory'. *South Asia Research* 27 (2): 187–204.

Scheper-Hughes, Nancy, 1992. *Death Without Weeping: The Violence of Everyday Life in Brazil*. Berkeley, CA: University of California Press.

Shah, Alpa. 2006. 'Markets of Protection: The "Terrorist" Maoist Movement and the State in Jharkhand, India'. *Critique of Anthropology* 26 (3): 297–314.

———. 2013, July. 'The Agrarian Question in a Maoist Guerrilla Zone: Land, Labour and Capital in the Forests and Hills of Jharkhand, India'. *Journal of Agrarian Change* 13 (3): 24–450.

———. 2014. '"The Muck of the Past": Revolution, Social Transformation, and the Maoists in India'. *Journal of the Royal Anthropological Institute (N.S.)* 20: 337–56.

Shah, Alpa and Judith Pettigrew. 2009. 'Windows into a Revolution: Ethnographies of Maoism in South Asia'. *Dialectical Anthropology* 33: 225–51.

Sprinzak, Ehud. 2000, September–October. 'Rational Fanatics'. *Foreign Policy* 120: 66–73.

Strenski, Ivan. 2003. 'Sacrifice, Gift and the Social Logic of Muslim "Human Bombers"'. *Terrorism and Political Violence* 15 (3): 1–34.

Sundar, Nandini. 2006, 22–28 July. 'Bastar, Maoism and Salwa Judum'. *Economic and Political Weekly* 41 (29): 3187–92.

———. 2016. *The Burning Forest: India's War in Bastar*. Juggernaut Books.

Suykens, Bert. 2010. 'Maoist Martyrs: Remembering the Revolution and Its Heroes in Naxalite Propaganda (India)'. *Terrorism and Political Violence* 22 (3): 378–93.

Taussig, Michael. 1987. *Shamanism, Colonialism and the Wild Man: A Study in Terror and Healing*. Chicago, IL: University of Chicago Press.

———. 1997. *The Magic of the State*. New York, NY: Routledge.

Trawick, Margaret. 2007. *Enemy Lines: Warfare, Childhood, and Play in Batticaloa*. Berkeley, CA: University of California Press.

Verdery, Katherine, 1999. *The Political Lives of Dead Bodies: Reburial and Postsocialist Change*. New York, NY: Columbia University Press.

Weinberg, Leonard, 1991, July. 'Turning to Terror: The Conditions Under Which Political Parties Turn to Terrorist Activities'. *Comparative Politics* 23 (4): 423–38.

Wilson, Kalpana. 1999, January–April. 'Patterns of Accumulation and Struggles of Rural Labour: Some Aspects of Agrarian Change in Central Bihar'. *Journal of Peasant Studies* 26 (2–3): 316–53.

8

Maoism and the Masses: Critical Reflections on Revolutionary Praxis and Subaltern Agency

Lipika Kamra and Uday Chandra

The Naxalite movement is not a movement of landless peasants and tribals seeking to overthrow state power. It is a project defined as such by those who are neither peasants nor workers nor tribals; but who claim to represent their interests.

—Dilip Simeon (2010)

We have taken up arms for the defence of people's rights and for achieving their liberation from all types of exploitation and oppression. As long as these exist, people will continue to be armed.
—Azad (2010), former CPI (Maoist) Spokesperson

Introduction

The Maoist movement in India has, broadly speaking, invited two responses that are mutually opposed to each other. On the one hand, there are those who believe that the movement merely claims to represent subaltern interests but does not, in fact, do so (Guha 2007; Nigam 2009; Simeon 2010). On the other hand, there are those who believe that the Maoists exist for the sake of subalterns (Azad 2010; Navlakha 2010; Roy 2011). The two epigrams above encapsulate the contrast between these two positions on Maoism in contemporary India. But there is also a curious common ground between these positions. Both speak unambiguously from the perspective of subaltern. Which one is correct?

In response, we answer that, although both positions tell us much about dominant tropes to represent subaltern politics in Indian civil society today, neither tells us why ordinary men and women outside privileged metropolitan centres joined the movement, and how they engaged with the internal contradictions of the movement. In this chapter, we wish to demythologise subaltern agency, which has been imbued with a transcendental ontology in India since the publication of Ranajit Guha's *Elementary Aspects of Peasant Insurgency in Colonial India* (1983). Myth making around the figure of the subaltern has become, in Bronisław Malinowski's sense, a 'charter' for a wide range of political projects. It is no surprise then that both defenders and critics of the Maoists have turned to the mythical subaltern in order to lend credibility to their arguments. For the defenders of Maoism, subaltern agency propels revolutionary praxis, whereas for its critics, Maoists mute the agency of subalterns and render them hapless victims.

Yet defenders and critics cannot be treated realistically as political equals. It is true that the imagined figure of the subaltern is believed by both sides to be 'caught between two armies' of the state and the Maoist revolutionary party (Guha 2010; Menon 2009; Mukherji 2012; cf. Stoll 1993; Sundar 2014). Radha D'Souza (2009) has labelled this portrayal of subalternity, the state and a revolutionary party as the 'sandwich theory' of Maoism. If this portrayal features prominently in propaganda put forth by Maoist leaders and sympathisers, it is because they can point to the Indian state as the principal perpetrator of human rights abuses, which, of course, justifies its affinities with subaltern communities. Equally, this convenient fiction permits Left-liberal elites in 'civil society' to characterise the Maoists as illegitimate for their use of violence and to remind the Indian state of its constitutional commitment to protect subaltern citizens. But, since the state and the

Maoists are not equally matched in any sense, an attempt at parity necessarily favours the state, of which civil society then becomes a handmaiden (Giri 2009; Shah 2013a). Indeed, we can clearly discern the statist allegiances of a number of academics and activists in a report published by the Planning Commission of India (2008), which presents Maoism as simply a 'problem' to be tackled through state-sponsored development initiatives in the so-called Red Corridor of Central and eastern India. This is, of course, how the mythological figure of the subaltern as victim has become the mascot for a fresh round of post-conflict statemaking in areas in which the Maoists enjoyed popular support. Much is at stake, therefore, in competing representations of subaltern agency, and the state ought to be recognised as a middle term in the equation between the Maoists and the masses in contemporary India.

In steering away from dominant representations of revolutionary praxis and subaltern agency, we rely on close-to-the-ground ethnographic perspectives on Maoism in contemporary India, focusing on how ordinary men and women have engaged with the revolutionary party-led movement. These bottom-up perspectives on Maoism push us to rethink the nature of both revolutionary praxis and subaltern agency. In this chapter, revolutionary praxis emerges less as a vanguardist imposition on the masses than a site of ongoing negotiations. By the same token, subaltern agency may be seen to be shaped by the structural constraints faced by a militant leftist movement. The dialectic between subaltern agency and revolutionary praxis is, of course, a key tenet of Maoist political thought. But since our task here is not to reinforce Maoist principles, we demonstrate in this chapter how subaltern agency operates as an unstable, even contradictory, force within the Maoist movement and steers it in unanticipated directions within Indian democracy.

Subalterns in the Maoist Movement

Since 2004, the Communist Party of India (Maoist; CPI
[Maoist]) has called for a New Democratic Revolution.
Rejecting democratic elections, the Maoists see the Indian
state as 'reactionary' and 'autocratic', and seek a 'worker–
peasant alliance' to overthrow 'imperialism, feudalism
and comprador bureaucratic capitalism' through an armed
revolutionary struggle of subaltern men and women. The
Maoists are active primarily in pockets of rural eastern
and Central India, where human development levels
rank among the lowest in the world, forest cover and
rugged terrain facilitate guerrilla tactics and protracted
low-intensity insurgency and Dalit, and Adivasi populations are preponderant. The Indian state has portrayed
the Maoists as the 'greatest internal security threat to
India since independence' (see Sundar 2011 for a sharp
critique of this claim). However, that portrayal sits oddly
with the fact that Maoist cadres are estimated to be any-
where between 10,000 and 40,000 in a country of around
120 crores (Harriss 2010, 11). These thinly spread cadres
are concentrated chiefly in what journalists, policy-makers
and scholars have termed the Red Corridor, running from
the Nepalese border through the states of Bihar, Jharkhand,
West Bengal, Odisha, Chhattisgarh and Andhra Pradesh.
In these areas, it should be noted, regular elections are held,
state and non-governmental organisations routinely participate in rural development and state police and forest
officials coexist with armed rebels and rural populations.
Just as the state's portrayal of the Maoists misleads us,
so, too, does the self-image of the Maoist movement as the
sole or leading political authority in areas swayed by their
influence.

In referring to 'subalterns' in the Indian Maoist
movement, we follow Ranajit Guha (1982) in defining
subalternity as a 'general attribute of subordination in

South Asian society' (see also Arnold 1984). The word, literally referring to subordinates in the pecking order of an army, follows Antonio Gramsci's (1996, 52) usage to refer to groups located outside of the ruling political classes that seek to exercise hegemony over them. In the annals of Subaltern Studies and its legacies today in India, the subaltern has typically been portrayed as a 'suffering subject' (Robbins 2013), which is forever condemned to resist the forces of modernity (see Bayly [1988] and O'Hanlon [1988] for classic critiques of this proposition). It is not surprising to see how in much recent scholarship on the Adivasis, for instance, they are made to fit the slot of the 'suffering subject' in order to represent them as hapless victims of state-directed development, dispossession and 'everyday tyranny' (see, e.g., Kela 2012; Nilsen 2010; Padel 2010). Such representations are problematic because, in the process of representing the suffering subaltern subject, they strip her of any meaningful political agency (Spivak 1988). Undoubtedly, the dearth of rigorous empirical studies of subaltern politics in India reinforces this problem. It is a deep irony, therefore, that subalterns are widely represented in Indian academia and beyond as suffering subjects even as both scholarship and activism end up silencing their voices (Chandra 2013a).

In the context of the Maoist movement, we find two dominant sets of representations of the suffering subaltern subject. One treats subaltern subjects as victims of Maoist vanguardism and seeks to rescue them from those who challenge the state's legitimate monopoly of violence within the nation state's territory. This perspective is seen most clearly in former Prime Minister Manmohan Singh's (2006) statement that the Maoist movement is the 'biggest internal security threat every faced by our country'. A later variant of this security-centric perspective may be seen in the Planning Commission report (2008) on 'Development Challenges in Extremist Affected Areas', which identified underdevelopment as the root cause of Maoism and urged development initiatives to wean subaltern populations away from the Maoists in the Red Corridor states. In this revised statist perspective that brings in the lens of 'development', endorsed by prominent activists and academics who contributed to the report, the Maoists appeared only as an 'epiphenomenon', merely a consequence of the state's failed development policies (Giri 2009, 466–68). Thus, security and development became two prongs of the Indian state's counter-insurgency strategy since 2009. P. Chidambaram and Jairam Ramesh literally became the two faces of this new strategy to save the subalterns from what newspapers commonly described as the Maoist 'menace' or 'problem'.

The Indian state's new strategy received support from an unexpected quarter when a number of prominent Left-liberal academics and activists based in New Delhi proposed the so-called 'sandwich theory' of Maoism (D'Souza 2009). The sandwich theory ought to be seen as a more sophisticated version of the 'human security' perspective (Chenoy and Chenoy 2010) outlined in the Planning Commission report. Whereas the 2008 report berated the state for its neglect of subaltern populations in Red Corridor states, sandwich theorists such as Dilip Simeon (2010), Nirmalangshu Mukherji (2012) and Aditya Nigam (2009; 2010) went a step further. These are representatives of the Indian Left who regard the more radical and militant Maoists as ideological enemies. Their interventions stemmed primarily from internal conflicts within leftist ranks. Notably, none of them has any first-hand empirical understanding of the relationship between subalterns and Maoists today. They criticised the state for its human rights abuses, besides its neglect of human development, but they also appealed to it to remedy these acts of omission and commission. Hence, although the Indian state was deemed to be a problem on par with the Maoists, sandwich theorists on the Left addressed the state in order to resolve their internecine conflicts with the Maoists.

The sandwich theory also came to be received enthusiastically by liberal defenders of human rights such as the Independent Citizens' Initiative, the People's Union for Civil Liberties (PUCL) and the People's Union for Democratic Rights (PUDR). It would be unfair to treat all of these diverse groups along with their complex histories (Gudavarthy 2008) as proponents of a single perspective. But, as Alpa Shah (2013b, 94–95) has recently argued, what binds them together is their commitment to 'working within the constitutional guarantees of liberal citizenship laid out in India, and with a claim to their own independence as activists'. It is in this spirit that we may read the activist-academic Nandini Sundar's (2014, 471) recent statement: 'The Indian state impersonates guerilla [sic] tactics in order to fight the Maoists, while the Maoists mimic state practices of governmentality'. Subaltern populations are represented, therefore, as 'innocent civilians' who are 'collateral damage' in a clash of 'mimetic sovereignties' (2014, 470). Compelling as it is, what is striking in Sundar's narrative is the absence of the voice of a single 'innocent civilian', in whose name she urges the Indian state to fulfil its constitutional obligation to protect its citizens. The only direct quotations in the chapter are attributed to a policeman and a sarpanch, both of whom have their own stakes in the conflict as local state representatives. The rest of Sundar's evidence, nestled amidst perfectly reasonable theoretical propositions adapted from recent cutting-edge work in anthropology and political science, does not examine the nature of the subaltern agency within the Maoist movement. In this most refined version of the sandwich theory, the liberal activist-academic reifies the suffering subaltern subject even as she renders the subject voiceless. The emphasis on competing 'sovereignties', moreover, posits a false equivalence between the mighty Indian state and the militant fringes of the radical Left. This serves no other purpose except to signal the independence of the author from either side. Lastly, it systematically depoliticises the contexts in which ordinary men and women negotiate the state and the Maoists in their everyday lives. While Nandini Sundar (2013) has been pushed to articulate a different view elsewhere, as we show further, the analytical sleights of hand in the chapter under consideration here, ultimately, appeal to the benevolence of the state towards the suffering subaltern subject. Such benevolence can, of course, be concretely demonstrated only via a 'humane' solution to the Maoist 'problem' from above.

If the Indian state and its allies among the Left-liberal elite deny the possibility of subaltern agency vis-à-vis the Maoist movement, a second set of representations ascribe an already existing revolutionary consciousness to subaltern agency. Arguably, the most poignant representation of the Maoists until date was the one penned by Arundhati Roy for *Outlook* magazine in 2011. Roy appealed to the 'liberal conscience' of her readers to recognise that the 'tribal people in Central India have a history of resistance that predates Mao by centuries' and that '[i]f they didn't, they wouldn't exist'. She then proceeded to highlight rebellions in colonial India by 'the Ho, the Oraon, the Kols, the Santhals, the Mundas and the Gonds' directed against 'the British, against zamindars and moneylenders'. If this triad of British rulers, zamindars and moneylenders sounds familiar, it is because we know it from Ranajit Guha's (1983) classic work on peasant insurgency in nineteenth-century India. The 'tribal' subject in Guha's account is the quintessential subaltern, exhibiting extreme suffering as well as an ever-present propensity to rebel against his suffering (see Chandra 2017 for a critique). The suffering tribal subaltern, in Guha's as much as Roy's account, is a victim and an insurgent. Comrade Azad (2010), alias Cherukuri Rajkumar, an ex-spokesperson for the Maoists, also articulated the same perspective in essays addressed to civil society prior to his death. In all of these accounts, the denial of agency curiously coexists with an excess of it, albeit in different historical moments. Implicit in such a proposition is a causal argument: extreme provocation incites tribal subjects to rebel against authority. For Roy, this causal sequence is repeated ad nauseam in colonial and post-colonial India to the extent that subaltern agency in the Maoist movement today is the congealed form of rebellions bygone. The birth of Indian Maoism, she asserts, took place in a 'tribal village' named Naxalbari, and since then, 'Naxalite politics has been inextricably entwined with tribal uprisings, which says as much about the tribals as it does about the Naxalites'. This assertion, too, has a source: it follows the work of the Australian anthropologist Edward Duyker (1987), who saw the Naxalite movement of an earlier generation mirroring long-standing tribal grievances in the foothills of north Bengal. It is worth noting that Duyker cites Ranajit Guha's *Elementary Aspects* and early Subaltern Studies approvingly in support of his own arguments in *Tribal Guerrillas*. Thus, we find an unspoken, uncited kinship between Roy's claims and those by Guha and Duyker that binds together the perpetually suffering yet revolutionary tribal subject with radical Left-wing insurgency in post-colonial India. The already existing revolutionary consciousness among tribal subalterns is, in other words, evident to these writers in multiple historical moments, but as Roy's essay shows us, its rhetorical appeal lies fundamentally in its ability to transcend history altogether.

A closely related claim put forward by Maoist sympathisers is that the armed movement is a direct response to the alienation of the Adivasi lands or development-related dispossession by the post-colonial Indian state. This is, simply put, an intellectual justification for taking up arms. The activist Gautam Navlakha (2010, 39), for instance, offered three reasons to explain why 'Adivasi peasants' in a Maoist guerrilla zone in Bastar had taken up arms: (a) the state was at war with them 'on behalf of big corporations to grab adivasi land'; (b) Adivasi land grabbed in this manner, along with its trees and livelihoods, could not be compensated merely in monetary terms and (c) 'development that the government talked of was bunkum (*bakwas*) having seen what was done in [the mines of] Bailadila'. Each of these three reasons is a part of Maoist propaganda in the Bastar region (see Azad 2010). They are reproduced faithfully not only by Navlakha but also by Arundhati Roy (2011) and Bernard D'Mello (2010). Roy, for instance, writes:

> Having dispossessed them and pushed them into a downward spiral of indigence, in a cruel sleight of hand, the government began to use their own penury against them. Each time it needed to displace a large population—for dams, irrigation projects, mines—it talked of 'bringing tribals into the mainstream' or of giving them 'the fruits of modern development'.

D'Mello writes, similarly, of 'neo-robber baron capitalism', which is both challenged by the Maoist movement and, in its latest avatar, a response to it. To argue that Maoism is a legitimate Adivasi response to the predations of the post-colonial state involves two moves: first, Maoist politics is inseparable from that of the suffering tribal subaltern subject, and second, the state's role in Adivasi suffering makes it a legitimate target of revolutionary violence in much the same way that tribal rebellions were justified as responses to colonial policies. Both moves are problematic. The former wishes away the relationship between the Maoist vanguard and tribal subalterns instead of elucidating it, and the latter fails to explain why the sites of major dams and mines across the scheduled areas elude Maoist control. If we scour the Narmada valley, the villages of the Dongria Kondh or the steel towns of eastern and Central India for Maoists, we will find that the Maoists are few and far between. Propaganda and reality are clearly at odds on this count. Why some Adivasis joined the Maoists, therefore, remains inadequately answered in the writings of their leading sympathisers in civil society. By overstating the nature of subaltern agency in the movement, ironically, the Maoists and their sympathisers overestimate their own influence over subaltern lives.

If we turn to social scientific explanations for why ordinary men and women join the Maoist movement, the anthropologist Alpa Shah's recent writings are a good starting point. Shah has not only been prolific but also attentive to issues of subaltern agency in the movement. Her earliest work dealt with 'markets of protection' that Maoists, analogous to the state, extended to rural Adivasi communities in Jharkhand (2006). This account, it ought to be noted, leaves no space for Adivasi agency. A subsequent essay described the uncertainty about future social relations in the minds of potential revolutionaries and how joining the Maoist movement produced relative certainty (2009). Arguably, this chapter marks a tentative moment in Shah's own trajectory in understanding Maoism in the Indian countryside. After another stint of fieldwork, she changed her mind. She argued now that kinship ties drew Adivasi women and men into the Maoist fold and could also potentially persuade them to leave it (2013b). Elsewhere, Shah (2014a) claimed that the Adivasis' distrust of an unresponsive, exploitative state attracted them to the Maoist movement. Combining the latter two explanations, she wrote: 'After more than two decades of the Maoist presence in these regions, kinship relations weaved in and out of the villages and the party, blurring the boundaries between the revolutionaries and the people' (2014a, 346). By moving from a portrait of no subaltern agency to one of subaltern agency subsuming revolutionary praxis, Shah now offers a sophisticated version of the perspective articulated by the likes of Roy, Navlakha and D'Mello. A recent essay goes further to compare the Maoists with Birsa Munda and his followers, encouraging the former to follow the latter in fusing together religion and political economy (Shah 2014b). She suggests that Ranajit Guha, much like the Maoists, did not go far enough to incorporate subaltern religious practices into his understanding of rural insurgency.

The intertextuality evident in Shah's or Roy's writings points to a shared canon of images and ideas about the agency of the suffering tribal subject in the Maoist movement. This shared canon permits individual writers to abandon their own misconceptions over time, as Shah appears to have done, in order to posit a seamless integration of subaltern politics and Maoist revolutionary agendas. Unlike most Maoist sympathisers who cling to simplistic notions of a pre-existing revolutionary consciousness, Shah is keen to suggest that an anti-state orientation may exist already among the Adivasis but it transforms into revolutionary agency within the movement. It is hardly surprising, under the circumstances, that Alpa Shah has clashed recently with Nandini Sundar over the Adivasis and their relationship to the Maoist movement. Whereas one appeals to the Maoists to take Adivasi lifeworld seriously, the other appeals to the Indian state to fulfil its constitutional commitment to Adivasi welfare. A knotty scholarly debate thus turns out on closer inspection to be little more than a sophisticated version of an ongoing propaganda war in Indian civil society.

To sum up, both sets of representations speak on behalf of subalterns, yet one depicts them as victims of Maoist politics and the other as victims of the Indian state's policies. The former may be associated with the state and its Left-liberal allies in civil society and the latter may be identified with the Maoists and their sympathisers in civil society. These competing representations are, of course, mirror images of each other, and to this extent, they sustain a false binary in the realm of political propaganda that has little space for subaltern voices. As such, a basic interpretive error seen in writings on contemporary Maoism in India is the inference that this binary opposition within civil society to reflect on-the-ground realities. Recent research on the micro-politics of 'civil wars' suggest that intense polarisation at the level of macro-political propaganda usually coexists with messy political realities at the local level and fuzzy allegiances on the part of subaltern actors (Kalyvas 2006). This kind of micro–macro disjuncture during insurgencies or civil wars often leads us to believe that subaltern populations targeted by both the state and insurgents are on neither side. In reality, however, as we shall see later, subaltern populations may be on both sides. Another key interpretive error noticeable is that the warring parties in the Maoist insurgency in India tend to be conceptualised typically as fixed, bounded institutional actors that are more or less comparable. Here again, the propaganda for the Indian state or the Maoists constructs a macro-level reality that distorts micro-politics on the ground. Whether in the Red Corridor or in insurgent zones in Kashmir and north-east India, democratic elections are regularly held and local government functionaries and NGOs coexist with armed insurgents and their supporters. The norm is thus shared, overlapping sovereignty, which sustains what Sanjib Baruah (2005) has termed 'durable disorder'. To cut through the thicket of propaganda and misinterpretation that dominates writings on Maoism in India today, we suggest an alternative theoretical lens on revolutionary praxis and subaltern agency in the insurgency and flesh it out in the light of recent ethnographic studies along the Red Corridor.

Rethinking Revolutionary Praxis and Subaltern Agency: Perspectives from the Field

By agency, we mean the capacity to fashion one's self or existence at the intersection of different sociocultural and political–economic forces. Conceptualising 'agency' vis-à-vis processes of self-making (Chandra and Majumder 2013), we understand it in intersubjective terms as a shifting property of social actors. To us, 'agency' does not necessarily imply a liberal–individualistic ethos or a propensity to resist social structures of power. Ours is a minimalist notion of 'agency', in other words, that avoids a common tendency in earlier iterations of peasant studies and Subaltern Studies to impute 'resistance' to acts of self-making, especially by subaltern actors (see, e.g., Guha 1983; Scott 1985). As Rosalind O'Hanlon (1988, 191) has argued:

> At the very moment of this assault upon western historicism, the classic figure of western humanism—the self-originating, self-determining individual, who is at once a subject in his possession of a sovereign consciousness whose defining quality is reason, and an agent in his power of freedom—is readmitted through the back door in the figure of the subaltern himself, as he is restored to history in the reconstructions.

For us, agency is 'non-sovereign' (Krause 2015) and 'socially structured' (Sangari 1993). We accept the Foucauldian premise that subjects are produced by the intersection of multiple discourses and structures of power (Foucault 1995), and hence, see the agency of subjects emerging within these structures of power rather than autonomously (Butler 1990). Moreover, insofar as agency may be associated with both self-making, it is also linked to 'worlding' in the Heideggerian sense through processes of 'structuration' (Giddens 1984; Sewell 1992). Thus, agency and structure are not opposed, as social scientists often assume, but mutually constitute each other. Yet there is a sense in which we also depart from these socially embedded conceptions of 'agency'. Self-making is far from coherent. Nor is agency free of internal contradictions. Agency and even resistance ought to be seen as embedded in structures and discourses of power, sometimes even reinforcing the very structures being challenged (Abu-Lughod 1990; Haynes and Prakash 1991; Mahmood 2005; Mitchell 1990). One may, in fact, exhibit 'agency' in ways that subordinate oneself to prevailing hierarchies. These 'antinomies of agency' (Kamra 2016), therefore, lie at the heart of our conceptualisation here.

These antinomies are particularly evident in subaltern interactions with political authorities. This is because the state, which is often taken to be a unitary actor, turns out to be a rather fuzzy entity that is hard to distinguish from the wider society in which it is embedded (Abrams 1988; Fuller and Harriss 2000; Hansen and Stepputat 2001; Migdal 2001; Mitchell 1991). The state is, of course, hardly unique in this respect. Insurgent groups, NGOs and religious bodies may be said to have similar 'blurred boundaries' (Gupta 1995) with society at large. Indeed, what is blurry here is the nature of sovereignty itself that is a property of states, but not exclusively so (Hansen and Stepputat 2005). We do not, of course, mean that states are somehow equivalent to all the other actors that exercise sovereignty over well-defined territories. Indeed, the sovereignty of the state is distinctive insofar as it is able to transcend scale vertically and to encompass society horizontally in ways that its rivals typically struggle to match (Ferguson and Gupta 2002). In a locality or region, the state may be equally matched by its rivals, but rarely throughout its entire territorial domain. This is especially relevant when considering the relationship between the Indian state and Maoist insurgents, both fuzzy rather than fixed entities, which are frequently treated by scholars and journalists as equivalent or comparable. In the uneven topographies of sovereign power that we find in the Red Corridor, for instance, the antinomies of subaltern agency are manifested in zones of negotiation with the state and the Maoists. These zones of negotiation seek to rework power relations and transform the conditions in which subaltern selves are produced. Zones of negotiation with subaltern agency, in turn, shape the nature and limits of revolutionary praxis for the Maoists. As such, those who deny subaltern agency in the Maoist insurgency as well as those who assume an excess of it are both misled into error. By mistaking the terms of propaganda to be descriptions of empirical reality, as we have shown, a vast swathe of

writings on the Maoists tends to paper over the complexity
of micro-political realities. To remedy this state of affairs,
the ethnographic evidence below fleshes out the theoretical
propositions sketched so far.

Let us begin in rural Jharkhand,[1] where Uday Chandra
has been conducting fieldwork for nearly a decade. The
modern state has a long history in the region dating back
to the 1830s, and successive waves of statemaking have
been intertwined with various forms of subaltern claim-
making (2013b). Here, as in other scheduled areas in India,
colonial and post-colonial states have collaborated with
Adivasi village headmen and elders to produce a body of
customary law that governs land and forests as well as
social relations within 'tribal' communities and between
these communities and resident aliens (*dikus*; cf. Cederlöf
2008; Karlsson 2011; Sen 2012; Sundar 2009). If the state
has been committed to an 'ideology of tribal economy and
society' (Corbridge 1988), its 'tribal' subjects have also
partaken of statist notions of 'primitivism' (Chandra 2013c)
in defining themselves and their communities. Class,
intergenerational and gender hierarchies within rural
Adivasi communities have emerged within the ambit of
these customary arrangements buttressed by a primitivist
ideology of rule (Chandra 2013d). While class differences
have arisen recently due to variations in educational
attainment, employment in the industrial economy and
reservation policies, Chandra also found during his fieldwork in Munda villages that class differences also emerge
from customary land ownership patterns that favour
earlier over later settlers and dominant lineages of the
village headmen and priests over others. Intergenerational
and gender hierarchies pit male village elders against
young men and women whose agricultural and domestic

---

[1] An extended version of this argument may be found in Chandra
(forthcoming).

labour sustain Adivasi villages. Challenging and reordering these intra-community hierarchies lie at the heart of the Maoist insurgency here.

In Jharkhand, over the past decade, the Maoists have offered non-farm, non-traditional livelihood options for young men and women. A young Christian Munda man, Benjamin, pointed me to widespread discontent with the elders in Munda villages:

> In every village, the young and the old are at odds with each other nowadays. Our tradition is simply to listen to what the elders say. We must farm for them, our wives and sisters must cook and prepare rice beer for them. What is so good about such traditions?

If customary law and tradition have been powerful resources in the hands of village elders, especially from dominant lineages, young men today are keen to move away from farming, and young women, who are prohibited by custom from even touching agricultural implements, have been especially keen to leave their patriarchal homes. Maoism and migration to megacities have emerged as the two principal alternatives for Adivasi youth. Victoria, an Oraon domestic worker in Delhi, pointed this out to a researcher recently: 'Young women like me only have two ways of coming out of the household before marriage, to migrate for domestic work to a large city or join the Maoist movement' (Wadhawan 2013, 47). Accordingly, young women have numbered a clear majority among the armed Maoist cadres in Jharkhand, a significant anomaly in its operations across Central and eastern India. Away from their homes in the Maoist movement or in distant urban environments, young women frequently find themselves in romantic liaisons across tribes (*jatis*) or within clans (*killis*) in the same tribe, both of which are prohibited in the customary gerontocratic order of their villages. By contrast, the Maoists not only do not object to, but actively encourage marriages across class, ethnic and religious lines. The simplicity of Maoist marriages, too, contrasts with the more

ritually elaborate traditional ceremonies overseen by the
pahan or village priest. In matters of domesticity and work
alike, therefore, powerful incentives have attracted young
women and men to the Maoist movement.

Within Maoist ranks, Adivasi youth enter a parallel
universe of 'modern' comradeship, in and of itself a critique
of 'traditional' village society. Maoist cadres participate in
campaigns to raise the minimum wage, to ensure Mahatma
Gandhi National Rural Employment Guarantee Act
(MNREGA) funds are paid fully and in timely fashion, to
help build homes for the poorer villagers and to redistribute lands illegally held by non-tribals among the poorest.
In Chatra district, at one point, the Maoists were even
offering cheap loans at 2 per cent interest per annum
(*Hindustan Times* 2009). NGOs working in central and
southern Jharkhand have rarely, if ever, been prevented
from working for grass roots development, even when
their activities dovetail nicely with New Delhi's counter-
insurgency plans. The fiscal structure depends almost
entirely from local forms of taxation (*rangdari*). The need to
resort to 'selective elimination' of an odd policeman, forester
or local trader is less common than is assumed. Fear of the
gun typically works just as well, if not better, than the gun
itself. Unsurprisingly, the greatest critics of Maoist youth
are the village elders, natural defenders of the traditional
Munda way of life. When discussing the raging Maoist
insurgency in rural Jharkhand in 2009–10, Soma Munda,
the Lohajimi-based leader of the well-known Koel-Karo
anti-dam movement, spoke to me of 'misguided youth' and
the 'romance of violence'. Others such as Sukhram Hao, a
retired school teacher in the nearby town of Khunti, adopted
a harsher tone to condemn Adivasi youth who joined the
Maoists:

> These party people are destroying our culture [*sanskriti*]. They
> don't care at all for the past or for us elders. When we were young,
> we always listened to our parents. But our children will not do
> so. This is the sad state of affairs today.

There can be little doubt that village elders, recognised by colonial and post-colonial states as bearers of customary or traditional authority, have found themselves under attack from young men and women who refuse to accept their authority as legitimate. The elders' politics must, perforce, be anti-Maoist.

The story of Masi Charan Purty, one of the best-known Maoist icons in central Jharkhand, neatly illustrates the aforementioned points about Adivasi youth politics and the desire to erect new forms of legitimate political authority. Masi's fame attained the status of folklore after he contested the Jharkhand state elections in December 2009. A shy, intelligent boy educated by Catholic missionaries in the highland village of Bandgaon in West Singhbhum district, Masi went on to the capital city of Ranchi to pursue a B.Com degree. By all accounts, he was a good student, and a bright future lay ahead of him. However, in 2003, a couple of years into his degree, he found his family embroiled in a land dispute with the village headman or Munda. With the headman's contacts in the local police, the Purty family faced the risk of losing its family plot. So, when the local Maoist unit offered its help, Masi could hardly refuse. He took on the village headman, literally, and ensured his family could hold on to their land. But there was no going back for Masi. He joined the Maoists in Khunti district and rose swiftly to become a key lieutenant of the area commander, Kundan Pahan.

A couple of years into his new job, Masi led a Maoist operation to rescue his female comrades from a detention facility for women in Hatia, barely 5 km from the state–capital of Ranchi. These young women, mostly Adivasis from nearby villages in Ranchi and Khunti districts in central Jharkhand, had been arrested for their participation in local Maoist party activities. Like Masi, they, too, had escaped the traditional patriarchal and gerontocratic set-up of their rural homes in pursuit of new forms of comradeship within the Maoist movement. One of the women arrested and then rescued in the Masi-led break-in at the Hati detention facility was his future wife, Protima, who hailed came from a faraway village on the Assam–Meghalaya border. Both Masi and Protima had seemingly entered the local Maoist ranks by accident rather than design, a fact that both repeatedly emphasised to me. Theirs was a shotgun marriage. Protima could not, as she put it, refuse him.

Masi, by this time, had run into a glass ceiling within the local Maoist organisation. He had served as deputy to the area commander, Kundan, who himself had not risen up the organisational ladder in nearly two decades. With his ambitions frustrated within Maoist ranks, Masi had been keen to find alternatives. Protima did not look forward to a life dictated by Maoist discipline and jungle warfare. She told me:

> We couldn't even talk to each other like we are now. We didn't feel a personal connection with them. One day, five of us, including Massi and me, ran away from the [Maoists] and came back to our village here in Bandgaon. We started our own [rebel] group, settling old scores with the local *munda* and ensuring people like us could hold onto their land without the elders deciding everything.

This new breakaway group was named the Jharkhand Liberation Tigers (JLT), though they now call themselves the People's Liberation Front of India (PLFI) to indicate their national ambition. In reality, however, the PLFI operates primarily in Khunti and West Singhbhum districts, where it enjoys an uneasy, fractious relationship with its parent organisation. Masi has been in jail since 2008; the PLFI supports his wife and two sons, paying for their daily expenses and school fees.

Many believe locally that Masi actually won the Khunti MLA seat on a Jharkhand Mukti Morcha (JMM) ticket in December 2009, but bribery and rigging helped his BJP rival Neelkanth Singh Munda win officially by 438 votes. Protima says,

[W]e were celebrating at the election center at 4.30 [p.m.], and
went off to the village to tell everyone. Later, we were told that
cash filled in boxes meant for sweetmeats were taken into the
office by BJP party workers, and the ballot boxes [sic] were
subsequently tampered with.

Four hundred and thirty-eight votes is a slender margin
of victory by Indian standards, and popular rumours of
electoral fraud say as much about how the Mundas today
see the state as about the actual course of events on election day. Today, Masi is a modern Munda youth icon:
he married whom he wishes regardless of ethnicity or
religion; he used the power of his gun to fight for the poor;
he settled land disputes extrajudicially against the interests of the rural elite and policemen in their pay and he
avoided what his followers call 'mind-numbing' rituals.
This is the example through which the PLFI endeavoured
to remake village communities in central Jharkhand today.
Despite being in jail, Masi remains confident of an outright
victory the next time he contests elections.

Masi is far from unique, of course, in rural Jharkhand.
During the 2009 national elections, I discovered that it
was common for the PLFI to campaign for the JMM during
elections. Pamphlets distributed by identifiable PLFI
members asked voters to choose JMM candidates over
their local rivals. So, when the PLFI second-in-command
Carlos, alias Lawrence Mundri, had earlier contested
elections on a JMM ticket too, it surprised none. On his
arrest in late October 2008, widely assumed to be the
handiwork of rival PLFI factions, Carlos defiantly told
his jailers that he had the 'blessings' of the JMM supremo
Shibu Soren, then the chief minister of the state (*One
News India* 2008). As Sukhram Hao, a retired headmaster
in Khunti, told me back then: 'Who are these Maobadis?
They are just the *netas* of tomorrow'. Sukhram's words
have turned out to be prescient. In December 2010,
panchayat elections were held for the first time in rural
Jharkhand. Protima explains how several of her husband's

ex-comrades contested the elections directly, themselves, or, indirectly, through their kin:

> They are now fighting these panchayat elections ... [name redacted] because there is so much money now in panchayats. The money comes straight from Delhi, you know, right? With Green Hunt [counterinsurgency operations], it is now possible to lay down arms and fight elections. ... Our fight against the village elites has succeeded.

What she did not mention is that those who fight and win panchayat elections also have the greatest incentive to provide intelligence to the police on their former comrades in rebel groups. Indeed, PLFI leaders such as Masi and Carlos were victims of precisely these games of ambition played by them and their rivals.

It is important to recognise that Masi and other Adivasi youth in rural Jharkhand are as much in dialogue with the post-colonial Indian state as with the elders of their own communities. Of course, as Philip Abrams (1988, 82) pointed out long ago, the state–society binary is itself illusory: 'the state is not the reality which stands behind the mask of political practice. It is itself the mask which prevents our seeing political practice as it is'. The same could be said for the Maoists, of course, though they cannot match the verticality and encompassment of the state. The state and the Maoists, far from being coherent macro-political entities, emerge in textured ethnographic narratives as fuzzy, socially embedded actors in a social 'field of struggles' (Bourdieu 1984, 244) and its contestation therein, whether on the basis of class, gender or intergenerational differences. Subaltern agency emerges from the interstices of rural communities and re-negotiates everyday power relations therein. Insofar as the Indian state and the Maoists may be said to share sovereignty in rural Jharkhand and beyond, they both define and limit the scope of subaltern agency and are, in turn, defined and limited by it. The contours of revolutionary praxis as well as statemaking today, as we have suggested, are shaped by subaltern agency. Yesterday's rebels may be tomorrow's legislators, and 'state' and 'society' are both transformed simultaneously in the radical upheavals of this historical moment.

In the Bastar region of southern Chhattisgarh, where Chandra has conducted stints of fieldwork since 2009, shared sovereignty is undoubtedly the norm. Here, in addition to the state and the Maoists, right-wing Hindu organisations also operate in Bastar's villages. Ordinary villagers, far from being sandwiched between rival political authorities, have grown accustomed over time to approach each authority with a particular set of demands and expectations. Hindutva is deeply invested in mass education, Maoists assist in raising the market rate for tendu leaves and the state provides heavily subsidised food grains via an efficient public distribution system. Nandini Sundar, despite laying out a sophisticated version of the sandwich theory on one occasion (2014), has reached a similar conclusion elsewhere.

> Against the view that being sandwiched or being only on the insurgent side exhausts the possibilities, my experience shows that people want both the Maoists and the state but for different reasons. They need open parliamentary parties and civil liberties groups who can help them when they get arrested, as well as a party like the Maoists who can help them keep their land. (2013, 366)

There are overlaps, of course, between different sovereigns. The BJP government in the state is certainly sympathetic to the grass roots educational and cultural agendas of Hindutva groups. But it is also striking that Maoist guerrillas and Hindutva groups do not clash with each other. Often, sovereignty shifts between night and day, and even overlaps within a single household. One of Chandra's interlocutors in Darbha tehsil, Hareram, is a school teacher who situates the Adivasis within a wider Hindu nation, weaving local folklore into creative retellings of

the Ramayana and the Mahabharata and recasting Bastar
as a Hindu kingdom under Muslim and British imperial
rule. His younger brother, however, is a key informant for
the Maoists in Darbha and, in particular, helps organise
nightly meetings in villages. Both subaltern agency and
revolutionary praxis are co-produced here under conditions of shared, overlapping sovereignty. This state of
affairs may also explain, at least partly, the BJP's puz-
zlingly impressive electoral performances in Bastar over
the past three state elections. Equally, Bastar's peculiar
circumstances may help us understand why the Maoists
are able to hold their ground over three terms of a BJP
state government. Betwixt and between lie the contradictory nature of subaltern agency.

In the Lalgarh region of the Jungle Mahals of West
Bengal, where Lipika Kamra conducted her doctoral
fieldwork, the contradictory nature of agency is similarly
apparent. In response to the high-handedness of the police
and the communist party-state in the area, ordinary men
and women, including those from Adivasi households,
participated in the People's Committee Against Police
Atrocities (PCAPA) under the leadership of Chhatradhar
Mahato. Over time, the membership of the PCAPA came
to overlap partially with the local unit of the Maoist party,
which, under the leadership of Kishenji alias Koteswara
Rao, had been expanding its organisation in and around
Lalgarh. The PCAPA also, however, came to be supported
indirectly by the Trinamool Congress (TMC), which set out
to replace the CPI (Marxist) government in Kolkata and
eventually succeeded in doing so. As popular fronts, party
politics and revolutionary praxis became oddly enmeshed,
subaltern agency played an ambiguous role in uncertain
times. Far from being sandwiched between rival authorities or led by kinship relations to one side or another,
subalterns committed themselves to multiple allegiances
and hedged their bets to ensure their physical security.
Although the Maoists proclaimed Lalgarh as a 'liberated

zone' and drew the attention of New Delhi to this remote forest region, these macro-political developments masked the micro-political calculations by which subaltern actors manoeuvred a political landscape characterised by shared, overlapping sovereignty. Those who had once supported the PCAPA and the Maoists subtly transferred their loyalties to the TMC in their fight against the CPI (Marxist) cadres. The TMC itself cast a blind eye towards Maoist operations in Lalgarh and, in fact, benefited from the decimation of the CPI (Marxist) in the region. By the time the new TMC government assumed power in May 2011, subaltern groups were keen to display their commitment to their new patrons, the TMC government and the local administration. From their role in creating a Maoist liberation zone, the people of Lalgarh subsequently turned into willing participants in counter-insurgency operations directed by the state and central governments. In the words of Durga, whose village of Netai that shot to prominence briefly during the Lalgarh agitation:

We would go to their [Maoists'] meetings at night then. The CPM cadres would harass us. We had to fight back. But now, it is different. We are looking for the government to help us.

Thus, subaltern agency proved to be slippery over time in Lalgarh. Insofar as it breathed life into revolutionary praxis at one moment and snuffed out the revolutionary flame in another moment, subaltern agency displayed its inherently contradictory character. Neither entirely autonomous nor wholly determined by macro-social forces, the agency of ordinary men and women in times of conflict ought to be recognised at the heart of social and political transformations in Lalgarh.

The ethnographic evidence presented so far pushes us to rethink the nature of both subaltern agency and revolutionary praxis in contemporary India. By laying bare the contradictory nature of subaltern agency and its relationship to shared, overlapping forms of sovereignty in the

Red Corridor, we have sought to avoid the problems that typically beset Maoism's critics and supporters in India today. For us, subalterns are not hyperreal or mythical beings available for political or theoretical appropriation. We refer to the flesh-and-blood narratives of ordinary men and women from our field sites in order to understand what Maoism means on the ground to them. The few existing ethnographic accounts of Maoism from Bihar and Telangana arrive at conclusions similar to ours (see Kunnath 2012; Suykens 2010). Yet empirical research that offers bottom-up perspectives on Maoism in India is remarkably limited. A large swathe of writings on Maoism has been simply armchair commentary by academics and journalists based in Delhi, and a number of promising fieldwork-based accounts have been unfortunately compromised by their reliance on either the state or the Maoist party for access. Accordingly, we call for further field research and reflection on Maoism and its impact on the Indian countryside today. Our knowledge at present is, at best, partial and fragmentary.

Conclusion

In this chapter, we have deconstructed the notion of subaltern agency and its relationship to revolutionary praxis in the Maoist movement in contemporary India. We have critiqued existing commentaries on Maoism and the masses in India for either ignoring subaltern agency or exaggerating its effects. We have further shown that both critics and supporters of the Maoist movement misrepresent subaltern politics in the Red Corridor, albeit in different ways. These dominant top-down representations of the movement fail to see revolutionary praxis as a site of ongoing negotiations between the party and the people. Equally, they fail to account for the shared, overlapping sovereignties that close-to-the-ground ethnographic narratives from the Red Corridor inevitably reveal. Thus, a focus on micro-politics helps us uncover the complexities and calculations that define subaltern politics in eastern and Central India today.

What does the contradictory nature of subaltern agency mean for Indian democracy? We believe that the Maoist insurgency has brought a renewed focus on these margins of modern India, paradoxically deepening democracy even as it is contested from the 'outside'. Local, state and national elections are regularly held in insurgent areas. Despite its stated antipathy towards Indian democracy, the Maoist movement has not subverted or diminished it in any sense. Indeed, as we have shown, some Maoists themselves may find the lure of democratic life to be inescapable. This state of affairs persists because subaltern agency is an unstable, even contradictory, force. On the one hand, it is shaped and constrained by a complex political environment in which multiple sovereigns overlap. On the other hand, it draws and redraws the porous boundaries between state and society as well as revolutionary praxis and everyday life. Insofar as modern 'democracy' retains its original meaning as the rule of the demos, the antinomies of subaltern agency ought to be regarded at the heart of popular democracy. Rather than destroying the so-called 'sham' of mass democracy in India, Maoist revolutionary praxis may have, in fact, revitalised it. Vigorous debates over mythical subalterns in the public sphere, however misled, have deepened the state's commitment to its putative margins. The Maoists, in turn, have proved to be able patrons of the masses, albeit not the only ones. If the militancy of Maoist revolutionaries has been transmuted into an unsettling force within the cauldron of a vibrant democracy, democracy, too, has thrown up radical possibilities beyond the constitutional limits that supposedly shackle it.

References

Abrams, Philip. 1988. 'Notes on the Difficulty of Studying the State'. *Journal of Historical Sociology* 1 (1): 58–89.

Abu-Lughod, Lila. 1990. 'The Romance of Resistance: Tracing Transformations of Power Through Bedouin Women'. *American Ethnologist* 17 (1): 41–55.

Arnold, David. 1984. 'Gramsci and Peasant Subalternity in India'. *The Journal of Peasant Studies* 11 (4): 155–77.

Azad. 2010. *Maoists in India: Writings and Interviews*. Hyderabad: Friends of Azad.

Baruah, Sanjib. 2005. *Durable Disorder: Understanding the Politics of Northeast India*. New Delhi: Oxford University Press.

Bayly, C.A. 1988. 'Rallying Around the Subaltern'. *The Journal of Peasant Studies* 16 (1): 110–20.

Bourdieu, Pierre. 1984. *Distinction: A Social Critique of the Judgment of Taste*. Cambridge, MA: Harvard University Press.

Butler, Judith. 1990. *Gender Trouble: Feminism and the Subversion of Identity*. New York, NY: Routledge.

Cederlöf, Gunnel. 2008. *Landscapes and the Law: Environmental Politics, Regional Histories, and Contests over Nature*. Ranikhet: Permanent Black.

Chandra, Uday. 2013a. 'Going Primitive: The Ethics of Indigenous Rights Activism in Contemporary Jharkhand'. *South Asia Multidisciplinary Academic Journal* 7. Accessed 25 July 2017. http://samaj.revues.org/3600

———. 2013b. 'Negotiating Leviathan: Statemaking and Resistance in the Margins of Modern India'. PhD dissertation, Yale University, New Haven, Connecticut.

———. 2013c. 'Liberalism and its Other: The Politics of Primitivism in Colonial and Postcolonial Indian Law'. *Law and Society Review* 47 (1): 135–68.

———. 2013d. 'Beyond Subalternity: Land, Community, and the State in Contemporary Jharkhand'. *Contemporary South Asia* 21 (1): 52–61.

———. 2017. 'Marxism, Postcolonial Theory, and the Specter of Universalism'. *Critical Sociology* 43 (4–5): 599–610.

———. Forthcoming. 'Intimate Antagonisms: Adivasis and the State in Contemporary India'. In *Indigeneity on the Move: Varying Manifestations of a Contested Concept*, edited by Eva Gerharz, Nasir Uddin and Pradeep Chakkarath, 297–310. Oxford and New York (NY): Berghahn Books.

Chandra, Uday and Atreyee Majumder. 2013. 'Introduction: Selves and Society in Postcolonial India'. *South Asia Multidisciplinary Academic Journal* 7. Accessed 18 July 2017. http://samaj.revues.org/3631

Chenoy, Anuradha M. and Kamal A. Mitra Chenoy. 2010. *Maoist and Other Armed Conflicts*. New Delhi: Penguin Books.

Corbridge, Stuart. 1988. 'The Ideology of Tribal Economy and Society: Politics in the Jharkhand, 1950–1980'. *Modern Asian Studies* 22 (1): 1–42.

D'Mello, Bernard. 2010. 'Spring Thunder Anew'. *Monthly Review Zine* July 3. Accessed 25 July 2017. https://monthlyreview.org/commentary/spring-thunder-anew/

D'Souza, Radha. 2009, 15 December. 'Sandwich Theory and Operation Green Hunt'. *Sanhati*. Accessed 18 July 2017. http://sanhati.com/excerpted/2003/

Duyker, Edward. 1987. *Tribal Guerrillas: The Santals of West Bengal and the Naxalite Movement*. New Delhi: Oxford University Press.

Ferguson, James and Akhil Gupta. 2002. 'Spatializing States: Toward an Ethnography of Neoliberal Governmentality'. *American Ethnologist* 29 (4): 981–1002.

Foucault, Michel. 1995. *Discipline and Punish: The Birth of the Prison*. New York, NY: Random House.

Fuller, C. J. and John Harriss. 2000. 'For an Anthropology of the Modern Indian State'. In *The Everyday State and Society in Modern India*, edited by C. J. Fuller and Veronique Benei, 1–30. New Delhi: Social Science Press.

Giddens, Anthony. 1984. *The Constitution of Society: Outline of the Theory of Structuration*. Cambridge: Polity Press.

Giri, Saroj. 2009. 'The Maoist "Problem" and the Democratic Left in India'. *Journal of Contemporary Asia* 39 (3): 463–74.

Gramsci, Antonio. 1996. *Selections from the Prison Notebooks*, trans. Quintin Hoare and Geoffrey Nowel Smith. Chennai: Orient Longman.

Gudavarthy, Ajay. 2008. 'Human Rights Movement in India: State, Civil Society and Beyond'. *Contributions to Indian Sociology* 42 (49): 29–57.

Guha, Ramachandra. 2007. 'Adivasis, Naxalites and Indian Democracy'. *Economic and Political Weekly* 42 (32): 3305–12.

———. 2010, 14 April. 'Unacknowledged Victims'. *Outlook*. Accessed 26 July 2017. https://www.outlookindia.com/website/story/unacknowledged-victims/265069

Guha, Ranajit. 1982. *Subaltern Studies I*. New Delhi: Oxford University Press.

———. 1983. *Elementary Aspects of Peasant Insurgency in Colonial India*. New Delhi: Oxford University Press.

Gupta, Akhil. 1995. 'Blurred Boundaries: The Discourse of Corruption, the Culture of Politics, and the Imagined State'. *American Ethnologist* 22 (2): 375–402.

Hansen, Thomas B. and Finn Stepputat. 2001. *States of Imagination: Ethnographic Explorations of the Postcolonial State*. Durham, NC: Duke University Press.

———, eds. 2005. *Sovereign Bodies: Citizens, Migrants, and States in the Postcolonial World*. Princeton, NJ: Princeton University Press.

Harriss, John. 2010. 'The Naxalite/Maoist Movement in India: A Review of Recent Literature' (Working Paper No. 109, National University of Singapore ISAS). Accessed 25 July 2017. http://www.isas.nus.edu.sg/Attachments/PublisherAttachment/ISAS_Working_Paper_10 9_-_Email_-_The_Naxalite-Maoist_Movement_in_India_12072010101317.pdf

Haynes, Douglas and Gyan Prakash. 1991. 'Introduction: The Entanglement of Power and Resistance'. In *Contesting Power: Resistance and Everyday Social Relations in South Asia*, edited by Douglas Haynes and Gyan Prakash, 1–22. New Delhi: Oxford University Press.

Hindustan Times. 2009, 21 May. 'Now Naxals Offer Hassle-free Banking for Poor', 7.

Kalyvas, Stathis. 2006. *The Logic of Violence in Civil Wars*. New York, NY: Cambridge University Press.

Kamra, Lipika. 2016. *The Politics of Counterinsurgency and Statemaking in Modern India*. DPhil thesis, University of Oxford, England.

Karlsson, Bengt G. 2011. *Unruly Hills: A Political Ecology of India's Northeast.* Oxford and New York (NY): Berghahn Books.

Kela, Shashank. 2012. *A Rogue and Peasant Slave: Adivasi Resistance, 1800–2000.* New Delhi: Navayana Publishers.

Krause, Sharon R. 2015. *Freedom Beyond Sovereignty: Reconstructing Liberal Individualism.* Chicago, IL: University of Chicago Press.

Kunnath, George. 2012. *Rebels from the Mud Houses: Dalits and the Making of the Maoist Revolution in Bihar.* New Delhi: Social Science Press.

Mahmood, Saba. 2005. *Politics of Piety: The Islamic Revival and the Feminist Subject.* Princeton, New Jersey: Princeton University Press.

Menon, Nivedita. 2009. 'Radical Resistance and Political Violence Today'. *Economic and Political Weekly* 44 (50): 16–20.

Migdal, Joel S. 2001. *State in Society: Studying How States and Societies Transform and Constitute One Another.* Cambridge: Cambridge University Press.

Mitchell, Timothy. 1990. 'Everyday Metaphors of Power'. *Theory and Society* 19 (5): 545–77.

———. 1991. 'The Limits of the State: Beyond Statist Approaches and Their Critics'. *The American Political Science Review* 85 (1): 77–96.

Mukherji, Nirmalangshu. 2012. *Maoists in India: Tribals under Siege.* London: Pluto Press.

Navlakha, Gautam. 2010. 'Days and Nights in the Maoist Heartland'. *Economic and Political Weekly* 45 (16): 38–47.

Nigam, Aditya. 2009, 27 May. 'Mass Politics, Violence and the Radical Intellectual'. *Kafila.* Accessed 25 July 2017. http://kafila.org/2009/10/27/mass-politics-violence-and-the-radicalintellectual/

———. 2010. 'The Rumour of Maoism'. *Seminar* 607. Accessed 26 July 2017. http://www.india-seminar.com/2010/607/607_aditya_nigam.htm

Nilsen, Alf Gunvald. 2010. *Dispossession and Resistance in India: The River and the Rage.* Abingdon and New York (NY): Routledge.

O'Hanlon, Rosalind. 1988. 'Recovering the Subject: Subaltern Studies and Histories of Resistance in Colonial South Asia'. *Modern Asian Studies* 22 (1): 189–224.

One News India. 2008, 27 October. 'Banned PLFI Claims to Enjoy Protection from J'Khand CM'. *One News India.* Accessed 26 July 2017. www.oneindia.com/2008/10/27/banned-plfi-claims-to-enjoy-protection-from-j-khand-cm-1225118133.html

Padel, Felix. 2010. *Sacrificing People: Invasions of a Tribal Landscape.* New Delhi: Orient Blackswan.

Planning Commission of India. 2008. *Development Challenges in Extremist Affected Areas—Report of an Expert Group.* New Delhi: Government of India.

Robbins, Joel. 2013. 'Beyond the Suffering Subject: Toward an Anthropology of the Good'. *Journal of the Royal Anthropological Institute* 19 (3): 447–62.

Roy, Arundhati. 2011, 29 March. 'Walking with the Comrades'. *Outlook.* Accessed 26 July 2017. https://www.outlookindia.com/magazine/story/walking-with-the-comrades/264738

Sangari, Kumkum. 1993. 'Consent, Agency and Rhetorics of Incitement'. *Economic and Political Weekly* 28 (18): 867–82.

Scott, James C. 1985. *Weapons of the Weak: Everyday Forms of Peasant Resistance*. New Haven, CT: Yale University Press.

Sen, Asoka Kumar. 2012. *From Village Elder to British Judge: Custom, Customary Law and Tribal Society*. New Delhi: Orient Blackswan.

Sewell, Jr., William H. 1992. 'A Theory of Structure: Duality, Agency, and Transformation'. *The American Journal of Sociology* 98 (1): 1–29.

Shah, Alpa. 2006. 'Markets of Protection: The Maoist Communist Centre and the State in Jharkhand, India'. *Critique of Anthropology* 26 (3): 297–314.

———. 2009. 'In Search of Certainty in Revolutionary India'. *Dialectical Anthropology* 33 (3): 271– 86.

———. 2013a. 'The Tensions over Liberal Citizenship in a Marxist Revolutionary Situation: The Maoists in India'. *Critique of Anthropology* 33 (1): 91–109.

———. 2013b. 'The Intimacy of Insurgency: Beyond Coercion, Greed, or Grievance in Maoist India'. *Economy and Society* 42 (3): 480–506.

———. 2014a. 'The Muck of the Past: Revolution and Social Transformation in Maoist India'. *Journal of Royal Anthropological Institute* 20 (2): 337–56.

———. 2014b. 'Religion and the Secular Left: Subaltern Studies, Birsa Munda and Maoists'. *Anthropology of this Century* 9. Accessed 26 July 2017. http://aotcpress.com/articles/religion-secular-left-subaltern-studies-birsa-munda-maoists/

Simeon, Dilip. 2010. 'Permanent Spring'. *Seminar* 607. Accessed 26 July 2017. http://www.india-seminar.com/2010/607/607_dilip_simeon.htm

Singh, Manmohan. 2006. Prime Minister's Speech at the Chief Minister's Meet on Naxalism, 13 April. Accessed 25 July 2017. http://archivepmo.nic.in/drmanmohansingh/speech-details.php?nodeid=302

Spivak, Gayatri Chakravorty. 1988. 'Can the Subaltern Speak?' In *Marxism and the Interpretation of Culture*, edited by C. Nelson and L. Grossberg. Urbana, IL: University of Illinois Press.

Sundar, Nandini, ed. 2009. *Legal Grounds: Natural Resources, Identity and the Law in Jharkhand*. New Delhi: Oxford University Press.

———. 2011. 'At War with Oneself: Constructing Naxalism as India's Biggest Security Threat'. In *India's Contemporary Security Challenges*, edited by Michael Kugelman, 48–58. Washington, DC: Woodrow Wilson International Center for Scholars.

———. 2013. 'Reflections on Civil Liberties, Citizenship, Adivasi Agency and Maoism: A Response to Alpa Shah'. *Critique of Anthropology* 33 (3): 361–68.

———. 2014. 'Mimetic Sovereignties, Precarious Citizenship: State Effects in a Looking Glass World'. *The Journal of Peasant Studies* 41 (4): 469–90.

Stoll, David. 1993. *Between Two Armies in the Ixil Towns of Guatemala*. New York, NY: Columbia University Press.

Suykens, Bert. 2010. 'Diffuse Authority in the Beedi Commodity Chain: Naxalite and State Governance in Tribal Telangana, India'. *Development and Change* 41 (1): 153–78.

Wadhawan, Neha. 2013. 'Living in Domesti-City: Women and Migration for Domestic Work from Jharkhand'. *Economic and Political Weekly* 48 (43): 47–54.

Epilogue: Populist Democracies, Failed Revolutions

The current political context seems to be one with democracies that are emaciated marked by growing social and economic inequalities, withdrawn and non-responsive states, revolutions that have failed to galvanise popular and idealist imaginations and thereby robust political mobilisation for waging armed struggles and deploying violent strategies. Political mobilisations have become sporadic and episodic instead of sustained and unifying. Whenever the political mobilizations gather momentum to become formidable, the State comes down heavily by invoking either the draconian laws or by using extra-judicial violence. Resistance to state violence has grave human and material costs to collectives. Where the costs are irreversible, resistance, including violent one, seems to be still a possibility. Resistance by the tribals in Central India, farmers in Bengal and peasants in Odisha has in the recent past demonstrated this. Issues mostly related to land acquisition in India have resulted in violent protests, and such protests have met with reasonable success, both because of sustained mobilisation and preparedness to use violence to resist the intrusion of the state. More militant kind of mobilisation requires clear target and a visible enemy; in the case of land acquisition, it was the state and it was also bound by law to be responsive to its citizens. Ironically, both the legal and democratic processes have, in fact, opened ways to make militant resistance a tangible option. It was the combination of the imperatives of the democratic and institutional processes and clear violation of citizenship rights that galvanised rural hinterlands to take recourse to militant modes of protest and reverse some of the impact of the ongoing process of 'primitive accumulation', including compensation and rehabilitation.

Maoist movement in Central India and the militant resistance of the Kashmiris in the Valley have been two formidable exceptions to the changing nature of political mobilisations across the political landscape of India, and also perhaps the world. The tribals resisting economic dispossession and Kashmir struggling for political sovereignty have demonstrated the continuing possibility of militant struggles holding value to the disempowered. The Maoists have been mobilising to create 'liberated zones' and 'Janatana Sarkar' based on an alternative imagination of development, as argued in the opening article by Varavara Rao, while Kashmir is struggling for *azadi*, more in political and cultural terms. However, beyond the portals of these 'war zones', militant mobilisation has not been this sustained, nor it has achieved the more immediate demands it has made, for instance, in the context of the struggles in Singur and Nandigram in Bengal. Relatively longer has been the struggle against POSCO in Odisha, demanding rehabilitation and compensation by a few and complete prohibition of mining by others. The Maoists have had fleeting presence in these struggles and according to the information available had to retreat once the immediate demands were achieved. What, perhaps, this kind of a changing dynamics establish is the point that to survive and become politically more self-sustaining, even the militant modes of resistance heavily depend on what kind of an equivalence would they be able to draw with democracy and the representational processes it has set in motion. It is imperative to recall that these militant moments have not transgressed into more sustained revolutionary mobilisations. The gap between revolutionary ideals and immediate imperatives has become too stark to ignore. The idea that 'revolutionary subject is made in course of revolutions' has either come to be circular or empty, leaving the subject to be contextually revolutionary but not necessarily in essence. There seems to be a growing need to recast revolutionary imagination from being outside of democracies to making it the inside of popular mobilisations that take place routinely within the available democratic spaces. How much of this interface can both democracies and revolutions sustain, will inform us the future story of revolutionary violence in India, in particular, and across the globe in general.

Democracies across the world are no longer the same. They are confined to operate within the limits set by neoliberal regimes; limits emerging from both withdrawal of the state and collapse of a collective imagination of an alternative. Political agency today operates within the limits of the neoliberal grid. Once a holistic imagination of an alternative is out of the equation, political agency is quarantined within the boundaries of pragmatism, it moves to realising demands that look feasible in the immediacy of the situation rather than in terms of altering the structures and imagining long-standing changes. Further, while state through both withdrawal and violence 'forces' through the neoliberal model, it also realises the limits of doing so due to the imperatives of popular politics, elections and more militant mobilisation. Politics of negotiation within the 'forced' limits of neoliberalism largely characterises the current phase of political mobilisation. In this context, even revolutionary violence can become a technology of bargain. Even radical acts of resistance can demand more effective service delivery system or reversal of some of the state policies. For instance, on more than one occasion, the Maoists have made demands such as inclusion of particular social groups in the Scheduled Tribe list, or mobilised for rehabilitation of those displaced by developmental projects or took part in local electoral processes. In such a context, radical ideals such as Socialism, as Nancy Fraser observes, becomes 'Cognitively compelling and experientially distanced'.

Confined politics of pragmatism do not then have a linear or a cause and effect relations with questions of inequality. In other words, even if inequalities are growing in absolute terms, this can be effectively abated either through relative mobility or through a discourse of hope and staggered inclusion. As Anne Phillips observes, 'Equality is now off the political agenda; Nobody these days believes people can or should be made equal' (Phillips 2000, 1). Retreat from economic egalitarianism has, in a sense, been replaced by political equality, referring to racial/caste equality or sexual equality. This separation between the economic and political equality marks the nature of political mobilisation. The arrival of this separation was ushered in, as I stated earlier, both due to the renewed concentration of power with the corporate and also growing ineffectiveness of mobilisations around issues of economic equality. Even if we realise that markets can exasperate economic inequalities, we really do not know a good way of correcting the situation. As Phillips argues,

> Everyone now knows that nationalized industries can become stultified and inefficient, that initiatives to end poverty can end up condemning people to a poverty trap, that when public authorities set out to protect employees wages and conditions from the harsher realities of the market they often do this at the expense of good service provision. We have even discovered, to our dismay, that the free health and education that was the great achievement of the welfare system can end up redistributing wealth from the poor to the middle classes. (Phillips 2000, 11)

It could well be possible that recourse to more violence could be an outcome of, not just state violence, but also a failed imagination. Politics that do not seem to work can be pushed hard to survive by deploying violence. It is, therefore, a constant worry with armed movements that they can possibly replace politics with mere militancy or militarisation of political struggles.

Democracy in such a context can become an attractive mode of pursuing demands, since the alternative is either not clear or costs of pursuing those are way too high. It is a context where the agents are aware of the limits, yet are hopeful for a change. It is a context where the discourse of formal equality has reached everyone but substantive inequalities in everyday life continue. Finally, it is a context where there is wide-scale despondency with flickering hope. This emergent social condition is in turn also driving the content and contours of democracy in India and the world. Can revolutions have any meaningful relation with such maverick democracies? Democracies have unplugged limits on participation and have opened the flood gates of populism, even as they emaciate the real-time possibilities of achieving substantive equality. Increasing popular participation and sense of claim combined with the imagination of relative mobility, with growing incapacity of the state to respond to issues of substantive equality and collapse of alternative visions has lead current democracies into a situation where,

> ... private troubles and pains do not add up and can hardly condense into common causes. What, under the circumstances, can bring us together? Sociality, so to speak, is free-floating, seeking in vain solid ground in which to anchor, a visible-to-all target on which to converge, companions with which to close ranks. There is a lot of it around—wandering, blundering, unfocused. Lacking in regular outlets, our sociality tends to be released in spectacular one-off explosions—short-lived, as all explosions are. (Bauman 2000, 3)

While revolutions are built on the basis of the structural locations of the actors, against clearly identified targets and antagonisms that are considered inbuilt, democracies on the other hand seem to be moving in the opposite direction. As Economist Jayati Ghosh argues, 'sadly, protests by people against injustice and inequality currently seem to end up producing governments that move exactly in the opposite direction' (Ghosh 2017). Mediatised politics partly has produced a new kind of 'reality' that has now come to referred to as 'post-truth', where a truth is constructed not necessarily on empirical facts, data or details but through the privileging of a 'felt' narrative that can be at odds with even basic and known empirical facts. This, perhaps, was always part of popular democracies but what is new is the fact that today not merely political rhetoric but also policy and governance seem to be driven by it. The recent pronouncements of Donald Trump regarding the Muslims or immigrants are clear examples of how 'post-truth' has come to dictate even global policy frame.

Do revolutions have the same levy to negotiate with reality as a fluid mass that can be constructed as relativism that changes its meaning based on the lens and context from which it is being viewed? Or does class/revolutionary politics and analysis demands gritty empirical details and facts? Construction of collectives need not necessarily be bound by what is but could well be driven by 'what must have been' and 'what should be', which are open to a wide array of symbolism. Cultural sociologist Jeffrey Alexander argues that 'From the perspective of a cultural sociology, the contrast between factual and fictional statements is not an Archimedean point. The truth of a cultural script depends not on its empirical accuracy, but on its symbolic power and enactment' (Alexander 2012, 4). The sense of what should be opens up both a wider space for political action, and political action can be forged through a range of causes instead of a single dominant reasoning. The sheer multiplicity of causal factors in reasoning can make collective action explosive and short-lived rather than sustain itself on the basis of established reasoning and empirical accuracy.

The new kind of collectives that we are witnessing in democracies across the globe, whether they are referred to as mobs or multitudes, seem to go beyond the discipline and singularity necessary for revolutionary action, especially in its violent form. Revolutionary violence needs singularity, prioritisation of preferences and stated consequences; however, a mob or a multitude is based precisely on multiplicity and simultaneity. A mob or a multitude, one could argue, is a social embodiment of hope and an urge for change with a realisation that things change only marginally setting in despondency. The urge for changes combined with disbelieve that change can actually be brought about leads to explosive action that is sporadic and eventful. Political action itself becomes symbolic in its self-realisation and self-representation that it is more to highlight the need for change than in bringing about the requisite change, since it is now conceded that mobilisations take place without the knowledge of how to bring about change. It is for the same reason that the new collectives are also marked by no clear agenda but more of the emphasis is on the process, which it is assumed by itself would contribute in very many indecisive ways to bringing about change. The sense of freedom that is perhaps available in random and contingent actions would be missing from the organised effort that revolutionary praxis requires.

Populism, in modern democracies, crafts such free multitudes unto the political landscape by converting them into meaningful subjects of political action. Laclau and Mouffe have for long argued on the open-ended nature of populist reasoning and why rejection of populism amounts to 'dismissal of politics tout court'. Laclau argues that 'populism' was always linked to a dangerous excess, which puts the clear-cut moulds of a rational community into question. He further argues that 'populism has no referential unity because it is ascribed not to a delimitable phenomenon but to a social logic whose effects cut across many phenomenon. Populism is, quite simply, a way of constructing the political' (Laclau 2005, x). In other words, populism is a process of contingent convergence of demands of varied social groups that could have conflictual social interests. For instance, the recent spate of movements against corruption such as that of Occupy movement in the United States, Brazilian Spring, Arab Spring and Anna Hazare-led movement in India, all of them had cross-class and cross-cultural alliances built into the social base of the movement. Corruption becomes an empty signifier that accommodates and accumulates a wide range of demands and anxieties that are in excess. They manifest a process of convergence at a symbolic level not necessarily at the social. Therefore, rationalism and interests do not exhaust the explanations that can be offered as to what brings collectives into the political landscape and why they get terminated before their demands get fructified into concrete programmes or collectives.

Revolutionary praxis is more closely tied to the idea of interests emanating from their social location. Similarly, it demands a fair degree of closure to push forward a concrete mode of action and programme in order to unravel the structural complexities. While it is driven by this logic of the structures, revolutions too seem to only partially and contingently arrive at those moments when actor's political action and interests are in a neat alignment. It is in this context that violence becomes the template through which bridges are built to hold those open-ended processes together. However, it also needs to be noted that where the actors converge with their structural location, state is more forthright and is using more repressive measures, both legal and extrajudicial. In much of the accounts of constructivism, populism and Cultural Sociology State becomes an empty or a missing category. It could well be argued that state manufactures 'populism', and publics can be orchestrated. What needs to be explained, even if state manufactures populism, is what helps them connect to the larger collectives.

Relevance of revolutionary praxis in future relates to the question of how sustainable are democracies in their populist mode, and how revolutionary praxis relates to populist democracies and also succeeds in foregrounding what cannot be achieved within the limits of populist democracies that are driven by neoliberal imperatives. Democracies are ostensibly addressing the immediate issues of mobility without actually delivering them in substantive terms, while revolutions are talking about distance dreams that promise to deliver more substantive equality. While democracies at other times are laying out future hope with existing despondency, revolutions seem to be more militant because they are pressing for more substantive changes in the near future. In this complex maze, political action is battered between various currents working at cross purposes. Revolutions have repeatedly failed, but so have democracies. What allows us to be patient with democracies and impatient with revolutions is for reasons of familiarity and prudence. It is also possible that violence of democracies is more hidden than that of revolutions and post-revolutionary societies as we witnessed in history. Democracies allow us the social gestation to falter and commit mistakes, while revolutions expect us to be more precise and accurate. The moot question regarding the relevance of revolutionary praxis is whether or not they can accommodate and include the democratic potential of populist democracies and yet overcome the limitations of populist democracies that have remained emaciated in achieving substantive equality for the majority of social groups. There seems to be an almost irreducible tension between these two streams of political praxis. It is of immense significance to ask if revolutionary praxis can continue with its militant and violent modes of mobilisation, or it needs to shift towards some form of 'Left populism' (Laclau 2005) or if it needs to combine a bit of both. In other words, can Populist rhetoric that offers wider space for popular politics be combined with more substantive social and economic demands?

Most of the recent sporadic mobilisations have had rhetorical impact in terms of consolidating floating imaginations about what is wrong in the system, though they have had limited success in terms of changing laws, policies, nature of economic model of growth and development, governance and growing state violence. If anything, one could argue based on the surprise win of Donald Trump in the United States that popular movements such as the Occupy have brought more clarity to what is wrong but since they offered no viable alternative, the field was left open to someone who could capture that imagination through an ultra-nationalist rhetoric that felt more assuring, concrete, doable and immediate. It had to do more with the 'will to act' rather than mere deliberation that Occupy seemed to stand for; it had to do more with closures than mere consensus. Movements such as Occupy seem to question the fundamentals of the system that short-changed the majority but a system in which the majority also had stakes. Paradoxically, more the public protest for equality more the space for demagogues who are occupying the space that such rhetoric routinely opens up. Similar is the story in India, populist mobilisation against corruption and demands for direct democracy lead to the rise of the current right-wing regime that has very little faith in public reasoning and participation. As participation is becoming ineffective, there is either faith in authoritarian regimes that look decisive or there is mobilisation where participation and consensus itself becomes the end of political mobilisation.

Mass movements today are driven by new ideals of direct democracy that translates into horizontal decision-making, where anybody who joins a protest 'could help set the direction of the movement'. In order to maintain such horizontal processes popular movements' aim for consensus, which then has a tendency to become an end in itself? Here, 'consensus stands in for is a participatory, egalitarian, self-determining movement, on the one hand, and, on the other, a society with the same characteristics' ('Is This What Democracy Looks Like?' 2015). Mobilisation spaces are imagined as prototype for the way society should actually begin to look. While this imagination holds immense democratic potential in terms of the alternative it presents, it nevertheless also drives the dynamics towards a stasis, since disturbing the processes of consensus building also strikes at the very spirit of the mobilisation. Consensus also leads to a minimalist agenda in popular politics, as each drive or direction has a counter-drive or consequence that is of equal significance in terms of democratisation. Fuller realisation of self-contradictory drives eventually opens up political space for normative suspension and suspended or deferred political action. Either we have restricted freedom or expanded freedoms that curb the will to act.

To conclude, the chapters in this book have revisited the question of the need and relevance of revolutionary violence in current democracies. Chapters in Part I of the book have pointed to various limitations of democracies in their promise to practice basic civil and political freedoms and rule of law necessitating more robust and militant mobilisations as a legitimate mode of resistance. Revolutionary violence and new revolutionary strategies such as kidnap open up the debate regarding the gap between the stated goals of the movement and its search for political power. Can they be equated or is it necessary to problematise the gap in order to democratise revolutionary praxis? Part II of the book raises significant dilemmas of using violence and the social fallouts and whether the dependence on violence springs more from resisting state or because of an un-nuanced and unchanging understanding of a social reality. Part III links it to some of the points we made in this epilogue, regarding the undercurrents of a revolutionary praxis such as the role of subjective emotions, politics in excess of the immediate stated goals and the question of 'non-sovereign agency' that opens up the debate of the necessity and possibility of forging links to the emergent populist democracies. It would be of continued interest to political observers, theorists and activists involved with both revolutionary movements and mainstream democracies to make better sense of the interface between populist democracies and revolutionary praxis in near future.

References

Alexander, Jeffrey. 2012. *Trauma: A Social Theory*. Oxford: Polity Press.
Bauman, Zygmut. 2000. *In Search of Politics*. Oxford: Polity Press.
Ghosh, Jayati. 2017, 21 January. 'The Majority at the Margins'. *Indian Express*.
    Accessed 18 July 2017. http://indianexpress.com/article/opinion/columns/
    donald-trump-brexit-demonetisation-globalisation-4484272/
Laclau, Ernesto. 2005. *On Populist Reason*. London: Verso.
Phillips, Anne. 2000. *Which Equalities Matter*. Oxford: Polity Press.
'Is This What Democracy Looks Like?' 2015. Accessed in May 2016. http://what-
    democracy-looks-like.com

About the Editor and Contributors

Ajay Gudavarthy is associate professor at the Centre for Political Studies of Jawaharlal Nehru University (JNU), New Delhi. He has taught earlier as assistant professor at the National Law School of India University, Bengaluru. He had been the visiting professor at the Centre for Modern Indian Studies, Göttingen University, Germany, in 2014. He had been visiting fellow at the Centre for Citizenship, Civil Society and Rule of Law, University of Aberdeen, in 2012. He was visiting faculty at the Centre for Human Rights, University of Hyderabad, in 2011 and visiting fellow at the Goldsmith College, University of London, in 2010. In 2008, he was Charles Wallace visiting fellow at the School of Oriental and African Studies (SOAS), London.

His published works include *Re-framing Democracy and Agency in India: Interrogating Political Society* (2012), *Maoism, Democracy and Globalisation: Cross-Currents in Indian Politics* (SAGE 2014) and *Politics of Post-civil Society: Contemporary History of Political Movements in India* (SAGE 2013).

K. Balagopal was a leading human rights activist of India. He was the general secretary of Andhra Pradesh Civil Liberties Committee and later founded the Human Rights Forum. He was a prolific writer in both English and Telugu. He contributed leading articles to the *Economic and Political Weekly*. He passed away in 2009. A collection of his writings titled *Ear to the Ground* (Navayana) was published in 2013.

Sumanta Banerjee is a senior journalist who is best known for his book *India's Simmering Revolution: The*

Naxalite Uprising. He contributes regularly to the *Economic and Political Weekly* on current affairs, including issues of political economy, right-wing politics and politics in West Bengal, among other such issues.

Neera Chandhoke was formerly professor of Political Science at the University of Delhi. She has worked on wide range of subjects, including civil society, secularism, revolutionary violence and secession. Currently she is trying to update her already existing work.

Uday Chandra is assistant professor of government at Georgetown University, Qatar. His research lies at the intersection between critical agrarian studies, political anthropology, post-colonial theory and South Asian studies. He has co-edited volumes and journal issues on the ethics of self-making in modern South Asia, subaltern politics and the state in contemporary India, caste relations in colonial and post-colonial eastern India and social movements in rural India today.

Chitralekha is assistant professor at JNU and Member, Institute of Advanced Studies, Princeton (2017–18). Her academic contributions, based on anthropological fieldwork in diverse contexts of political unrest in India, include work on contemporary histories of participation in the Maoist insurgency in Jharkhand and Bihar, right-wing extremism and violence in Gujarat and the unarmed 'militancy' in Kashmir.

G. Haragopal is currently visiting faculty at the Centre for the Study of Social Exclusion and Inclusive Policy, National Law School, Bengaluru. He earlier taught at Tata Institute of Social Sciences (TISS), Hyderabad, and University of Hyderabad. He is a well-known civil rights activist and was one of the team members that negotiated with the Maoist Party during three kidnappings and successfully got the captives released.

Lipika Kamra is visiting assistant professor, Georgetown University, Qatar. She holds a DPhil from the University of Oxford. Her research interests crisscross political anthropology, gender studies, development studies, and South Asian history and politics. She is currently writing a book, based on her doctoral research, on the politics of counterinsurgency and development in the margins of modern India.

Varavara Rao is a well-known revolutionary poet and a long-term member of the Revolutionary Writers Association (VIRASAM). He earlier taught Telugu literature at Kakatiya University, Warangal, in Telangana. He regularly contributes to various Telugu dailies and is a known public intellectual in the Telugu world.

Anand Teltumbde is a civil rights activist, political analyst, columnist and author of many books. His recent books are *Mahad: The Making of the First Dalit Revolt* (2016), *Dalits: Past, Present and Future* (2016) and *The Persistence of Caste: India's Hidden Apartheid and the Khairlanji Murders* (2006). He writes a column 'Margin Speak' in *Economic and Political Weekly*.